# THE HITLER VIRUS

Other Books by Peter Wyden

*Conquering Schizophrenia: A Father, His Son, and a Medical Breakthrough*

*Stella: One Woman's True Tale of Evil, Betrayal, and Survival in Hitler's Germany*

*Wall: The Inside Story of Divided Berlin*

*Day One: Before Hiroshima and After*

*The Passionate War: The Narrative History of the Spanish Civil War*

*The Bay of Pigs: The Untold Story*

# THE
# HITLER
# VIRUS

## The Insidious Legacy
## of Adolf Hitler

# PETER WYDEN

Arcade Publishing • New York

Arcade Publishing books may be purchased in bulk at special discounts for sales promotion, corporate gifts, fund-raising, or educational purposes. Special editions can also be created to specifications. For details, contact the Special Sales Department, Arcade Publishing, 307 West 36th Street, 11th Floor, New York, NY 10018 or arcade@skyhorsepublishing.com.

Arcade Publishing® is a registered trademark of Skyhorse Publishing, Inc.®, a Delaware corporation.

Visit our website at www.arcadepub.com.

10 9 8 7 6 5 4 3 2 1

Library of Congress Cataloging-in-Publication Data is available on file.

ISBN: 978-1-61145-322-5

Printed in the United States of America

# CONTENTS

# PUBLISHER'S FOREWORD

As is the case with many books, there is a story behind this work, one that needs to be told so that the reader will understand the events that led to its publication.

In mid-February 1997, Peter Wyden called me and said, "Dick, I have a manuscript I want to send you. I've taken it as far as I can without editorial guidance. But I know you're an editor who doesn't mind wielding a harsh blue pencil when it's called for. May I send it to you?"

"I'd be delighted to read it," I said, and the more he described its contents the more excited I became. I had the highest respect for Peter Wyden, both as an author and publisher. I had recently read his *Stella,* a stark but tremendously moving account of his return to Germany to research the fate of one of his close schoolmates, a teenage girl who, as a Jew, had agreed — after having been tortured and promised that her parents would not be sent to Auschwitz — to collaborate with the Nazis. Peter was obsessed to know what had impelled her not only to collaborate but become, in a sense, a pro-Nazi monster. But if he was a fine writer, he was also a stellar publisher. Both of us had, in the 1970s, an editorial imprint, I at Viking, Peter at Morrow, and we used to meet irregularly to compare notes on the virtues and frustrations of having your own imprint. As Peter focused increasingly on his writing we had seen each other less, but whenever Peter and I did meet in the corridors of publishing, the mutual respect and basic friendship was always there intact.

A week or two after our conversation, I received the following letter from Peter, dated February 20, 1997:

Dear Dick:

As we discussed, THE HITLER VIRUS, just under 400 mss pages, needs one helluva lot of work: new writing, also cutting, polishing, updating. Be assured that 1) I'm fully aware of the patient's woeful clinical condition and 2) I'll work as long as it'll take to unreel this case effectively. Your suggestions are more than welcome; I solicit them. . . . The middle sections — Joachim Fest et al — need pruning. I'd appreciate your thoughts on whatever strikes you as long-winded.

My personal life shows up here and there, as you'll see — my memories of Hitler's birthday, for example — but this dimension could be deepened so the book would take on more of a My-Life-With-Hitler cast. Again, guidance would help.

New developments have left some of my case histories incomplete. Just this month, the village-wide arson conspiracy in Dolgenbrodt — see Chapter 3, [manuscript] page 13 — broke open with new indictments. Gerhard Lauck, of the Nebraska propaganda factory, is in prison in Germany. Anna Rosmus, the "nasty girl" of Passau, has moved to the U.S. and works for the Holocaust Museum. I'll tidy up all this, of course.

You're entitled to know why this body bleeds from so many wounds. I abandoned it, hastily and temporarily, for a more perishable project: CONQUERING SCHIZOPHRENIA. . . . It's partly history of the illness; partly case record of my younger son, Jeff, schizophrenic for 25 years; and partly history of revolutionary new medications, just out on the market, and the race for their development. I still need to sweat hard over the final editing.

As I've mentioned, I have a carton of recent documentation to be incorporated in the final HITLER chapter. A few examples from the top of the box: last December, a small revolution broke out in western Berlin over efforts to re-name a side street for Marlene Dietrich because she is still perceived as a traitor. A committee of U.S. doctors is campaigning against a physician, still practicing in Dachau, who was implicated in the murders of retarded children in World War II. A university president was unmasked as a former SS Hauptsturmführer who altered his identity.

Major war criminals, including the commandant of the Theresienstadt concentration camp, were lately revealed to live comfortably, protected by fellow-citizens in the know.

So while the Hitler Virus is losing strength as new generations take over, plenty of developments keep it alive for the present.

All the best,
Peter


I read the manuscript and found it fascinating, often brilliant: though it needed some serious cutting and pruning, as well as updating, it was far from in the "woeful clinical condition" Peter had described. Over the next three or four weeks, Peter and I talked on the phone, and on April 2, I wrote him a letter making him a formal offer, adding that I understood his prior commitment to finish, publish, and promote *Conquering Schizophrenia* had to take precedence, even if that meant pushing back publication of *The Hitler Virus* a year or more. Not atypically, Peter accepted my offer but preferred not to formalize it or take an advance until he felt the manuscript was ready for publication. "I'm familiar enough with the economics of independent publishing to know you can't, you shouldn't, be paying me an advance two or three years before we bring this child of mine out," he said in a phone conversation that summer. "If it makes you nervous not to have a formal contract, know that you *are* the publisher of *The Hitler Virus.*"

That was good enough for me. Though other, more pressing manuscripts took priority, I constantly went back to Peter's, read and reread chapters, tinkered, made notes, and talked to him on the phone every few weeks.

*Conquering Schizophrenia* took him more time and energy, both real and psychic, than Peter had anticipated, but we kept in touch, and by early 1998, I had gone as far as I could without Peter's further input. Increasingly, he felt he needed one more trip to Germany to follow up on some of the more virulent manifestations of the Hitler virus, and, during an exchange of letters in January 1998, I heartily agreed.

When would he take the trip? Peter was vague, but thought "sometime in the spring or summer" of that year.

What I never knew, because he carefully refrained from telling me after it happened, was that in February Peter had suffered a severe heart attack. But, robust and hearty as he was, he had apparently fully recovered. To me, he simply said that, until he could make the German trip, I should put the book on hold, assuring me however that once the trip was over, it would be a matter of weeks before we could finalize the "monster" (his term).

Peter never made that final trip to Germany. In June 1998, he died within days of suffering a cerebral hemorrhage. I didn't learn about the sad event until months later, for I was out of the country when it happened, and when I returned I made no immediate contact, since in essence he had told me that until his return from Germany, "don't call me; I'll call you."

Saddened and upset, I didn't even look at the manuscript for several weeks, assuming there was no point. Then, one weekend, almost on a whim, I scooped it up and shoved it, almost belligerently, into my briefcase. By Sunday night I knew I had to publish Peter's last work. We would have to do the updating he had intended to do himself; the notion was daunting but not impossible. On Monday I wrote Elaine, Peter's widow, who had "lived" much of this book with him, and informed her of our decision to go ahead. I asked her if she knew the whereabouts of the "carton of documentation" he had been hoarding up to his death. Yes, she said. She had never delved into it, but she could send it on. It was Peter's repository, his cardboard box file into which almost daily he dropped any reference he came across to the Hitler virus. Fine, I said, we would start with that. We also had a number of contacts in Germany whom we could ask to follow up on various manifestations of the virus and see how they had developed over the intervening two or three years. Thus, in the present manuscript, there are probably as many as fifty-five to sixty pages of new material. Doubtless the prose is not as scintillating, the thinking not as cogent, as Peter's would have been, but throughout we have tried to emulate his style and respect his viewpoint as much as humanly possible. We have also asked Elaine Wyden to review the completed manuscript and make any changes, of style or substance, that she thought inconsistent with her knowledge or memory of the events, many of which she witnessed. Had he lived to see this book through, the author would doubtless have thanked the many people who helped shape it over the years. As Elaine Wyden has assured me, they will know who they are.

From our end, I would like to thank especially Alessandra Bastagli and Gregory Comer, who spent literally hundreds of hours following up on Peter's notes and suggestions and verifying facts. Thanks, too, to Rebecca Morrison and David Martyn, who from their respective homes in Berlin and Bonn answered many questions.

So, Peter, if I may address this last thought to you: Your absence made this project difficult, and personally painful in more ways than one, but I also feel that, inadequate though it may be compared to what you envisaged, *The Hitler Virus* is a work that does you great honor.

Richard Seaver

# HOW TO USE THIS BOOK

This is a not collective indictment of a most complex people. It is a highly personal investigation into a loose alliance of opinion-shapers, intellectuals, rank-and-file old-timers, and younger neo-Nazis who hanker after their Führer and apparently cannot let his spirit die. For the most part, they are respectable citizens, worlds removed from the neo-Nazi hooligans marching and heiling on television. They are more surprising and could become dangerous if the German economy were to go into serious decline.

I once believed that as the aging German population disappeared, the Hitler virus would die with it. And yet, at the dawn of a new century, more than fifty-five years after the death of Adolf Hitler, there are still alarming indications that the virus is still very much alive and that his "Political Testament," dictated on April 30, 1945, the day before his death, predicting that "the consolidation of the Nazi state represents the work of centuries to come," was frighteningly accurate.

Documenting the manifestations of this "virus" is the point and purpose of this book.

P.W.

# BOOK 1

## THE END
## THAT NEVER WAS

# 1

## WHEN THE PAST BECOMES

## THE PRESENT

It was in 1993 that I learned of the audience response to a TV documentary on Auschwitz, shown the previous year on the German network equivalent of *Sixty Minutes*.

The program had focused on the memorial that was installed after the Holocaust at the most notorious of the Nazi extermination camps, reporting that the remnants of remembrance were by now decaying and encouraging atonement in the form of contributions for repairs. The feedback from some viewers, however, did not exactly reflect sentiments of generosity.

One wrote, "I'd be happy to make a sizable contribution if it would make Auschwitz functional again." Another took offense at pictures showing shoes worn by slaughtered Jews and piled up as booty for transport to the Reich. "I was a soldier in the Wehrmacht long enough to know German orderliness," this viewer protested. "Taking those confiscated shoes and throwing them into a random pile, such a thing would never have been allowed."

I thought I wasn't reading right, even though I was hardly a stranger to German anti-Semitism. With my parents, I had fled from Hitler in 1937, not too long after *Kristallnacht* (Crystal Night, or Night of the Broken Glass). I was thirteen. Along with all other Jewish kids, I had been expelled from my junior high school because the Führer wished Jews removed from "public life."

This disgrace was just as well, because I had lived in fear of my environment for some time. My homeroom instructor quite seriously taught in our "racial hygiene" course that the Jews were descended from the devil. My fellow students glared and checked me out for horns; on class excursions they bunched up behind me to sing a popular tune about the joy that comes when Jewish blood spurts from their knives.

Such boyhood experiences seemed very distant indeed in the 1990s, for in the intervening half century I had watched the Germans undergo a radical transformation, or so I thought. I had returned often, first in American uniform with the U.S. Military Government in 1945, and later as a tourist and author, roving widely to research books about the Holocaust, the Berlin Wall, and the divided lives in the two Germanys.

In my adult years, I had felt comfortable among the Germans, never quite at home but not unsympathetic. I made a lot of new friends, mostly younger men and women from the media and politics, my usual crowd, and they struck me as enlightened democrats, often more appreciative of their freedom than many Americans because of the repressive regime under which their parents had been forced to live. Yet there were a number of signs and statistics that I found disturbing.

Some poll results caught my eye as soon as I began to acquaint myself with up-to-date efforts to take the collective German pulse. In 1992, nearly forty-seven years after Hitler's suicide, 42 percent of German voters, nearly one-half, declined *all* responsibility for wartime treatment of Jews. Some 32 percent went further: they said they believed that "the Jews are guilty of complicity when they are hated and persecuted."

A novel thought: Were Jews now doomed to be implicated in their own mass murder? There probably were more believers in this bizarre notion than the overt poll statistics showed, because more than the reported number of voters were likely to hold poisonous convictions; no doubt they just didn't want to disclose them to poll-takers.

Another poll in the new millennium revealed that 79 percent of Germans see May 8, 1945, as a day of liberation rather than of defeat. However, if one considers different age groups separately, 87 percent of people under the age of thirty think of May 8 as a day of liberation, while only 67 percent of those over fifty do. On a more positive note, 95 percent reject the "Auschwitz-lie" that the Allies invented the Holocaust in order to demonize defeated Germany.

The poll findings helped me understand what I had been reading concerning a certain school of thought that was expanding into a cottage industry. It was nurtured by "revisionist" history books, propaganda tracts camouflaged as academic journals, sensationalist telecasts, political assemblies, "news" headlines. They chorused denial that the Holocaust ever took place or else they found ways to dismiss events long documented beyond reasonable argument.

"Hoax," concluded these accounts. "Myth," they insisted. "Where did the smoke go?" cried one young man direct from the Auschwitz catacombs during a grisly TV program I saw. "Ja," he kept demanding, "where did the smoke go?" He was striving to legitimize the *Leuchter Report,* a popular tract by Fred A. Leuchter, Jr., a German citizen who was raised in Canada and was living in Boston. An "engineer" without an engineering degree or training, Leuchter informed audiences of his findings that nobody was executed in Auschwitz.

The cause had other prominent spokesmen. "A shell game" — so the British "historian" David Irving told large audiences in flawless German. The murdered millions? "They were whisked into new homes, lives, and identities in the Middle East," he declared, "leaving their old, discarded identities behind as 'missing persons.'"

For years, Irving functioned as the well-paid mouthpiece for Dr. Gerhard Frey, the wealthy head of the right-wing DVU — the Deutsche Volksunion, or German People's Party — and publisher of the *National-Zeitung,* whose red banner headlines, "What Really Happened at Auschwitz," "What Really Happened at Dachau," and similar revelations, were a weekly diet for some 100,000 subscribers.

To keep from withering in today's democratic German society, such extremism, however marginal, required an underpinning more respectable than the heiling, shaved-head neo-Nazi hooligans I had watched marching on American television. And, behold, at least one impressive source of credibility wasn't hard to find.

As a class, German professors occupy an unusual status, simultaneously revered and mainstream, and the buzz among intellectuals punched up a history professor, Ernst Nolte, of whom I had just begun to hear. My regular reading, the liberal *Spiegel* magazine and the weekly *Die Zeit,* obviously did not think highly of him. The conservative *Frankfurter Allgemeine Zeitung,* the daily whose readers like to compare it to the *New York Times,* was, however, a staunch advocate of Nolte. Fan and foe alike accorded him the treatment of a hot property, a VIP. Respectful attention and lots of printed space was his. Radio and TV also catered to Nolte's views.

His picture showed a ramrod figure, bespectacled, austere in a vested dark suit that fit like a uniform. He had lately turned emeritus from the faculty of Berlin's Free University, a liberal-oriented creation of the American occupiers. His thick books about the rise and philosophy of fascism and communism had enjoyed applause from academics. These works ranked too highbrow for popular consumption, however — the language was too convoluted, the bite too antiseptic. His latest 500-pager, *Streitpunkte (Points of Contention),* was said to whip up new waves about the very basics of National Socialism.

The reviewers were right: there were fresh interpretations here. The Nuremberg Laws of racial discrimination were described by Nolte as a statesmanlike move to restrain anti-Semitic violence. The gassings were likewise acts of moderation, surely more humane than shooting naked people in front of their newly dug graves, as had been customary. Hitler, moreover, deserved admiration for having produced an economic miracle and for creating a military machine without equal.

All this seemed thought-provoking, especially since it did not originate with the likes of David Irving and Fred Leuchter. It was a trend known as "the Intellectualization of the New Right." And did the "New Right" live only in an ivory tower of self-delusion? Was it a small, isolated elite? I picked up the hint of an answer in the breathtakingly beautiful Bavarian mountains, where I had once gone to summer camp. It suggested otherwise.

In Berchtesgaden, so I was reading, some 340,000 pilgrims a year still trooped to the Führer's sacred mountain, his "Eagle's Nest," paying $12 per ticket for their homage. They were known as "brown tourists," and 70 percent were Germans.

I concluded that attention needed to be paid to the outward as well as the clandestine manifestations of what by then I had dubbed in my mind "the Hitler virus," and decided to return once again to Germany.

# 2

## THE JOURNEY BEGINS

For a moment I thought my hearing was playing tricks on me. I was talking with Professor Ernst Nolte, the historian, at seventy-one my contemporary, in his gloomy, cavernous apartment off Kurfürstendamm in Berlin. Our topic was Adolf Hitler. Nothing remarkable about that. The Führer remains a popular ghost in German conversation, sometimes as a demon, sometimes as a quasi-member of one's family, a father figure who made it big in Berlin.

"I don't consider him the embodiment of evil," said Professor Nolte pleasantly. He was the same grave, old-school figure in his gray vested suit, the picture of decorum and scholarly rectitude that I had spotted earlier in his author photo.

In his low-key manner he kept on chatting in the same vein, much as one contemplates the weather. Nothing so flagrant was said as to deny that the Holocaust occurred; merely that, as he had written, the gassing of Jews proved to Nolte that "painless death was intended." On balance, National Socialism did not seem such a bad idea to the professor. It incorporated "positive elements" that nowadays tended to get overlooked. His concern was apparent: the world was being unfair to the Führer.

Geographically, I was at home. Literally. I was born under enormously high ceilings, much like those in Nolte's residence, only a few minutes distant on Kantstrasse 128 in Charlottenburg. From childhood I also remembered how awed the Germans are by ranking academics and reminded myself not to fall into that trap.

It is a slippery task to respond to Nolte and his breed in any surroundings, including the United States. The outrageousness of their
views takes one's breath away. My profession taught me long ago not
to act shy or stand silent, yet some defining encounters with bigots
can paralyze one's speech. The afternoon with Nolte — his Frau
Professor served the obligatory *Kaffee und Kuchen,* along with homey
small talk — was one such occasion.

It reminded me of a snowy winter in the wheatfields of western
Kansas. As a young reporter for the *Wichita Eagle,* I was interviewing
a farmer who could have stepped out of a Norman Rockwell magazine cover. Oil had been discovered under his fields and he was suddenly rich. In the line of duty, I inquired how it felt to have so much
money.

"OK," he grumped, "but the Jews got it all."

Even after pausing to collect myself, I was regrettably unable to
squeeze out a word; nor could I summon a reaction to Professor
Nolte in 1994.[1] My Kansas farmer — I still see his sly face in front of
me more than forty years later — had lost his shirt through his own
stupidity. He had gambled away his millions by uninformed speculation on the volatile Commodity Exchange. Apparently, that institution was equated in his mind with "the Jews."

Nolte's *Weltanschauung* springs from more ideological sources, but
did such archconservatives share something that transcended traditional anti-Semitism? And was this something — or someone —
rooted in a peculiarly German phenomenon?

At a guess, Hitler was the common denominator. Surely he was
more than a vague symbol in today's turbulence. He had made it
materialize to begin with; was he still making waves? When Nolte
put forth his creative circumlocutions in order to "renegotiate and
diminish the national mortgage of guilt" (in the memorable phrase of
a sharp British observer), was the professor appeasing a great German
psychic hunger? Was the denial of the Holocaust more than an

---

[1]The speechlessness was a truly physical reaction. The Berliners have a marvelous
colloquialism for becoming so tongue-tied. They say, "Da Bleibt einem die Spucke
weg," meaning, "One's spittle freezes."

invention and a lie? Was it perhaps a need, because if the Holocaust didn't happen one did not have to feel guilty?

Perhaps these ever-pending psychic leftovers from Nazi rule helped to explain why a Hitler apologist like Nolte was being invited to write articles for leading newspapers, why even magazines that opposed him and his views published pages and pages of interviews with him, and why this dry and forbidding figure was such a popular guest on television.

I thought back to my first return to Germany as a soldier in the spring of 1945. It seemed a time of closure. In the Führer's dank Berlin bunker shortly after 3 P.M. on April 30, 1945, the Hitler phenomenon appeared to have come to a most inglorious end. The finality of the dictator's death seemed immutable and the scene frozen for all time.

Face swollen, hands trembling, Hitler had startled his friend, the architect and armaments minister Albert Speer, by shuffling about, looking for once vulnerable. Fifty steps below the ground, under sixteen feet of concrete topped by an additional six feet of earth, he gave a start every time a heavy Soviet bomb detonated in the real world outside and made the entire fortress shudder.

The Third Reich was tumbling down at that moment and the Führer was about to vanish. Or so it was then assumed by everyone — except Hitler himself.

At 2 A.M. the previous day he had asked the youngest of his four secretaries, a war widow named Gertrud (Trudel) Junge, to come with him from the map room where he had just married his longtime mistress, Eva Braun, in a makeshift ceremony lasting only a few minutes.

Together, the Führer and Frau Junge withdrew into a smaller nearby conference room, and Hitler, trembling and speaking from notes, began dictating the document he wanted labeled "My Political Testament." Frau Junge would remember how her hand shook as she bent over her steno pad.

Consulting his notes, he named a new government of twelve henchmen and charged them with responsibilities extending into infinity: "Our task, the consolidation of the National Socialist state, represents the work of centuries to come. . . ."[2]

Centuries. The dream of the Thousand-Year Reich would not die that day after all. Hitler orated the following prediction to Trudel Junge: "Out of my personal commitment, the seed will grow again one day, one way or another, for a radiant rebirth of the National Socialist movement in a truly united nation." A day later, in a court-yard littered and deserted, shaking under artillery drumfire, two SS bodyguards hurriedly poured gasoline over Hitler's corpse. He had eluded the fate he had feared most: a Moscow show trial "run by Jews."

Bleeding from a self-inflicted bullet wound to the right temple and wrapped in a blanket, the body was torched by the flame from a cigarette lighter while nine of the Führer's close aides, led by Propaganda Minister Joseph Goebbels, so briefly his successor, came to attention and silently offered the supposedly final Hitler salute.


Was it all an illusion?

"I can hear Hitler laughing in hell now." Thus reflected George Shultz, President Reagan's poker-faced secretary of state, a low-key diplomat not given to fantasy, in his 1993 memoirs.

Shultz was reconstructing the strange 1985 affair at the military cemetery in Bitburg, where the enduring memory of Hitler maneuvered Reagan and Chancellor Helmut Kohl into canonizing departed Waffen-SS fighters who might well have been guilty of hideous war crimes — thereby further immortalizing the Führer, if in another world.

Uncannily, Hitler had predicted his durability earlier, at a time and place subsequently well documented.

It happened on a dazzling, euphoric day in June 1940, in Paris, shortly after 6 A.M., and he had just conquered the city he loved and envied. Viewing Napoleon's tomb, he noted that its design forced him to look downward in order to glimpse the emperor's remains. He

---

[2]The new chancellor, Goebbels, also looked ahead, even though he would shortly commit suicide himself. At one of his last staff conferences, he told his assistant, "Perform now so you will look good on color TV in the year 1999."

deemed this poor public relations. As he told Albert Speer, his own memorial would ensure that he was looked *up* at, not down, and remembered forever.

Fittingly, Hitler's posthumous quasi-survival emerges from the shadows each April 20. That was his *Ehrentag,* the day of honor, his birthday, and I remembered the occasion vividly: banners, parades, and no school.

During my visit to Germany in January 1994, a headline in the Berlin afternoon newspaper *BZ am Mittag* said, "*Times:* Hitler Stops British Soccer." The *London Times* was reporting that a championship match between Germany and Britain had been called off because it was set for April 20, the Führer's birthday, and riots were feared. An Italian sports journal was also quoted. "Hitler won," it said. "The cancellation grew from fear of right-wing extremists."

German sports functionaries were indignant, and one official, Wolfgang Niersbach, blamed American interests. "Eighty percent of the American press is in Jewish hands," he explained. He singled out the *Washington Post,* whose owners, the Graham family, if they heard about the incident, were presumably startled by their sudden change of religion.

Later, the cancellation was confirmed, and Sir Bert Millichip, president of the British Football Association, declared, "We had hoped that these risks might have receded. Unfortunately, in our opinion, they have not."

"It's an outrage," responded Otto Jöhne, the Berlin head of the German Soccer Federation. "It's bad for sport when a tiny minority of extremists succeed like this."

A tiny minority of extremists? That sounded familiar. That was what my father had called the rising Hitler movement when I was growing up.

# 3

## "THE BLOOD OF GERMANS

## IS A SPECIAL FLUID"

Since a nation's raw realities tend to find their mirror images in its courts, I decided to pursue my mid-1990s explorations with a quick look at several relatively current trials in widely separated cities where a number of very different types of judges were presiding over cases that had striking characteristics in common. The defendants were young, of the post-Nazi generation, and yet their crimes were rooted in the Hitler ideology.

Only one of the judges was a throwback to the courts of the Third Reich, and he was finding much to enjoy in the case before him. Judge Rainer Orlet, fifty-nine, of the Mannheim State Court, was a self-confessed introvert who lived alone, without telephone or car. His social life was confined to an occasional outing to a Chinese restaurant with his mother. And ever since he became famous in the summer of 1994 by, in effect, finding the notorious neo-Nazi party boss Günter Deckert not guilty of being a neo-Nazi, the judge felt "persecuted."

Like Deckert, Judge Orlet stuck to his guns. This defendant was an "unusually interesting and appealing personality of firm principles" — so Orlet insisted even after his verdict unleashed an international firestorm. He and the defendant had so much in common that they might well have become friends, the judge said. Orlet, like Deckert, had quit Chancellor Kohl's conservatives because they were too friendly with the Communists. And the judge compared his Deckert dictum with the gentle treatment that was accorded Hitler because of the Führer's "selflessness" in the deadly Beer Hall Putsch of 1923. "I see Deckert that way, too," he told a reporter admiringly. And popular approval reached the delighted judge in a flood of applauding letters in his mail and to the newspapers.

Orlet viewed himself as an idealist like Hemingway's partisan hero in *For Whom the Bell Tolls*. The judge waxed rhapsodic as he recalled that romantic figure: "His leg was shattered, but he fought on. I would have fought on the Franco side, but I was incredibly impressed."

His defendant/hero, Günter Deckert, a man then in his mid-fifties, described himself as a revisionist and compared himself to Galileo and medieval martyrs. He hoped to assume Hitler's defunct title of *Reichskanzler* and he delighted his audiences by expressing his "doubts" that Jews were gassed during what he derisively minimized as "the Holo."

Deckert was fired from his high school teaching job in 1988 as an "enemy" of the German constitution. He started the Germania travel agency and remained a city councilman in Weinheim, a pretty tourist spot in the Bergstrasse district of the Rhineland. Fame came to him as chairman of the National Partei Deutschland, an ultra-right-wing party of 5,000 members specializing in agitation against foreigners. According to the party's literature, "The blood of Germans is a special fluid, very different from foul-smelling slime."

In the summer of 1994, Judge Orlet wrote a sixty-six page opinion, which the prosecutor denounced as constituting "instructions" for getting away with denying the Holocaust (illegal under German law).

The root cause of Deckert's joy and subsequent headache was Fred A. Leuchter, the "engineer" and ranking Holocaust denier. At Deckert's invitation, Leuchter had spoken to an enthusiastic audience at a Weinheim inn in 1991. While Deckert, who used to teach English, translated approvingly, Leuchter asserted it would take sixty-eight years to gas six million Jews and another thirty-five years to cremate them. The Weinheimers applauded and laughed heartily when "the Holo" was made the subject of dreadful jokes.

In 1992, Deckert was sentenced to one year in prison, but in March 1994 the Mannheim State Court ordered a new trial, complaining that the lower court had failed to ascertain all the necessary facts. And so the case wound up before Judge Orlet, whose amiable chief judge let him run the show in his court because Orlet's pains-taking opinions tended to be "revision-proof" — precisely what was needed in the Deckert case.

Orlet's notoriety for hating left-wingers went back to the 1969 university riots in Heidelberg, where his harsh rulings stood out. He once let a student defendant testify for three hours without allow-ing him to be seated. Thereafter, Orlet was considered somewhat unstable under stress. In 1974, he had suffered what the press called "a nervous breakdown" and was moved to the gentler atmosphere of Mannheim.

Two decades later, a full-page color magazine photo of Orlet offered an unusual appearance, possibly revealing and certainly incongruous for a judge: short, corpulent, trim, sport coat several sizes too long and too wide. He is clutching a briefcase like a security blanket, his round, bland face glistening with perspiration.

In the Deckert case, Orlet's opinion downgraded the historical realities of the Holocaust murders to a "thesis" and a "conviction." It criticized the fact that Germany was still subject to "extensive demands" to make good for the persecution of Jews "while the mass murders of other nations remain unatoned" — a common German allusion to Israeli treatment of Palestinians.

About Deckert, Orlet held reassuring views. The defendant was "no anti-Semite"; he merely considered it "desirable that research constantly rechecked even historical theses that are considered valid." Deckert "left a good impression upon the court" as a "responsible personality of strong character" whose "political conviction is a mat-ter of the heart."

Orlet and his two fellow judges conceded that Deckert had vio-lated German law when he told his 1991 Weinheim audience that the Holocaust was a myth perpetrated by "a parasitical people who were using a historical lie to muzzle and exploit Germany." The judges found him guilty again, and again sentenced him to one year in jail, but suspended the sentence in the expectation that he would be careful to "avoid punishable involvements" in the future, even though "changes in his political views . . . were not to be expected."

The ensuing storm was fast in coming. Jewish spokesmen cried foul. The German justice minister called the verdict "a slap in the face of all Holocaust victims." The prosecutor in the case said he thought he was caught drunk when he read Orlet's opinion. The Association of German Judges called it a "slip of the footing." Orlet's chief judge regretted "unfortunate formulations that might be misunderstood."

Initially, Orlet remained unmoved. "I don't understand all the excitement," he said. "When the verdict is considered objectively, it follows that it is in order as it stands."

The political establishment disagreed. Another trial was ordered. Orlet was furloughed because of "long-term illness." Yet in a matter of weeks his judicial colleagues closed ranks behind him, and after a leisurely journey of homage to patriotic sites in eastern Germany, Orlet resumed his seat on the bench.

However, when the media started accusing Orlet of being a neo-Nazi and Holocaust denier himself, he distanced himself from the Deckert verdict and claimed that the media had misinterpreted his words. When he was asked if he could imagine being friends with a man like Deckert, he said that his positive reply had been purely theoretical. He maintained that he was not an anti-Semite, admitted that the Holocaust really did occur, and added that he fully supported the state of Israel. Despite these assertions, Orlet was threatened with arrest as a Holocaust denier, at which point — being sixty and severely handicapped — he asked for and was granted his pension in July 1995.

At his third trial in April 1995, Gunther Deckert was sentenced to two years in prison without probation, for *Gefährliche Politische Brandstiftung* — literally, "dangerous political incendiarism" — by Judge Wollentine in Karlsruhe.

While still in prison, Deckert wrote a provocative, dangerously inflammatory letter, which was published in the NPD newspaper, to the then chairman of the Central Council of Jews, Michel Friedman, strongly urging him, as a Jew, to leave Germany. Again, Deckert was accused of "incendiarism," and at his trial in Mannheim in 1997 he was found guilty and sentenced to another two years and three months in prison. His lawyer in this case, Ludwig Bock, based his defense on the fact that the Holocaust was a "legend" invented by the Jews. In his argument to the court, Bock claimed that German politicians legitimized their "unique political incompetence" through the "uniqueness of German guilt" and called President Herzog and Chancellor Kohl to the witness stand. In 1999, Bock himself was fined 9,000 German marks for this statement, which was declared to be *Volksverhetzung* — sedition. He refused to pay, claiming that he had not denied the Holocaust but simply used the argument to defend his client. He was brought to trial in Mannheim on April 4, 2000, the issue being whether he, or any lawyer, had the right to deny the Holocaust for the sake of his client's defense. Bock's own defense lawyer, Norbert Wingerter, claimed that a defense lawyer's job was to *verharmlosen* — to make harmless or to play down. The jury decided that though a defense lawyer is protected when he tries to "play down" the defendant's crime, this protection ends when the act of *verharmlosen* is "foreign" to the case. Bock's fine of 9,000 marks was upheld.

"It's like a kindergarten here," Judge Hans Blumenstein in Stuttgart Youth Court blurted out at the sight of seven giggling, whispering, nail-biting young men, the defendants in my second case.

The youths were on trial for murder. Shortly after 2 A.M. on a hot July night in 1992 they had beaten Sadri Berisha to death with a baseball bat. The victim had been asleep in his home. A well-regarded construction worker, resident in Germany for twenty years, he was offensive to the slayers simply because he was a foreigner, an outsider, an inferior element.

"To make a little noise, raise a little ruckus, to provoke a little so maybe he'd attack us." That was what the killers had in mind, or so Klaus-Dieter Angelbauer described their original intentions in court a year later. Angelbauer was twenty-one but looked seventeen.

The deadly caper had started innocently over some beers at the Kegler bar in Kemnat, an industrial town of 5,000 near Stuttgart, amid the picturesque scenery of Swabia. When the Kegler closed, the group repaired to the home of some friends. There, the mood had initially been mellow, remembered Thomas Wede, their unappointed leader, until two outside elements infiltrated the beery gathering.

Someone put on some LP records. The first was hard rock music: celebrations of violence by a band of skinheads known as Kahlkopf

(Shaved Head). And then came the shrieking, importuning voice of the Führer himself on LP, delivering some of his mesmerizing speeches, his calls to arms of half a century ago. At once, dramatically, the mood changed, so the defendants testified. The air turned tense.

"Plözlich war's da," one of them recalled. "Suddenly, there it was." A catchword ran through the room: "Asylanten!" — asylum seekers. It was the standard war cry, the red flag that often goaded neo-Nazi bullies into action.

Off the soon-to-be killers trooped, armed with baseball bats, air pistols, and a metal bar. The door to the bungalow where Sadri Berisha rented a room was open, and the group stormed in. Berisha was barely awake when two blows on the head by Thomas Wede's baseball bat killed him on the spot.

The official reaction was predictably defensive. "We're no nest of rightist radicals," said Mayor Herbert Rösch. "We've been living for years with foreigners, just like other towns." The police report stated, "It cannot be disputed that no political background existed."

That was not quite true. In Thomas Wede's room, swastikas decorated the walls, as did newspaper clippings of extremist violence and slogans such as "Foreigners Out!" and "Germany for Germans." Yet neither Wede nor any of his fellow killers were affiliated with political groups of any kind. Theirs was a case of "*Stammtisch-Radikalismus,*" said one of the police investigators, a statement that tried to make the event look almost homey, routine, for the *Stammtisch* is a venerable German institution in pubs and cafés where a big table is set aside for the regulars, the steadfast indigenous clientele gathering for gossip and hilarity and the comfort of the like-minded.

Judge Blumenstein and some — possibly most — of the spectators at the trial were not among the like-minded. Thomas Wede received a life sentence. His principal confederate got nine years, and two of the other perpetrators were each given seven-year sentences. The rest were sentenced to various lengths of probation. And if Hitler had the first word, he was also given the last. As one of the court spectators said of the defendants, "Them people should have their heads off, like Hitler."

*    *    *

My third case was triggered by treasured possessions of Volker L.'s parents: old-style recordings of Hitler and Joseph Goebbels. To Volker, eighteen, these speeches were not memorabilia but the foundation for his everyday beliefs. "Information material," he called them in court. As he listened to them more and more often, his enthusiasm for the ideas of the departed leaders grew.

"They were to my taste," he testified.

It was a taste already conditioned by annual garden parties and campfires celebrating Hitler's birthday in Volker's native village, Hünxe (population 1,420), in Westphalia, and by his contacts with a noisy extremist neo-Nazi party, the FAP (Freiheitliche Deutsche Arbeiterpartei). Though tiny, the party was another powerful motivating force propelling Volker into action.

"Ausländer Raus!" ("Out with Foreigners!") was its principal slogan. And: "No voting rights for foreigners, no multicultural society!" And: "The rising numbers of foreigners are threatening the existence of Germans!" These were Volker's sentiments exactly, and he knew how to boost the cause.

On the night of October 3, 1991, Volker and two like-minded cronies, Jens G. and André C., both eighteen, were drinking heavily at a party given by a friend. Later, the police picked up FAP literature in Jens's room. André's father was known to celebrate Hitler's birthday regularly.

The boys found their party boring, so toward midnight the three-some drove to Volker's home and, in the garage, prepared Molotov cocktails. Volker later told the police that he might have been inspired by a well-known recent arson against foreigners in Hoyerswerda. In court he said, "Suddenly the idea was there." His friend Jens agreed: "It all ran automatically."

They knew just what to do. Without speaking, they filled three bottles with motorcycle fuel, placed parts of a flammable rag in the neck of each, and drove off in André's car to the obvious target, the home for asylum seekers on Dorstener Strasse.

Their recollections of what took place there were shrouded by either alcohol or guilt, probably both. Volker and Jens admitted that they heaved their missiles against the wall of the home, "thinking nothing" at the time. André claimed that he deliberately aimed his cocktail at a car. They drove away without turning on their lights.

The Juvenile Court of Duisburg was already in session on April 28 of the following year when the mother pulled her fiercely resisting ten-year-old daughter to the front of the defendants' bench, pulled off the girl's sweater, and spit on the floor. From behind, the father shouted, "They must see what they did to my children!"

The presiding judge, though clearly revolted by the acts of the defendants, nonetheless warned the child's father that any further outburst would result in the entire family's removal from the court-room. But everyone there had caught a glimpse of the girl's upper arms, which her mother had exposed to the three defendants, who seemed completely unmoved: both the girl's arms were covered with horribly mutilating scars. Her injuries, which had been life-threaten-ing, had required repeated surgery.

The victims of the three neo-Nazis, their anonymous and arbi-trary targets in the dark, were the Saado family: Faozi, Zeibeide, and their six children, Lebanese refugees long resident in Germany. The parents and four of the children escaped injury. Zeinab was the daughter badly hurt; her sister Mokadass sustained lesser burns.

For attempted murder, arson, and the associated offenses, the judge imposed prison sentences of five years on Volker and three and a half on his colleagues. He also made certain the defendants would remem-ber for life. They were ordered to pay the equivalent of $150,000 in compensation, as well as a lifetime pension of $240 a month to Zeinab.

Reactions to the verdict reflected a diversity of interests. The de-fense attorneys pronounced themselves pleased. The sentences were better than they had hoped for, they asserted. Hopefully, too, the convicted men would find work after their release from prison, so that at least "a fraction" of the awarded compensation would perhaps actually be paid.

Mr. Saado, on the other hand, was disgusted. "Money is only money," he said. "My daughter will be marked for life." Both of the injured girls were still waking up at night, he said, terrified, bathed in perspiration.

On behalf of the defendants, Martin Duscha, the evangelical pastor of Hünxe, who knew all three, was sad. The young men were not right-wing extremists, he said. They were only "misled" by the "information material" left behind by the Third Reich.


The locale of my next exhibit of justice at work, the pretty village of Dolgenbrodt — 270 souls, mostly farmers, fishermen, and retirees — slumbers on its narrow peninsula in the pine woods and lakes twenty-five miles southeast of Berlin, in what not long ago was Communist East Germany. It has no store, no post office, no local police. It does own a collective secret: a conspiracy of silence that speaks loudly about the Nazi notion of racial purity still poisoning German life and death.

Death, in this case barely avoided, could easily have been the fate of eighty-six African refugees who were to have been moved within hours into the abandoned children's vacation home at the Dolgen-brodt lakefront. The county authorities, anticipating trouble, had already instituted a guard service, placed bars over the windows, and surrounded the building with a barbed wire fence. "It looked like a concentration camp," recalled the mayor, with no irony intended.

The villagers had fiercely opposed the coming of the Africans. A citizen committee was formed. Angry letters were sent to the county chiefs in Königs Wusterhausen. Protest meetings were held. Finally, at a citizen assembly in the village inn on October 22, 1992, a spark flew that hinted of a violent solution to Dolgenbrodt's emergency. Someone — later nobody was able to recall who — suggested that the home be burned down.

It was. On the night of November 1, two Molotov cocktails were thrown across the fence. The guards were unaccountably not present. Of the fifteen Dolgenbrodt volunteer firemen, only five managed to pull themselves awake, arriving in time merely to prevent the fire from spreading to other buildings. This inefficiency is all the more surprising in that these same firemen, when they were part of East Germany, had won the "speed competition" — a multi-city race to see which fire brigade could respond most quickly to an emergency. The Dolgenbrodt brigade came in first, with a response time of just over four minutes. This time, however, the local firemen would clearly have finished last: the condemned homestead for the Africans burned to the ground while the fire sirens wailed. Hardly anyone seemed to have heard them. The fire burned its lonely way as if it had been a long-awaited and welcome guest. One old-timer, Willi Schulz, eventually appeared on the scene to hoist the old Reich War Flag in victory.

During the ensuing investigation, the silence of those interrogated was proverbially deafening. Several people said they had had a lot of beer, in order to sleep soundly that night. The innkeeper could not recall any of the talk that had swirled around in his bar only ten days before. He swore he hadn't even been in the room during the October 22 meeting when the fate of the home was sealed. Schulz's son said his father advised him not to go to the fire scene, because he might be called an arsonist. The rule of see no evil, hear no evil grew to include remember no evil.

Yet evil will out, especially about crimes organized and executed at the hands of amateurs who are moved by ideology. In May 1993, a nineteen-year-old skinhead, Silvio Jackowski from Königs Wusterhausen, was arrested after he bragged in a local bar that he and three skinhead friends had committed the arson. And in August, the leftist Berlin newspaper *taz* reported that the equivalent of $1,200 had been collected in the village to contract the job and that a "victory celebration" had been held in the inn afterward.

Judge Klaus Przybilla, who heard the case in Potsdam in June 1994, expressed himself extraordinarily frustrated. More than thirty witnesses were heard, but nobody said one incriminating word. Jackowski and his three friends acknowledged that they were happy the home had been torched, but denied the crime. Jackowski testified that he had merely been boasting, and he accused the other three. The girlfriends of that trio all testified that the men had spent the night of the fire with them. And that was that.

Jackowski was convicted and sentenced to four weeks in prison for driving without a license and carrying a weapon, but was released because he had already served more than a month while awaiting trial.

Judge Przybilla, visibly angry, found fault with the superficiality of the pretrial investigation. He said that an arson expert should have been consulted, and ordered the prosecutors to review their efforts. His strongest censure, however, was directed at the villagers, whom he accused of acting as a cohesive force. While he felt compelled to exonerate Jackowski of arson on the basis of reasonable doubt, he placed the townspeople in another category.

"This chamber is not in a position to acquit the village itself of complicity," he said. "The climate for the arson was created there. Only the enforcer was lacking." Complaining that "the court has run into a wall of silence," he found "the deep sleep of the Dolgenbrodters on the night of the fire" particularly "surprising."

The *taz* headline read, "No Acquittal for Dolgenbrodt," and media attention was strong, so the case could not be shelved. Though the wheels of justice did grind slowly, the facts are finally coming out. In April 1997, several other people were accused of the crime. One, Pierre S., aged twenty-three, was accused of committing perjury during the original 1994 trial, for not disclosing that he knew Silvio Jackowski was one of the arsonists and that the local florist, Thomas O., had paid him. Pierre S. was put on probation for three years and ordered to pay a fine of 4,500 marks. In 1999, Silvio Jackowski was given a two-year probation for his part in the Dolgenbrodt arson. But through the new trial the facts began to emerge.

On the night of the fire, Silvio and a man known in court records as Marko S. had entered the town meeting and accidentally heard mention of the possibility of burning down the future asylum seekers' home. Later that night, the two young men, Silvio and Marko, heard from the latter's stepfather that there were people willing to pay for the arson. Thomas O., who lives near the site of the arson, had apparently collected money to pay for the crime, and he too is now under arrest.

In the early hours of the morning following the arson, Pierre S. and Silvio Jackowski returned to the site of the fire, where, after bantering with the members of the press who had come to cover the story, they went to pick up the promised money from Thomas O., who had collected a total of 12,000 marks,[1] 2,000 of which was to be

---

[1]Roughly $7,650 at the time.

an award for the deed and 10,000 hush money. In court, Silvio claimed that all he did was take the money from Thomas O., while the fire was lit by twenty-seven-year-old neo-Nazi Renato P., who is also now under arrest. Thomas O. and three other men, whose names remain as yet undisclosed, are still due to be tried for having collected the money.

In these later trials, another interesting fact came to light. In the early 1990s, a real estate firm had shown interest in the land where the children's vacation home stood. The firm had approached Ute Preissler, who was then mayor of Dolgenbrodt, for a possible deal, and serious negotiations ensued. A secretary of the real estate firm testified that a couple of hours before the arson, Mayor Preissler had called the firm's boss and begged him to do something: "*They* want to move in there now!" she is claimed to have said, clearly meaning the dreaded Africans. Already back in November 1992, the mayor had been the subject of a major scandal when she reacted to the arson by saying, "No one here was sad about this solution."


On July 23, 1994, a hot summer day, twenty-three skinheads from Erfurt, between the ages of sixteen and twenty-four, had wanted to take a bus to a skinhead concert (oi music) in Thuringia. But the concert was cancelled. Since the bus (which was rented) had cost money, they decided to go on a tour of the region. They ransacked the bus and urinated around gas stations where they stopped, already drunk, in the morning. One tore the moneybox from the hands of a Turkish flower-seller, spilling his earnings all over the floor. At noon they stopped for a couple of hours at Hohenwarte-Stausee, where one of the skinheads grabbed a parasol from a bar and jumped off a wall into the lake with it. Others damaged a boat. Another started a fight with a twenty-year-old Austrian who would not give him a cigarette, not even for money. "Not for you," the Austrian had said. The skinhead punched him in the face and lifted five cigarettes from the pack.

It was four in the afternoon when a member of the group mentioned that someone was throwing a party at Weimar that evening, so the name Buchenwald came up (the former concentration camp is not far from Weimar). Some wanted to go there to pass the time up to the party, others were indifferent, others still were asleep (as they testified in the ensuing trial). Those who wanted to go prevailed, and the bus driver was ordered to take them to Buchenwald. Doubtless, given the nature and actions of his passengers, the driver should probably have refused, but he decided to follow orders.

Thus it was that late that afternoon around seventeen young right-wing extremists (the other six remained on the bus, later claiming they "were asleep") ranged over the wide field of the camp committing various acts of violence and vandalism. A woman working at the camp called the police, who responded, arresting three of the seventeen. As they were being taken away one of them shouted to the lady who had called the police, "I'll burn you myself!"

Within a couple of days all the others who had visited and desecrated the camp were arrested, but they were soon released, except for the man who had stolen the cigarettes. He was sentenced to twenty months in jail because he had a record of previous arrests. When news spread of the vandalism at Buchenwald, the Israeli ambassador in Bonn went to visit the camp, and Ignaz Bubis, chairman of the Central Council of Jews, was furious. "I would lock them up until they come to their senses," he said.


The recent history of the city of Lübeck is notable for a series of disturbing neo-Nazi events. On March 25, 1994, four young neo-Nazis set fire to the Lübeck synagogue. They were tried and found guilty by the court in Schleswig. It was the first attack on a Jewish house of God in Germany since *Kristallnacht* in 1938. That year, the Lübeck synagogue had not been burned down because it was near the "German-Aryan" museum of Saint Anne, the Nazis limiting themselves to destroying cult objects inside it. In 1995, the same synagogue was again set on fire to mark the fiftieth anniversary of the fall of the Third Reich. As in the 1994 case, the neo-Nazis were tried and found guilty.

A year later, again in Lübeck, a home for asylum seekers was set on fire, on January 18, 1996, killing ten people and injuring thirty-eight. Four young neo-Nazis from Grevesmühlen were arrested at the time, but were quickly released when a former resident of the home, Safwan Eid, a twenty-year-old Lebanese, was arrested because he had allegedly told first-aid attendant Jens Leonhardt, "Wir warns" — "It was we [who did it]." At the time, Safwan, a recent arrival, had but a rudimentary grasp of the language: he had taken only six months of German lessons. During his trial, which began in September 1996, when asked to say and write what he had told Mr. Leonhardt on the night of the arson, he said and wrote, "dir waren das": he confused the word *dir* — "you," with *wir* — "we," and *die* — "they." Furthermore, according to the files, Safwan had reported to his friends and neighbors that people from outside the house had set fire to it — this prior to his conversation with Jens Leonhardt, who was the principal witness for the prosecution. There is also a dispute regarding the exact location of the start of the fire, as Mr. Leonhardt gave inconsistent versions of what Safwan had said on the matter. Finally, it is hard to believe that Safwan, who lived in the home with his family, would set fire to it unless he had suicidal as well as homicidal intentions.

The four young neo-Nazis from Grevesmühlen had no alibi for the night of the arson and were found, during a medical examination following their arrest, to have scorched hair, eyebrows, and eyelashes of very recent origin. These young men already had extensive criminal records for violence and theft, and one of them is currently charged with the desecration of Jewish graves. On April 8, 1998, one of the original suspects, Maik Wotenow, confessed to the crime and claimed that the other three suspects were jointly responsible. Three days later, Wotenow retracted his confession.

Finally, in another disturbing display of Lübeck's political leanings, on March 14, 1998, three hundred uniformed Nazis marched through the St. Lorenz Nord section in Lübeck carrying black, white, and red flags.[2]

On February 13, 1999, in the early hours of the morning, a fight broke out in front of a disco in Guben, a former East German town near the Polish border, where a group of locals attacked the guests of

---

[2]Swastika flags being illegal, right-wingers have adopted a relic, the battle flag of World War I, featuring the Prussian eagle at the center and a picture of an iron cross on the upper left.

the club, most of whom were foreigners. During the brawl, a black man took out a machete and slightly injured one of their group. Ten to fifteen young people, among them skinheads, set out in a car to find the man and take revenge. At a gas station they came across three foreigners, two Algerians and an asylum seeker from Sierra Leone. The two Algerians ran off in opposite directions, the man from Sierra Leone following one of the two, whose name was Omar Ben Noui. Less than half a mile from the gas station, Ben Noui and the man from Sierra Leone broke into a house, seeking safety. However, in smashing through the glass door, Ben Noui injured himself so badly that he bled to death. The neo-Nazis drove away. Shortly thereafter, eleven neo-Nazis between the ages of seventeen and twenty were accused of negligent homicide, dangerous bodily harm, disturbing the peace, and sedition.

Again in the city of Guben, on March 21, 2000, six men and two women between the ages of sixteen and twenty were accused of vandalizing a Jewish cemetery during the night of March 19. A chapel, several graves, and the cemetery walls were damaged and sprayed with anti-Semitic propaganda and swastikas.


On May 29, 1993, the house of a Turkish family was set on fire in the town of Solingen. Five Turkish women and girls died. It took two years for the crime to come to trial, but in 1995 four neo-Nazis between the ages of twenty and twenty-five were tried for the murder of the five people and the attempted murder of fourteen others who were in the house at the time. They were sentenced to ten to fifteen years in jail. Bekir Genc, aged twenty-two, who was very badly burned, received 250,000 marks (almost $174,000 at that time) compensation for pain and suffering as well as a monthly pension of 360 marks (then about $250). Genc has already undergone twenty-two operations, as one-third of his skin was burned and his head severely damaged. Ahmet Ince, whose wife died in the fire, was awarded 8,000 marks (then roughly $5,500) and his injured daughter 10,000 (about $7,000). Altogether the offenders will be paying a quarter of a million marks in restitution as well as providing for the reconstruction of the damaged house.

One of the jailed neo-Nazis, Christian Reher, aged twenty-three, was sentenced to ten years in prison. From jail he has been writing to Ursula Müller,[3] leader of the Hilforganisation für Nationale Politische Gefangene und deren Angehörige (HNG) — the Aid Society for National Political Prisoners and Their Kin — complaining that the prison authorities had refused to provide him with information material on the NPD and failed to forward his application for admission to the party.

It is to be noted that most of the crimes described in this chapter were committed in the former East Germany, where after World War II all right-wing movements were forbidden and thus forced to go underground. This had the effect of preserving the most extreme and radicalizing the more moderate right. In West Germany, the right was demonized only for the first fifteen years after the war, after which the debate regarding it was reopened and the Christlich Demokratische Union (CDU) — Christian Democratic Union — successfully managed to integrate the more moderate right into the party.

Nevertheless, in the last five years a rise in Nazi-related crimes has been recorded in western Germany, indicating that right-wing extremism is extending its boundaries. In August 2000, alarmed by an expanding wave of anti-immigrant and anti-Semitic violence, Germany's foreign minister, Joschka Fischer, warned his country that right-wing extremism must not be underestimated, as this was precisely the mistake made in the 1930s. Fischer went on to say that a majority of the population seems to remain silent in the face of the increasing violence but that they must learn to speak out. Chancellor Gerhard Schröder also declared forcefully that radical right-wing tendencies must be fought with all means — the police, the justice system, and also with the cooperation of the entire population — and in August 2000 he made a personal visit to a number of cities in eastern Germany to confront the problem personally.

The defendants in all the cases mentioned above, Deckert aside, were young men and women. Their crimes were violent, their

---

[3]More on Ursula Müller and her husband, Curt, in chapter 5.

organization impulsive and weak. Generally speaking, these young German neo-Nazis have no real knowledge of National Socialist ideology, and the motives behind their violent acts are unclear even to themselves. Their knowledge of contemporary revisionist theories — those of David Irving, Nolte, et al. — also appears to be minimal. In most of these eight widely different cases and trials, the only true inspiration one can pinpoint is Adolf Hitler himself.

For Judge Rainer Orlet the slap-on-the-wrist verdict against the Führer in the case of the historic Beer Hall Putsch lived on as an admirable judicial model, waiting to be perpetuated in the Deckert nonverdict.

For the baseball-bat murderers of Kemnat, Hitler personally issued their marching orders through his recorded harangues.

For the gang at Hünxe, Hitler's speeches allowed, if not ordered, arson.

For the villagers of Dolgenbrodt as well as the young men and women from Kemnat, Hünxe, Grevesmühlen, Guben, and Solingen — plus the Buchenwald desecration — Hitler's race laws remained in force.

Judge Orlet's orientation clearly placed him within a minority of his colleagues on the bench, but how large was it? Even the angriest commentators on his ruling in the Deckert case carefully refrained from asking how many judges like Orlet were still on the bench.


At first I found these proceedings puzzling. How could these defendants — and Judge Orlet — be reconciled with my young friends, the New Democrats?

But then, all societies are infected by criminal elements. Only the ideological undertow was directly German: Hitler as a seemingly timeless motivator and Nolte as his intellectual renewal. How pervasive were they?

# 4

## HOT TICKET: UP THE FÜHRER'S

## MOUNTAIN

Feeling the need for a change of pace, I decided to investigate a cheerier scene. Berchtesgaden, in Hitler's starkly lovely vacation country, seemed promising. Indeed, the famous mountain resort proved a lighthearted romp, starting with a happy cry thundering across the parking lot for the "Eagle's Nest":

"We need a Führer!"

The shout came from a crowd of tanned tourists milling about, momentarily lost, trying to find the right bus in the confusion of the jammed parking area.

The response to the shouter's joke was mixed. Some of his fellow travelers burst out laughing. Some chuckled knowingly. Some looked startled, pained, slightly embarrassed. Obviously, the Führer was a delicate subject to them. He was the reason they were assembled at the starting point of the one-way private road winding precipitously up the mountain, sometimes at a 27-degree grade, to 6,017 feet.

They were among the 300,000 pilgrims a year, the majority of whom are German or Austrian, who pay roughly $12 each for a ticket to Hitler's Eagle's Nest. During the five-month snow-free season, the road is open to his Shangri-la in the Bavarian Alps at Berchtesgaden (population 8,000), the sunny tourist mecca 150 kilometers southeast of Munich.

It is, to my surprise, a jovial scene, this show of remarkable engineering, ruins, and remembrance. The air resounds with laughter, bonhomie, and, yes, approval.

29

The tourists who are lost on the parking lot need a Führer all right. But why, really? Again, answers vary. Many decide to go up that mountain simply because, like Sir Edmund Hilary's Mount Everest, it is there — a singular attraction, a curiosity waiting to be explored. They are like the poker-faced American and British couples on our guided tour by minibus. Or are they? On Hitler's mountain, the Obersalzberg, there is no way to be certain about motives. No marketing surveys exist, which is just as well, because the truth would doubtless not come out. Most people with $12 to spend for a ticket to guzzle beer in a mountaintop restaurant are smooth enough to act politically correct.

Hitler, as everyone knows, is incorrect, at least overtly, in much of society. This also brings out nervous ambivalence in the authorities of the Berchtesgaden tourist office. The unmentionable Führer is of course their star. He is also their migraine. They prize him but cannot officially admit it. Tantalizingly, here more than anywhere, he is the big man who wasn't there, producing nothing but cash and trouble.

Just a couple of weekends before my wife and I briefly joined the Hitler fans to reconnoiter the Eagle's Nest for ourselves, an ideological alarm had jolted the tourist people. On the mountain and at stands all over Berchtesgaden, a profusion of Hitler trinkets, color postcards, brochures, and souvenir books in several languages had always been hawked for up to $40.

They depicted the Führer as jovial host to prime ministers, generals, the Duke of Windsor and his new wife, Wallis Simpson, and such favorite dictators as Mussolini. Here he was paterfamilias to enthralled blond children and playmate to his beloved Alsatian, Blondi, and, naturally, to his "Tschapperl," the humble mistress Eva Braun, who had to scurry into hiding whenever outsiders approached. (She was so intimidated — as she confessed to Albert Speer — that she was afraid of running into the Hermann Görings in the corridor.)

One souvenir booklet was called "Obersalzberg and the Third Reich." By 1994, finally, some members of the media had come to criticize the profiteering from "brown tourism," and one journalist/watchman had spied illegality within, literally, a dot on the cover title: a minuscule swastika that had previously eluded everyone. The display of swastikas being illegal under German law, the tourism authorities hustled the offending tract off the shelves, at least those under their control on the mountain.

The "brown tourists" had no occasion to notice. Piles of other Hitler propaganda remained stacked up: "Adolf Hitler and Eva Braun on the Obersalzberg," "The Eagle's Nest from Adolf Hitler to the Present Day," and many more to satiate the appetite of the junketeers for the Führer and his greatness.

"They're interested but don't dare admit it," said our guide, the personable American-born David Harper. That is, they won't admit it to guides or inquiring researchers. We found an inside source, however, an elderly caretaker whose years of eavesdropping on the beer drinkers had told him a different story:

"I hear a lot of comments about what a great man he was and 'How wonderful he built this!' Especially from Austrians."

The full meaning of Hitler's alpine stronghold may be felt but remains invisible to tourists, brown or otherwise. It is the message of power then and power now, and this helps to explain why the legend lingers.

The breathtaking views from the summit, the feat of access through sheer rock via a 400-foot brass-lined elevator for forty people and accessible only through a 400-foot marble tunnel spacious enough for Hitler to drive through — the sum total suggests conquest of unconquerable forces, victory for a king of the world, precisely as the showman Hitler saw himself in the mirror and as gullible rubberneckers still perceive him. So as they ascend his mountain, they happily look up for him — sometimes at the summit, majestically above the clouds.

The Berchtesgaden countryside, with its towering, craggy mountain ranges, appealed to the thirty-two-year-old Hitler from the moment in late 1922 when he was introduced to its grandeur by his mentor, Dietrich Eckart. A pamphleteer, poet, and translator in Munich, Eckart was on the lam from the police there and roomed in a small pension as "Dr. Hoffmann." An intemperate drunk and a cocaine addict, he would die of alcoholism in Berchtesgaden within the year. Though he was never a household name anywhere, his influence was enormous as godfather to Hitler and midwife to the still embryonic

Nazi movement. Hitler looked up to Eckart as he did to no one else, and made him editor of the party battle sheet, the *Völkische Beobachter*. In years to come, the Führer's eye would moisten whenever the master's name came up.

In Munich, Eckart had shown Hitler how to be less of a provincial bumpkin, taught him how to converse in polite society, introduced him to notables and sources of money. In the bracing climate of Berchtesgaden, where Hitler became known as "Herr Wolf," the two conspirators walked and talked during that winter of 1922–23, planning the future of the world; how to conquer it and wipe out their enemies, especially the Jews. Eckart said he would cage them into boxcars and dump them in the Red Sea. Together, the pair decided to adopt the swastika as their emblem.

In 1923, Berchtesgaden became the playground of their cronies, those very first settlers of what would become the *Altkämpfer,* the old fighters with their Bavarian accents: the ever-amusing "Putzi" Hanfstaengl[1]; the officious, one-armed Max Amann, who ran the business affairs; and all the rest who made Hitler feel so at home. The beer flowed at the Dreimädlerhaus, pretty blondes smiled, and as an enemy of the state Hitler valued the security of the border location. Surrounded on three sides by the independent republic of his native Austria, Berchtesgaden made a getaway easy.

It was a watershed year for the Nazis, 1923. With Bavarian politics in rioting disarray and the German economy pounded by runaway inflation, Hitler decided to attempt his first play for government: the Beer Hall Putsch. Heinrich Himmler marched with him to the Feldherrnhalle in Munich, and so did Rudolf Hess and Hermann Göring. Eckart, already too close to death to march, had to watch from the sidelines. The police opened fire, twelve Nazis fell dead, and Hitler crawled off with a dislocated shoulder and served eight months in Landsberg prison.

It was a country club life. Hitler was served breakfast in bed, dreamed his dreams of power, and posed imperiously for photos.

---

[1]Harvard educated Ernst Hanfstaengl was a man of two countries, his father from Munich and his mother American. Splitting with Hitler in 1937, he wrote a book: *Hitler: The Missing Years.*

Refusing to join the other prisoners in exercises, he began to dictate *Mein Kampf* into the typewriter of his cellmate Rudolf Hess. It was this trusted deputy who anointed Hitler with the title of Führer at that time, and by November 1924 Hitler was back in his beloved escape hatch, Berchtesgaden.

He lived at the Pension Moritz, then in the Hotel Deutsches Haus, and in 1928 rented and eventually bought a wealthy north German businessman's comfortable vacation home in the hills, 3,281 feet high, Haus Wachenfeld. It would become his island of seclusion, a place where he sometimes spent weeks preparing his speeches for party congresses in Nuremberg. He always referred to the place, forbiddingly, as the "mountain." It would become his celebrated home, officially known as Berghof, the nucleus of what blossomed into a giant Hitler compound in the 1930s.

The Berghof name was phony, deliberately deprecatory, for propaganda reasons. Normally, this term described a snug mountain farm. The Führer's roost had been nothing of the kind to start with, although when Albert Speer, his friend and architect, was first admitted for a visit in 1933, he was struck by its petit-bourgeois ambiance. A canary chirped in a cage. Pillows and knickknacks were adorned with swastikas.

The humility ceased in the summer of 1935 as Hitler took sketchbook and even drafting tools in hand to design the first of numerous enlargements to his property. A floor was added. So were several extensions and outbuildings. A Gothic marble hall arose and became the lobby for a large conference room. Even the trusted Speer was banished to an upper floor when the Führer turned architect.

In the meantime, the whole area's expansion had turned explosive. Hitler was a mighty magnet. Göring built a spread with a (then very rare) swimming pool. Joseph Goebbels constructed a chalet, as did Hitler's right-hand man Martin Bormann. Speer put up an elegant "studio" at a choice spot. A hotel was added, guardhouses, a theater, SS barracks, homes for the service personnel, garages, and more and more until an almost unbelievable half a billion Reichsmarks had been sunk into the compound.

Hitler was ambivalent about his impact on this rustic environment. He basked in the attention, yet he disliked seeing nature disrupted on such a scale. After his election as chancellor in 1933, seemingly unending streams of delegations began to visit the mountain. These official (and loyal) sightseers, thousands almost daily, many of them women and children, lined up hoping for a glimpse of him. He did not want to turn them away; he also did not wish to be constantly on display, compelled to smile at strangers.

His turf became a showcase, and in 1939, when he was at the pinnacle of power and shortly before he ignited World War II, Hitler's vacillation between pomp and environmental piety was put to a heroic test. Pomp won.

The occasion was the Führer's fiftieth birthday on April 20. With his acolytes throwing all restraint to the wind in their eagerness to demonstrate allegiance, Martin Bormann, arguably the world's most ambitious secretary, came up with the most elaborate and expensive birthday present in history. He hustled up the required 34 million Reichsmarks from industrialist well-wishers and sent 3,000 workers into the sheer rock to crown the Shangri-la with the Eagle's Nest, its breakneck road, the shiny brass elevator, and the other amenities so admired by tourists today.

"It's like a gold miners' town," said wits at the Führer's court. "Only Bormann doesn't find any — he throws it away." The fantastic costs didn't trouble Hitler. "That's Bormann's business," he told Speer. "I don't want to interfere."

Today's visitors generally are convinced that they are touring Hitler's home. Actually, he did not spend very much time there. He said his heart couldn't tolerate the altitude and the entrance tunnel made him claustrophobic. The catchphrase "Eagle's Nest" was promoted by the PR-conscious U.S. military after the war. In Hitler's time, it was the peaceable "Tea House" where Bormann liked to impress visiting foreign diplomats and Eva Braun was permitted to entertain girlfriends out of sight.

Hitler did enjoy the ritual of taking tea and cake there in the afternoon, surrounded by Eva Braun and an entourage of about twenty. Lapsing into his repetitive monologues, he sometimes droned himself to sleep until 6 P.M. The others talked in whispers, hoping he would awake in time for dinner.

These days tourists are far from bored. The Tea House views could not be more spectacular, the beer is excellent, and the pilgrims are crazy about their commanding perch. Our guide, however, had been oblivious to all this history and its ramifications when, in the mid-1980s, he pursued a German girlfriend, followed her to her native Berchtesgaden, and became the modern version of *The Man Who Came to Dinner.*

First, the U.S. Army hired him to guide GIs around the Eagle's Nest and handed him 400 words of local history to parrot on the bus. Next, the Berchtesgaden tourist people retained him to serve their audience, so he expanded his script and parroted 800 words for English-speaking sightseers. Finally, he incorporated himself, along with his new American wife, Christine, who is from Montana, as "Berchtesgaden Mini Bus Tours" and crammed to make himself a walking encyclopedia of his beat. Who else would know that Hitler used to arrive at Berchtesgaden in a red private train named *Amerika?*

David Harper's sympathies are beyond question. One of his aunts was involved in Allied espionage and was shot in Dachau. But he is a businessman and, as such, discreet and caring about his international clientele and their affinity for his popular sponsor, Adolf Hitler.

"It's a powerful marketing tool," he says, yet his flyer, "Eagle's Nest Historical Tour," merely mentions a "former residence" to be toured. The resident remains anonymous. Hitler's name is nowhere in his printed material. In his spiel on the bus, the Führer may, by instructions from the tourist office bosses, be mentioned no more than twice.

Harper also still works for the tourist office and has learned to step nimbly around German sensibilities. "German tourists feel uncomfortable," he observes, tactfully ignoring the many that we had heard about who feel comfortable indeed. Says Harper: "They haven't gotten over feeling they're responsible for *him.*"


Hitler's memory is still nurtured around Berchtesgaden primarily because the demand for his ghost is a money-maker. Things almost didn't work out that way. For years, the survival of the relic assets hung in the balance. Twice they were doomed, only to be reprieved.

The process of abortive obliteration commenced four days before Hitler's suicide. On April 25, 318 Royal Air Force Lancaster bombers rained 1,232 tons of bombs on the area. The war was all but over. The raid, planned since the previous fall, was something of an after-thought designed to kill off a possible rallying point for resistance by Nazi "werewolves" from a "redoubt" that never existed.

The bombing results were curious. Preparations had been rigor-ous. The "target information sheet," dated October 5, 1944, was remarkably informative in its detail of "Target A," the Eagle's Nest, and "Target B," Wachenfeld, the Führer's "Berghof." Damage was extensive. Hitler's home suffered three direct hits, and part of the main building went up in smoke. One SS barrack was wrecked by a direct hit. Yet "Target A," the Eagle's Nest, escaped unscathed, as if by divine command.

With victory in hand, the U.S. military preserved the remains as a symbol of Nazi defeat. Cheering GIs posed in front of the Berghof's ruins. General Eisenhower posed in the tea room of the Eagle's Nest, hands clasped behind his back, and added his name to the surface of the round conference table where visitors recorded their names for posterity.

In 1952, the "end" recurred. At American instigation, sappers were assigned by the Bavarian state government to blow up all the remain-ing evidence of Hitler's personal Reich. The "death sentence" was actually signed — but again, the Eagle's Nest survived by a last-minute reprieve. The regional governor intervened with the highest authori-ties. Times were still hard, the sightseers and the restaurant were excellent sources of income. Why blow up a calf that gave so much milk? Eventually, ownership was transferred to a local trust, the income assigned to unnamed local charities.

Besides the Eagle's Nest and its charmed life, not much of Hitler is left to be seen. Directional signs chastely point only to "Kehlstein," the mountain in the immediate vicinity. The old Platterhof Hotel, saved for a U.S. Army recreation center, survives as the "Hotel Gen-eral Walker." Of the sainted Berghof, only the wrecked garage remains, graced by the graffiti (in German) "Hitler Lives in our . . ." and completed by drawings of two hearts.

In respectable surroundings around the country, the preservation of the memory is deplored these days. "On the Obersalzberg, the Third Reich Is Glorified," scolded a headline in the travel section of the newspaper *Welt am Sonntag* in the mid–1990s. In critical language, the article describes the Hitler literature being huckstered and continues, "Not a word about war crimes and holocaust; instead, elegies for the so-called 'true' Hitler."

# 5

## A DAY TO REMEMBER HITLER

Hitler was my bogeyman when I was small, too close for comfort, his hysterical voice screeching out of every radio. I confess, however, that every April 20 lightened my view of this palpably villainous character. The occasion was *Führergeburtstag,* the Führer's birthday, and I had the day off from school. Jews were not asked to attend the parades and assemblies, so it was a liberation, a play day, almost enough to wish Hitler happy birthday.

For some Germans, the day remains a traditional, even revered, occasion, and on April 20, 1994, some two hundred were assembled for the event, belting out the song that I recalled my schoolmates singing about Jewish blood spurting from their knives. That year the scene was "Valhalla," the barn of Curt and Ursula Müller, nursery owners in suburban Mainz-Gonsenheim, near Frankfurt. Both are longtime right-wing leaders of prominence.

It was hard to believe, this déjà vu of spurting Jewish blood, but I had secured an inside source about the Müllers and it was reliable. My informant was Inger P., then twenty-two, a recent defector from the neo-Nazi ranks, which she had joined at the tender age of twelve. With her delicate figure, high cheekbones, satin skin, full lips, and black hair flowing far below her shoulders, Inger looked positively angelic, a youthful Madonna.

On *Führergeburtstag* in 1993, this adult child had stood vigil by the table in the Müllers' Valhalla, where the partygoers were being registered. Eager to measure up to her boyfriend's expectations, she mustered her briskest command tone to shout, "Next!" I had learned this much from the ten-page story of her hectic life, assembled by Otter

38

Jenner, an editor for the magazine *Tempo*. Jenner arranged for me to talk to Inger in greater detail about the celebration from which outsiders were banned by a wall reinforced with barbed wire. The barrier surrounds the Müller property and is patrolled by a "security service" whose identities are disguised by ski masks.

Within this bizarre oasis from another age, "Sieg Heil" and "Heil Hitler!" were the proper greeting; the "Horst Wessellied" and other Nazi marches, though forbidden by law, were rendered routinely and with gusto; the oratory exalted the Führer and the erstwhile triumphs of his Reich; forbidden swastika stickers and other Nazi paraphernalia were for sale in quantity; and the outlook for the future was upbeat, although legal reprisals were on the rise.

Valhalla, the Müllers' shrine to Hitler, had burned down in 1984 — according to gossip it was arson committed by rival right-wingers. In those earlier days, the barn had been awash with pictures of Hitler. These days, the walls of the rebuilt barn were bare except for a Reich War Flag. Since Hitler T-shirts were prohibited, quite a few celebrants wore shirts bearing a picture of his deputy, Rudolf Hess, and the legend "Martyr for Germany."

Speeches not being subject to restrictions, Müller extolled Hitler for about an hour as the greatest leader of all time, which made the audience restless, even though the message was what these zealots had come to hear. "My party has been forbidden since 1945," Müller called out, "but we will bring it back again."

The most welcome speaker was another regular, Otto Riehs, a veteran without title or overt competence, except that he was said to have earned the Knight's Cross in World War II. Year after year, the crowd lionized Riehs because he was at least in his seventies or older — nobody could be certain. He was a star without peer, because he could glow with firsthand memories of the Third Reich. He had been there.

And so Adolf Hitler still marched along in spirit at the Müllers,' as the lyrics of the "Horst Wessellied" phrased it, and in an alcove of the bar in the living room of their private home — which only selected birthday guests were allowed to enter — where a shrine to the Führer was maintained. His picture was on the wall, along with the slogan "The chosen people of Satan killed Jesus Christ, Martin Luther, and

Adolf Hitler." In case anyone might wonder who Satan's people are, Müller once explained to Craig R. Whitney of the *New York Times,* "We believe America is the long arm of world Jewry; Germany has become the crown colony of Judas."

Müller, who was then sixty-four, wore a brown toupee and formidable metal-framed glasses. He ran the birthday party like an excitable field marshal — issuing commands loudly and brooking no violations of his house rules. When a skin band struck up their rock tunes, Inger watched Müller stop the music and bark reprimands. He wanted only traditional accompaniments for his Führer's annual day of honor.

As anticipated, some 2,000 left-wing opponents marched up for a protest counter-"demo," and a skirmish ensued under another Reich War Flag, this one fluttering in the breeze. Müller's security men, some armed with truncheons and baseball bats, summoned reinforcements over their walkie-talkies. From Valhalla everyone came running and shouting, "Reds die!" Nearly all were fit-looking males between seventeen and thirty-five. At the wall, they fired flares and heaved rocks. But the police stepped in, so the engagement was brief and bloodless.

Long tables had been set up in the barn and impressive quantities of hot dogs and beer were consumed. Further songfests of "traditional" marches and folk tunes heated up the atmosphere, until, around 3 A.M., the last celebrants staggered, thoroughly tipsy, into the attic and the sleeping bags everyone had brought along.

The host's wife busied herself with housekeeping details and appeared to be under Herr Müller's thumb in a way that their guests, being German traditionalists, could be expected to approve. In the couple's home, out of sight of the crowd, Inger observed a different relationship: Ursula Müller came across as an authoritarian in her own right.

Inger was not surprised, because she also knew Frau Müller in her other incarnation: director of the HNG, which regards itself as "ultra-militant." *Kamaradin* Müller, known as the mother of the movement, collects money for jailed neo-Nazis and finds them jobs when they are freed. At the dawn of the new millennium, Ursula, sixty-six, still leads the HNG. The organization has a Web site that denounces the violation, in Germany, of one of the fundamental human rights (the right to a different opinion) and describes contemporary neo-Nazi crimes from a completely different perspective from that of the German press.

Herr Müller had been arrested a few times since he became politically active in the early 1970s, and his wife had once been fined for neo-Nazi activities, but largely the pair had been left free to pursue their accustomed political practices, including that outstanding annual event, the commemoration of Hitler's birth.

They had a long, rich history, these occasions, heavily weighed down by symbolism and remembered agony.

It was April 20, 1989, the hundredth anniversary of Hitler's birth, and Simon Wiesenthal, the oldest and fiercest of the Nazi hunters, was still shaken as he remembered how close to death he came on another Hitler birthday, the fifty-fourth, in 1943. Wiesenthal had been an inmate of the concentration camp at Janowska in Lvov, then in Poland and now in the Ukraine, doing slave labor as a sign painter in the nearby railroad yards of the *Ostbahn,* the Eastern Railway.

It was a glorious, sunny spring day — "Führer weather" — and Wiesenthal was rushing to finish painting banners for the big SS birthday celebration. Again and again, he kept painting "Wir lieben unseren Führer" ("We love our Führer"). It was routine duty, for the birthday was jubilantly celebrated as a national holiday every year. It was an occasion laden with emotion, the opportunity to offer homage to the beloved leader — thanksgiving to him as a person, not merely as a symbol.

His picture graced shop windows, framed in twig-and-flower garlands. Swastika flags fluttered from every loyal home. Ten thousand and more well-wishers paid their respects at night before the Chancellery. The afternoon parade in Berlin showed off the Wehrmacht's new weapons to a proud populace, and not so incidentally to the military observers from the foreign embassies. Hour after hour, the Führer beamed and saluted indulgently to acknowledge the tributes.

"He gets more and more like a Caesar," a disgusted young American news correspondent, William Shirer, had written prophetically in his diary for April 20, 1937.

Two years after Shirer's prescient diary entry, on April 20, 1939, Hitler's fiftieth birthday, he was being acclaimed a genius. His followers had much to be grateful for. Unemployment had vanished. Rearmament was steaming ahead. Austria had been annexed without a shot fired. "Peace for our time" had been proclaimed only shortly earlier by the appeasing British prime minister Neville Chamberlain at Munich, after Hitler marched unopposed into Czechoslovakia.

Six army divisions — 40,000 men and 600 tanks — now passed in review before him for four hours, and everyone marveled at his stamina.

According to Propaganda Minister Joseph Goebbels's diary, two million faithful roared "Heil Hitler!" to inaugurate the five-mile East-West Axis; it was the first stroke toward the new capital, Germania, which the Führer was planning with his proud architect, Albert Speer. "Jubilation without equal," wrote Goebbels. "Never were the people so happy and cheerful."

That night, the cream of Nazi society, 1,600 hand-picked leaders and their women, crowded the Mosaic Hall of the Chancellery to drink, preen, hear speeches, and be dazzled by the piles of gifts. "The number and value of this year's presents is quite staggering," wrote Hitler's secretary, Christa Schroeder, the following day. "Paintings by Defregger, Waldmuller, Lenbach, even a magnificent Titian, wonderful Meissen porcelain figurines, craftwork, globes, radios, clocks, etc. . . . Of course there are model ships and aircraft and other military paraphernalia, too — those are the things he's happiest about. He's just like a boy with them."

World War II was still almost half a year away.


On that same day four years later, in the Polish railroad yard where Simon Wiesenthal was furiously painting signs, his work was interrupted by two SS men. He and a group of fellow Jews were ordered to march to the sand pit at the Janowska concentration camp where executions took place.

Along the route, they passed by Wiesenthal's supervisor, *Oberinspektor* Adolf Kohlrautz. Wiesenthal had grown to like Kohlrautz. They had long, personal talks. But as the condemned men trudged by, Kohlrautz caught Wiesenthal's eye, lowered his head, and shrugged helplessly.

In his 1989 birthday reminiscences, Wiesenthal recorded, "Nobody had to say a word. We knew: the SS wanted to make the Führer a present of some dead Jews."

As the victims lined up before the pit, it began to rain. All had to disrobe. Their clothing had to be piled up neatly in waiting trucks. The pit was about one hundred-fifty feet long and still about six feet deep. Limbs were visible, because the last layer of corpses was only thinly covered with sand. The first row of condemned men was ordered to the rim. The first shots rang out. More shots. Petrified, resignedly awaiting his turn, Wiesenthal, deafened by the driving rain, did not immediately hear the shrill whistling and shouts of "Wie-sen-thal! Wie-sen-thal!"

He was told to put on his clothes. Only after he was taken to *Oberinspektor* Kohlrautz did he comprehend that something had miraculously saved him. Kohlrautz had called the camp command and complained. He needed Wiesenthal to finish painting the birthday banners!

"So in a way, the Führer's birthday is your birthday, too, Wiesenthal," said Kohlrautz.

After the war, Wiesenthal tried to locate his savior but learned that he had died in the final battle for Berlin. In his 1989 reminiscences, this hunter of Nazi war criminals noted that Kohlrautz was one of numerous decent Germans he encountered during the Holocaust; because of them he had always rejected the idea of a collective German national guilt for Hitler and his crimes.

Voices of compassion, voices of hate — Wiesenthal had dealt with both, and in his comments on Hitler's hundredth birthday in 1989 he noted sadly that talk of hatred was rising again, this time mostly against people who were like brothers to him, foreign asylum seekers with dark skin.

"One can hear it around the tables of perfectly civilized inns," he noted.

Wiesenthal recorded his experience in a book published by *Der Spiegel* magazine on the centennial of Hitler's birth. Other notables reminisced in the same volume; their observations were mostly angry or doleful.

Former chancellor Willy Brandt, bemoaning Hitler as an "immeasurably underestimated devil," told how he and his friends during their wartime exile in Sweden had laughed and laughed as they watched Charlie Chaplin playing "Hynkel" in *The Great Dictator* and eating a carpet. Brandt now saw Hitler not as a clown but as "a highly talented mental patient" who should have held sway not in a chancellery but in "a closed institution."

Lord Bullock, the author of *Hitler: A Study in Tyranny,* marveled at the unlikely development of Hitler's becoming a greater international preoccupation in recent times than he had been in the first twenty years after his suicide.

Henryk M. Broder, a German-Jewish historian, warned of the remark by the black American racist Louis Farrakhan that "The man fascinates me. In my youth I went to see all the Hitler films."

My friend Guido Knopp, the television impresario, could not resist rubbing it in that TV "in certain countries" loved showing images of swastikas, Hitler diaries, or, "best of all," Hitler himself: "the Wagnerian aspects of the Third Reich, my God, how it fascinates!"

The various publishers of the "revisionist" historians Joachim Fest, David Irving, and Werner Maser used the opportunity of the *Spiegel* volume to advertise their own Hitler biographies. And the John Jahr publishing enterprises, alert as always, purchased space to market five different recordings of Hitler oratory (*Hitler Speaks*) and two more records of proceedings from the Nuremberg war crimes trials, entitled *Not Guilty within the Meaning of the Indictment.*[1]

In the streets that year, the celebrations took a more active turn. In Bremen, thirteen were arrested during Hitler birthday riots, and about a hundred in Berlin, where thirteen policemen were injured.

---

[1] The exaltation of this occasion was still available as an audio and visual experience in the 1990s. For $50, the John Jahr enterprise in Hamburg was marketing a twenty-minute video as a "historical rarity" recording the event that had "impressed the world."

One of the officers was shot with a gas pistol when he trailed two men who were painting "SS," "SA," swastikas, and "Golden 100" onto house walls and shop windows in the Wedding district. In the Neukölln area, the baseball bats used by right-wingers to attack eight foreign workers were spiked with nails.

When five hundred left-wingers countered with a protest march, bottles and glasses flew from a third-floor window, and a woman in front of a pub told a reporter, "Someone should throw a bomb on that gang!"

Violence on April 20 had become such an ordinary occurrence every year that it was no longer noted in the statistics. Nor was it exclusively a big-city phenomenon.

The population in the farming hamlet of Jamel, to the north of Berlin in rural Mecklenburg province, numbered exactly forty-one. More than a week beforehand, large black lettering at the only bus stop announced: "April 20, 1992 — the Führer's birthday — Giant Party at Obsty's." Obsty was the nickname of the local *Obsthändler,* the fruit merchant.

The event commenced on April 19 when gangs of youthful skinheads arrived and piled up wood for a campfire. A Reich War Flag and an illegal swastika flag were hoisted. Bottles of schnapps circulated. Nazi songs reverberated around the village square.

On the great day, many more neo-Nazis arrived. Drunkenness spread. Rocks and bottles went flying. No foreign workers lived in Jamel, and for some reason the birthday celebrants surrounded the home of the Goscensky family. Mayor Fritz Kalf had gone there with a shotgun hidden under his coat to join the defense forces, which included two neighbors and policemen in three patrol cars. The skinheads threatened to storm the home. A shot was heard and one of the defenders clutched his bleeding head. Finally, more police arrived to lift the siege.

A reporter hiked to the manor house where the local leader of the right-wingers lived. The runic lettering of the "SS" greeted him from the garage wall. Underneath was scrawled, "We are the people." A man in an army cap came to the door and shouted the words often heard during the final battles of Hitler's war: "We're going to hold out to the last drop of blood!"

Such extremist diehards were few. Many Germans made fun of them, called them "the eternal yesterdays." But Hitler personally was durable and contemporary, loved and living on in the hearts of ordinary citizens who would never dream of throwing a rock or a bottle. He was almost a member of the family, so celebrations of his birthday were cozy, closeknit homestyle affairs, as evidenced by testimony from the Berlin residential districts:

*Tempelhof.* "We sat around in the garden until dawn telling ourselves stories of old times," said Lucie F., owner of a lot in the bungalow colony "Happiness." She had invited all her neighbors to a "joyful festival" for Hitler's birthday.

*Tiergarten.* "We got together in front of the old parliament building (Reichstag) and drank a few bottles of champagne," reported Detlef K., a driver for the Opel works.

*Schmargendorf.* "Jupp always used to give a speech about Hitler, but he died in January," mourned Milly F., seventy-eight, resident of a home for the aged. "So this time it was hard to work up the right mood. We put on old records and offered toasts with liqueur."

*Kreuzberg.* In the Pückler-Corner pub, Willem P. suddenly remembered around midnight: "Hey, it's April 20 — Hitler's birthday — I'll spring for a round!" Four others later bought rounds for everyone, while Erwin Y. told about his war experiences.

*Schöneberg.* A group of workers from the Osram electric factory got together in the home of Karl B. and reminisced about "the advantages of the Nazi time." Karl summarized later: "The workers were allowed in the opera, there weren't so many foreigners, and the world was giving us recognition."


As the 1990s moved along, politics was becoming an uncomfortable pursuit for the more fanatical old-timers like Curt Müller in Mainz-Gonsenheim. He had been a steadfast Nazi since 1944 when, at age fourteen, he narrowly escaped death in an American bombing raid on Mainz. By 1993, his convictions had left him with a hard burden. In twenty-eight years, the police had raided his nursery twenty-eight times in search of weapons and Nazi propaganda. More hurtfully, the bartender of the Dorfschänke restaurant, a few blocks away, had lately blocked the door to him and his wife, Ursula. Like most in his trade, this barkeep was an excellent barometer of neighborhood sentiment.

"You can't come in here," he told the couple. "If I let you in, all my other customers will boycott the place."

The Müllers had become pariahs on their own turf, and in 1994 the police finally moved in massively to close down the Hitler love-fests. The Müller property was cordoned off. Outsiders were not allowed to pass. The great Hitler birthday game appeared to be up for the folks in Gonsenheim, at least for the time being. For the country at large, however, and even for Great Britain, April 20 had not lost its fascination.

# BOOK 2

## FROM MY
## CASE HISTORY FILES

# 6

## REEDUCATION: THE VACCINE

## THAT DIDN'T TAKE

Billy Wilder received the news in the summer of 1945. "They made soap out of my mother," he remarked bitterly to a colleague of his and mine. We had recently arrived as victors in Germany, assigned to the Information Control Division of the U.S. Military Government. Formerly, the outfit had been known as Psychological Warfare Division, but peace had broken out and this sounded too aggressive. Our mission had also been renamed. It used to be called "propaganda"; now it was "reeducation."

That was the word of the year, reeducation, and in the 1990s the Germans were, understandably, still brooding and complaining about this effrontery. The plan was, in retrospect, preposterous. We were going to sit the Germans down in our laboratory, all 67 million of them, all brainwashed by Hitler, and inoculate them, from a bottle marked "Democracy" against a future Hitler. I played a footnote role in this well-intentioned but megalomanic enterprise; Billy Wilder was a star.

A refugee from Vienna and Berlin, Wilder, who was then only thirty-nine, had already made nineteen films in America. Celebrated as an entertainer, a cynic, and a funnyman, he was also a closet social critic, a disturber of the status quo. His 1939 champagne comedy *Ninotchka,* starring the soulful Greta Garbo and advertised with the tag line "Garbo laughs," was actually a lampoon of Stalinist Communism. His *Lost Weekend,* shown just before he left for Germany as the war ended, was a devastating exposé of alcoholism.

Reeducation was a very deliberate and personal mission to this secret reformer. He had volunteered for the work at $6,000 a year, something of a comedown from the then astronomical $2,500 a week he had been earning in Hollywood. Stubbornly determined to convert those crazy Krauts into civilized humans, he had been given the final push into this self-assignment by his mother's fate in Auschwitz.

Seemingly hard-bitten, Wilder was fervently sentimental about his adopted homeland. So, by no coincidence, had been his mother, Eugenia, known as Genia. The family hailed from Sucha, a village south of Kraków, where Oskar Schindler protected the Jews of *Schindler's List,* but Genia had fallen in love with exotic America during a visit there when she was a teenager (which explained Wilder's first name, originally spelled Billie).

When he last visited her in Vienna not long before Hitler decided upon the Austrian *Anschluss,* the famous son had tried to persuade his mother to come to the United States. It was too late. Genia, like many elderly Jews, could not bring herself to cut loose from her accustomed surroundings.

In 1945, she was soap. It was a year of foreboding, endings, and beginnings. Of my family, my aunt Marie had disappeared in Terezin (Theresienstadt), my uncle Max had been gassed in Auschwitz just weeks before the camp was disbanded. On the bright side, the U.S. Army, which loved to ship German-speaking soldiers to Burma, had miraculously selected me for its ill-starred campaign to reeducate Germans.

This was a project I felt I had invented at the age of nineteen in 1943.

Before sending me to Europe with my propaganda troop, the Second Mobile Radio Broadcasting Company, the army had sent me to the University of Illinois for an academic booster shot, and there I had composed a seventeen-page paper, titled " 'Re-Educating' Germany." I had placed the buzzword in quotation marks at the time, which seemed prescient later, and my reflections were based on my personal experiences as a boy in Berlin.

The term "brainwashing" had not yet been invented when I was a teenage army scholar in peaceful Illinois, but my early experiences in Berlin had convinced me that the Germans were suffering from something like a powerful psychic virus, a mania, and I perceived that curing it would be an overwhelming and probably unrealistic job. In my paper, I pointed out some beginnings that might be made here and there, but to *reeducate* the whole people, really to persuade millions to cast off their past and adopt a new mind-set, seemed to me, at age nineteen, too much to expect.

In this belief I was ahead of our government, which, as I learned much later, was then only beginning to explore in innumerable secret conferences of many committees whether it would be able to agree on any policy at all. The confusion was such that no direction was in place when the war ended. Plato's dictum on democracy ruled — "a charming form of government, full of variety and disorder."

The State Department, with modest hopes for a civilized Germany, advocated a reconstructionist course. The Treasury Department, under Secretary Henry Morgenthau, was lobbying for an essentially pastoral society. The War Department, seeking instructions because its Military Government had to do the running of the country, faced frustration. The bottleneck was at the top. President Franklin D. Roosevelt had received much of his early education in Germany and hated the place. Morgenthau, stern and Jewish, hated the Germans even more. In declining health and facing crucial decisions to shape the postwar world, the president let this annoying matter of how to deal with a postwar Germany slide.

To deal with the vacuum, the Germany Country Unit (GCU) of the War Department's pragmatists spent six months in 1944 working up a preliminary "Handbook for Military Government in Germany Prior to Defeat or Surrender," including rules on education that followed moderate reconstructionist lines. Morgenthau got hold of a copy and took it to the president. Both hated it, and the president ordered its distribution banned.

In September 1944, Morgenthau proposed an alternative plan for postwar Germany. His main idea was that the Germans had to be made aware of their crimes against humanity and that the best way to achieve this was by deindustrializing the country. Complete deindustrialization, according to Morgenthau, meant reducing Germany to a purely agricultural economy, but the plan also included complete demilitarization and overall border changes. When this plan became public, Goebbels used it as propaganda against the Americans, and it turned out to be a strongpoint for the *Durchhalte-Propaganda* — resistance-propaganda.

Roosevelt actually signed off on the draconian and impractical Morgenthau Plan. At the end of the same month, however, Churchill and Roosevelt met in Quebec and agreed that the plan in this form went too far. The incredulous public reaction in the United States had caused Roosevelt to back down without a policy to take the scheme's place, and this is where reeducation stood when we occupiers reached the first German towns.

If my colleagues and I in psychological warfare had known about the chaos among the cooks in our policy kitchen, our morale would surely have suffered. But in blissful ignorance, we reformers — civilians in uniform who detested the army's greasy food and scratchy clothes — were delighted to help with what we regarded as a crusade against Hitler, meaning the man quite personally.

As the occupation inevitably moved ahead, my work was with the press in Berlin and did not require me to face the crucial issues of reeducation. Along with the rubble of the bombings, we were supposed to clean out the minds of our conquered subjects, to have the rank and file recognize the misery *they* had brought forth upon innocent people and persuade them to accept some share of responsibility for these acts, to show a measure of guilt.

Our main instrument for bringing all this about was a film made by one of my colleagues, Lieutenant Hanus Burger, under the guidance of the great Billy Wilder. It was to be our psychological atom bomb. Beginning in the spring of 1945, I watched the project's rocky progress with growing fascination, and in time I talked to Burger about the experience in some detail. Born in Prague, he was an experienced director of documentaries and a congenial fellow. We wrote surrender leaflets together in Normandy. These were far more effective than the Burger/Wilder film about concentration camps, which came to be named *Todesmühlen* (Death Mills).

The awesome ambition of the project was not lost on our chiefs in Psychological Warfare. They knew that such a film could not be allowed simply to end up as a "high-grade newsreel," confronting Germans only with piles of emaciated bodies. So a cautionary memo from Davidson Taylor, chief of the Film, Theater and Music Control Branch and an astute former executive at CBS, staked out ambitious goals.

"The film must let the moviegoer participate in the sufferings of which he was witness," he wrote, and "should generate a feeling of personal responsibility that he permitted them to happen."

A very tall order indeed!

It was also directed that the film be "factual and documented to the last detail." This memo even foresaw the rise of future Holocaust deniers: "We have to count on the Nazis to try denying the evidence in a few years or to assert that the events being shown were rare exceptions."

Burger did not care for Billy Wilder and his Hollywood mannerisms. The little lieutenant had worked with devastating footage from the newly opened concentration camps; films of German civilians who were more or less compelled to go through the camps as witnesses;[1] and new footage he had shot of surviving Germans whose reactions would enable audiences to identify with the millions of bystanders who had "permitted the atrocities to occur" (as Davidson Taylor had phrased it).

Burger's account spared nobody. The script was so unyielding that in the end the word "Nazi" was changed throughout to "German"; that would emphasize the presumed guilt of *all* Germans. When Wilder first viewed the production at the American film office on North Audley Street in London, however, it was eighty-six minutes long and obviously had to be greatly shortened. The supreme propaganda authorities in Washington had already issued such orders. Wilder was the hatchet man; Burger was crushed.

"I guarantee that, at the most, he [Wilder] looked at two and a half minutes of the film," Burger would remember.

"Twelve hundred feet [twenty minutes] is the limit," Wilder grumbled at the production man. "From the horror scenes, only the most essential! I can't even look at it anymore."

---

[1] General Eisenhower had personally ordered such tours, and after one of these, through a camp at Ohrdorf near Kassel, the mayor of the village and his wife hanged themselves.

Burger, who did not know how Wilder had lost his mother, interpreted the famous man's behavior as shocking callousness.

The film vanished so fast from occupied Germany that I did not see it; it was never shown in the United States. So I did not view it until in 1993 I found a copy at the National Archives in Washington. Its power had not faded.

I saw barely stirring bodies placed on stretchers by medics ("Help came too late for many") . . . Sacks of hair ("Methodically packed for sale to manufacturers") . . . The commander of Bergen-Belsen ("What kind of humans did these things?") . . . SS witnesses being interrogated ("They can explain everything") . . . Surviving children ("Walking skeletons who had forgotten their names").

A sequence at Weimar showed citizens during the occupation being marched off to see the remains of Buchenwald. Some families were picnicking nearby. ("It was only a short walk to the nearest concentration camp.") The picnickers were having fun. ("These Germans, who said they didn't know, they were responsible too. They had put themselves into the hands of lunatics.")

Families emerging from the camp's artifacts were shown with their faces ashen. They were dabbing at their eyes with handkerchiefs. Suddenly, the scene switched to mobs cheering, smiling, shouting, their arms outstretched under seas of swastikas. Said the commentator, "They are the same Germans who once heiled Hitler."

The film had no life in Germany because it found no audiences. At a sneak preview in Würzburg, a light operetta film had been advertised. When the lights dimmed, *Todesmühlen* came on. The audience had been asked to record its reactions on cards, using pencils provided in the lobby.

Billy Wilder told me how he witnessed the disaster in the lobby. Of the four hundred or so moviegoers, only about twenty stayed until the end. Not one preview card was filled out. The visible reaction: all the pencils were gone. Those were hungry times.

The many official reports and analyses tended to run much like the following from Bavaria in January 1946: "Everyone depressed, some women cried, expressions of regret about the reported conditions, but little feeling of responsibility." The Germans did not wish to be reminded of what most said they didn't know in the first place. And as for the starving of people, the beating of people, the gassing of people, that was done by others, strangers whom nobody seemed to know.

# 7

## BOB AND JACK LAUNCH

## THE HITLER REVIVAL

Hitler's afterlife received its initial jump-start from two impecca-
bly accredited flag-bearers of the American establishment. First to
appear, right at the birth of postwar Military Government in Berlin,
was Ambassador Robert D. (for Daniel) Murphy.

When the genial Bob Murphy retired from the State Department
in 1959, he had risen to undersecretary, the first career diplomat to
attain number two rank in the vast and competitive hierarchy. In 1923,
at the age of twenty-seven, when he was the senior American at the
tiny consulate in Munich, he was already considered a promising talent, though just why is hard to make out. In fact, Murphy's rise remained a lifelong paradox, for this engaging figure — tall, rangy, with
a photogenic smile, conservative tailoring, and views to match —
often bet on the wrong horse.

Back in Murphy's Munich of 1923, Hitler was already beginning to
make a name for himself. Yet after attending some Nazi rallies Murphy
dismissed the Führer as "unconvincing" and reported to Washington
that he doubted the fellow "would ever amount to much."

During Hitler's war, as General Dwight D. Eisenhower's political
adviser for the Allied invasion of Africa in 1942, the articulate Murphy counseled against General Charles de Gaulle, who was capable
and popularly adored, in favor of fascists and has-been hacks whose
rightist politics he preferred. (De Gaulle wisecracked that the Germans, in Murphy's eyes, consisted of people whom Bob would find
congenial as dinner companions.)

During his semi-retirement in 1960, as member of the president's Foreign Intelligence Advisory Board, Murphy was still holding to his steady course. Repeatedly and vehemently, he demanded that the CIA be ordered to assassinate Ho Chi Minh. The Vietnamese leader was adored in the rice paddies, but he was giving Washington too much trouble.

Murphy's upside-down diplomacy was most prominently on view during his years as the principal governing force behind the West German scene: political adviser in the precedent-setting first postwar period, 1945–49. Again he kept close to his own — Germans fit to be his dining companions — confident in the faith that well-tailored gentlemen of conservative bent, fine manners, and a nose for business would appreciate freedom and detest the common enemy, Communism.

In the vivid phrase of Supreme Court justice Felix Frankfurter, Murphy looked "grottier than the Grotties" (meaning the graduates of the blue-nosed Groton prep school). And yet Bob Murphy grew up as a poor Irish lad in Milwaukee, Wisconsin, laboring at menial jobs to put himself through school on a scholarship.

Catholicism ruled the parental household, the favorite epithet of Bob's often unemployed father being, "You blue-nosed Presbyterian SOB!" So it was natural for Ambassador/Conqueror Murphy to feel warmly about Catholic dignitaries like Michael Ritter von Faulhaber, the autocratic cardinal of Bavaria, who resisted the faint attempts to liberalize his turf as "another form of dictatorship."

Although few still remember him, Murphy's pro-Nazi influence was pervasive and endures today.

In Germany as elsewhere, he worked quietly. Yet the first postwar West German leaders, both the politically acceptable and those of tainted past, recognized him as the nuclear power behind his friend, the military governor, General Lucius D. Clay, an upstanding engineering officer with up-front ways. Murphy pulled private wires backstage, especially in Washington, whereas Clay was perceived as a choleric nuisance.

Murphy's maneuvering became self-sustaining because his prejudices and poor judgments represented the life-giving energy of the occupation powers at a crucial historical turn. The Germans still call it *Die Stunde Null,* zero hour, when life after the war began. The victors were rich and almighty; the vanquished were destitute, seemingly impotent, dependent on their muscle and wits.

Murphy was present at The Creation. Indeed, he personified it and his signal was unmistakable. Effectively, it gave the fledgling German leadership permission to downgrade or ignore the surviving Nazi influence. Murphy set the direction and the tone and his history is an open file.

Within this history, "denazification" stood out as the reigning, if unloved, buzzword of 1945 (and for many years beyond), though right from the start everybody wished it would go away. The Germans sabotaged his crucial military government program because it kept the nasty past alive, while the simultaneous nosy American *Fragebogen* (political questionnaires) threatened to create a future caste of untouchables.

To Murphy and his fellow Cold Warriors in Berlin and Washington, denazification would deprive the West of allies who would soon be needed to fight the Soviets. We wanted Nazis as comrades, not outcasts.

Murphy all but wished away the program by unilaterally declaring it over. "The immediate objectives of denazification have been achieved," he messaged the State Department on August 25, 1945, when he had been on his Berlin post for little more than a month. By 1948, with the West spending $700 million a year on the German occupation, not counting Marshall Plan support, the U.S. Congress refused to continue paying for denazification even at its foot-dragging pace.

In February, the House Appropriations Subcommittee on Foreign Aid recommended full amnesty for remaining Nazi offenders. When General Clay protested, the Pentagon summarily instructed him "to conclude all denazification trials by the end of April." Clay obeyed reluctantly, noting that 28,065 cases remained, including not a few "bad actors."

Of course Murphy well knew that denazification had not been "achieved" in 1945. He took charge of this chronic headache and found a partner in a trusted old friend, the congenial, pipe-puffing

Allen W. Dulles, who headed German operations for OSS (the Office of Strategic Services), the forerunner of the Central Intelligence Agency. The two men had been fellow spies at the famous listening post, the American Legation in Bern, Switzerland, during the war, and in his 1964 autobiography Murphy loyally called Dulles "brilliant." This wasn't too long after the long overrated "master spy," as director of the CIA, had botched the Bay of Pigs invasion on an epic scale and been fired by President John F. Kennedy.[1]

Dulles was not enamored of detail work. This was handled for him by his principal assistant, Frank Wisner, a rising superstar in intelligence, who told his boss, "Forget the Nazis and get in there and find out what the Commies are up to instead."

And so this triumvirate rehabilitated such talent as Karl Blessing, who would become head of the Federal Bank although he had joined the Nazi Party in 1937 and inspected concentration camps as a generous financial contributor to the secret "Himmler Circle."

It was Murphy who sneaked Gustav Hilger and his family into the United States "under assumed names" in 1948. In Washington, this ranking alumnus of the Nazi Foreign Office became unofficial ambassador from Konrad Adenauer's Christian Democratic Union and led negotiations with the U.S. government.

Hilger's past had by then been laid aside. A diplomat in the German embassy in Moscow, he became a member of the personal secretariat of Foreign Minister Joachim von Ribbentrop and during the war was the chief political officer for the Eastern Front in the Foreign Ministry. As the liaison with the SS during its genocidal missions in the Soviet Union, he had — at least — processed documents about killing operations. In Italy he had participated in the capture and murder of Jews by the SS. In 1942, Hilger had coordinated and obtained sanctuary in Germany for several Hungarian army officers responsible for the murder of Serbs and Jews. Charles Allen, a Nazi

---

[1]Only with the recent declassification of once secret documents did word surface that Dulles's wartime bosses in Washington were not high on their man in Bern. They cabled complaints about "the degeneration of your information which is now given a lower rating than any other source." They called some of his output "most inaccurate and misleading," "outdated," and of "minor interest."

hunter, found Hilger in 1962 in Washington, D.C., where he was in close communication with the State Department, which maintained a telephone contact service on his behalf. After the war, American war crimes investigators had sought him for "torture," according to his "wanted" notice. Hilger died a free man in Munich on July 27, 1965.


Bob Murphy's choice of congenial spirits also ran true in his affinity for Fritz Schäffer, the deputy minister–president of Bavaria (and close friend of Cardinal Faulhaber). Schäffer had just been fired by an infuriated General Eisenhower. "I was favorably impressed with Schäffer," Murphy reported after a pleasant dinner. Eisenhower's independent investigators were not pleased. They called Schäffer's regime "only a little better than the Nazis it replaced" and found it loaded with militarists, ultra-nationalists, and intimates of former top Nazi officials.

In the end, it was Murphy's gross misjudgment that prevailed. In 1949, Schäffer became the Federal Republic's first finance minister.

Initially, Schäffer had come to power under the auspices of the Bavarian military governor, General George S. Patton, who espoused the anti-Soviet Murphy-Dulles-Wisner ideology, albeit in more martial language. "What do you care about those goddamn Bolshies?" he demanded. "We're going to fight them sooner or later."

Before a press conference on September 22, 1945, Patton blustered once too often. He said the American occupation would run better if it employed "*more* former members of the Nazi Party." Egging him on, one of the reporters asked, "After all, General, didn't most ordinary Nazis join their party in about the same way that Americans become Republicans or Democrats?"

"Yes," said the general, "that's about it."

Tormented with regret and guilt, Eisenhower fired his old friend. "Georgie" had been such a good man.


Like Ambassador Murphy, his even more powerful — and equally respectable — successor, John J. McCloy, would have been appalled to find himself classified as a Naziphile, much less a camp follower of the Führer. Absurd! Both would have smiled dismissively or sued for libel. Yet the facts are plain. Murphy's record as an advocate of many players from the old Hitler camp is unmistakable, as even the preceding very brief summary shows; and the decisions of "Jack" McCloy, the next American proconsul, carried on the unwritten policy: a German wheeler-dealer was entitled to protection even if he had profited from the Nazi regime, as long as he possessed useful talents and hadn't murdered Jews with his own hands.

No one wrote or said this. There was no need. Bob and Jack's actions, particularly their personal decisions, made it superfluous. Indeed, the Germans have a neat phrase for such broad signaling. They call it "a wink with a fencepost." Bob and Jack were accomplished winkers.

McCloy governed under a rarefied new title, "High Commissioner for Germany" (HICOG), and the inside of his almost billiard-bald head was considerably more complex and brighter than Murphy's. His résumé thundered of stardom: assistant secretary of war, negotiator and confidant of four presidents, president of the World Bank, president of the Chase Manhattan Bank, Wall Street's lawyer-in-chief, and on and on. When his biography was finally published in 1992, it was titled *The Chairman*. Underneath was the explanatory reading line: "John J. McCloy — The Making of the American Establishment."

Nevertheless, "Jack" McCloy was charmingly lacking in self-importance. He was too smart for puffery and could even joke about his authority over the Germans. "It was the nearest thing to a Roman proconsul that the modern world afforded," he later recalled. "You could turn to your secretary and say, 'Take a Law.'"

Like Bob Murphy, Jack McCloy would naturally never muster anything but total disgust for Adolf Hitler. Like Murphy, however, he had the Cold War frozen in his bones. Anti-Communism was not policy to him. It was religion, and events like the Soviet blockade of Berlin and the crude verbal aggression of the Kremlin clique, notably the bellowing and shoe-thumping of Nikita Khrushchev, made the hymnal swell ever more fervent. By nature, therefore, all who stood against Communism were welcome in his tent, and that automatically included a lot of Nazis.

Unlike Murphy, McCloy was not easy to puzzle out. He was no "Grottie" manqué. He was a "Peddie" from the exclusive Peddie

Institute, whose headmaster aped Groton's illustrious headmaster, Endicott Peabody. And from this cocoon, Jack McCloy, an appealing class act, carried forward a well-hidden disdain for his ethnic lessers.

Nobody ever came right out and called him a bigot. He maintained delightful friendships with many Jews, all of them of his own social class.

He did not, however, dine with any Japanese. Before the war they were generally considered shifty little people who cheated American consumers with junk merchandise that quickly fell apart. And when this "inferior race" suddenly stabbed the United States in the back at Pearl Harbor, McCloy joined in the instant hysterical hatred for the 120,000 Japanese Americans and Japanese on the West Coast, almost all of them demonstrably loyal citizens and taxpayers. As number two man in the War Department, McCloy was primarily responsible for the decision to intern them in primitive camps for the duration of the war, more than three and a half years.

Only in 1981 did the American Civil Liberties Union call this "the greatest deprivation of civil liberties by Government since slavery." McCloy, then eighty-six, stuck to his ancient guns. "We didn't attack Pearl Harbor," he fumed. "They did." And he was incensed when Congress voted to pay to every surviving internee $20,000 and to apologize to each.

The Holocaust was another personally distasteful topic to him. He was again the pivotal official when, at last, it dawned on Washington that Jews were being systematically exterminated by the millions and it was proposed that Auschwitz or the railroad lines leading to the death camp be bombed. Jewish groups and several ranking officials, especially the aggressive (and Jewish) Treasury Secretary Henry Morgenthau, Jr., pushed for the plan. McCloy vetoed it.

In one typical memo he called such a mission "impractical." Besides, it could be executed only by the diversion of considerable air support essential to the success of our forces. When lobbying for the mission continued, McCloy countered that the distance from British bases, 2,000 miles unescorted over enemy territory, made it too risky. No mention was ever made of the U.S. planes based at Foggia, Italy, a round-trip of under 1,300 miles.

To be fair, the reports of genocidal crimes were so sweeping and so gruesome that a great many Americans, including some Jewish leaders, simply refused to believe them. As late as December 1944, McCloy took aside the president of the World Jewish Congress, Leon Kubowitzki, and said, "We are alone, tell me the truth. Do you really believe that all those horrible things happened?"

Yet there was more to McCloy's refusal to act on behalf of the Auschwitz inmates. They were a faceless, shuffling mass, an unimaginable number, and they were mostly from the East, impecunious cogs in shawls and wide-brimmed black hats and long sideburns, speaking Yiddish. Not dinner partners like Felix (Frankfurter), the justice, and Benny (Buttenwieser), the financier. Expendable.


Although McCloy's reign in Germany coincided with tumultuous events — the Korean War, West German rearmament, the rattling of genocidal new nuclear weapons by the Soviets — nothing produced greater long-range resonance than the clemencies he granted to dozens of war criminals, the most visible symbols of Nazi evil, now excused by American bumbling and expediency.

German pressure on McCloy could hardly have been more intense. Led by repeated entreaties from the first chancellor of the newly born Federal Republic, the imposing Konrad Adenauer, the official lobbying came close to blackmail. A delegation from the West German parliament called upon the American viceroy and told him in no uncertain terms to go easy on the convicted Nazi mass murderers in view of the "political and psychological factors at a time when Western Germany was being called upon to make a military contribution to Western defense."

The most sensational (and consequential) case was that of Alfred Krupp von Bohlen und Halback, the armaments king, whose 175 companies had been leading suppliers of panzers, artillery, and ammunition for Hitler's war machine. During the war, Krupp's empire had employed as many as 200,000 slave laborers and had even set up a munitions factory within Auschwitz. Krupp had been a rabid Hitler enthusiast. He had personally signed contracts with the SS allowing its killers to punish his workers, and so they had died by the thousands of malnutrition, disease, and beatings.

At the Nuremberg trials, Krupp had been sentenced to twelve years in prison and the loss of his personal fortune, possibly worth as much as $100 million. He had served only three years and got all of his money back. McCloy had listened to the Germans and they had listened to him. When Krupp walked out of Landsberg prison — Hitler's erstwhile lockup — into the bitter cold at 9 A.M. on February 3, 1951, he was, according to the *New York Times,* "greeted like a returning hero."

The newly enfranchised German voters got McCloy's message: a mere five years after the end of the slaughter unleashed by Hitler, the pushover Americans were already willing to forgive and forget in exchange for the services of German soldiers. If a leading headliner like Krupp, whose very name stood for Nazi aggression as practiced by the Führer, could get away with so much guilt for mass deaths, then certainly less prominent believers could feel amnestied as well.

In his zeal to lure German loyalties to the American side, McCloy lavished mercy upon killers with records of culpability remarkable even by the standards of the SS. One case in point was SS lieutenant Heinz Hermann Schubert, an assistant to SS general Otto Ohlendorf, commander of Einsatzgruppe D on the Eastern Front.

Ohlendorf, responsible for the slaughter of 90,000 men, women, and children, mostly Jews, was hanged, but Schubert's death sentence was reduced to a prison term of ten years with the curious justification that he was "a relative subordinate" who "did not know why the individuals were being executed."

This could not have been true. As Ohlendorf's adjutant, Schubert had access to his chief's correspondence and other files. He was one of three officers to whom Ohlendorf regularly entrusted the supervision of mass executions, and Schubert remembered the scenes with precision.

"When the people who were to be shot were already standing in their positions in the tank ditch," he had testified, "I supervised the actual shooting."

Kai Bird, the American historian who followed up on these matters in the 1990s, correctly pinpointed in *The Chairman* the consequences of McCloy's insistence on playing God. "Tampering with the individual sentences handed out to *Einsatzgruppen* killers allowed many Germans to harbor doubts about the truth of all the Nürnberg judgments." That was half a century ago. Half a century later, resentment against the Nuremberg brand of "victor's justice" was still afoot. The extremist right-wing journal *National-Zeitung* inveighed against it every week in exactly the style Hitler had used to harangue against the "shame dictate" of World War I, the Treaty of Versailles.

To the degree that the hand of Nuremberg could still be stayed, McCloy had on his own reversed international judgment, a titanic feat that played conveniently into the hands of Konrad Adenauer. Although the chancellor had won election in the parliament by only one vote in 1949, he soon maneuvered the American high commissioner so skillfully that jokesters in Bonn began calling him "the real McCloy."

# 8

## U.S. INTELLGENCE AND THE CLERGY
## HELP NAZI LEADERS TO ESCAPE

Hitler was gone; his ethics survived. As if afflicted by a lingering contagion, representatives of mainstream institutions went systematically out of their way to protect and aid genocidal killers who clung to undeserved freedom after World War II. At considerable expense, reputable officials spirited war criminals to safety so they could get away with mass murder.

This reprehensible intervention still requires an accounting. The subjects of the following case histories survived beyond whitewash or redemption. In the permissive climate of post-Hitler society, their evil did them little harm. Indeed, it ensured their comfortable lives for decades.

*"Heil Rauff!"*

During the spring of 1942, SS *Standartenführer* Walter Rauff operated under extra pressure at the RSHA, Himmler's Gestapo headquarters at Prinz Albrecht Strasse 8 in Berlin. The mass executions of Jews in the eastern territories were moving too slowly to suit Hitler and Himmler. It was cumbersome to wipe out so many people one by one. Complaints from commanders of the execution squads were also piling up on Rauff's desk. Too many SS shooters were getting too drunk or had dropped out with nervous breakdowns.

"The most important consideration for me was that the shootings were a terrible ordeal for the men concerned," Rauff recalled thirty years later in prosperous exile at Santiago, Chile; he was of course referring to the perpetrators, not the victims.

To relieve the distressed executioners, Rauff designed and procured fifty "S trucks." The "S" meant "Special." The chassis were standard and were routinely supplied by the Saurer truck works. But custom-made extra-wide and airtight superstructures were required to turn the vehicles into mobile gas chambers so they could asphyxiate approximately fifty Jews at one push of the gas pedal.

Rauff sent two agents from his department IID 3a to the Glaub-schat vehicle works in Berlin's Neuköln district with the cover story that the trucks were needed to evacuate typhus victims. Eventually, Glaubschat delivered enough vehicles to — in the language of Rauff's reports — "process" a "cargo" of 97,000 bodies in 1942 alone. Un-happily for Rauff, this bonanza triggered a flood of new technical hassles, mostly from the truck drivers. Suddenly, Rauff's office was inundated with correspondence from indignant field inspectors who complained that the hoses transmitting carbon monoxide fumes from the engine exhaust into the personnel chamber were not airtight, which gave the German operators headaches. Other complaints: the chamber's metal floors rusted rapidly; disposal of "thin fluids" and "thicker filth" had to be speeded up. Death came more slowly than planned, so that faces were reported "horribly distorted." The vehi-cles were "packed solid" and so the front axle became overloaded. At Chelmno near Lodz, the first of the extermination camps, where the killing units went into operation in December 1941, one truck actu-ally exploded because of an operator error.

While Rauff did his best to deal with his clients' complaints — once he even traveled east to inspect his improved vehicles in action — some problems were beyond his power: the stench, which official reports de-scribed as "hellish," and the desired secrecy. At one point, the vehicles had been camouflaged as "Kaiser coffee trucks," supposedly deliver-ing beverages. But no one was fooled. Wherever Rauff's vehicles appeared, civilians referred to them as *Todeswagen* (death trucks).

By mid-1942, the pressures relating to these mobile operations had lessened, because the final refinement of the death machine was com-ing into use: mass exterminations in the huge crematoria at Auschwitz and other big camps. For Rauff, this meant promotion from *Schreib-tischtäter* ("desk perpetrator") to hands-on murder.[1] Appointed Gestapo chief in Tunis, he directed killings of Jews and partisans, winning praise from his superiors in Berlin. At his next post, Gestapo director for all of northern Italy, he built a further record for ruthlessness and became known as "the murderer of Milan." At the same time, anticipating German defeat, he formed secret alliances with his eventual lifesavers: the Catholic clergy.

In late 1944 and early 1945, Milan was a warren of high-level conspiracies. Working with Himmler's chief of staff, SS general Karl Wolff, Rauff enlisted the city's archbishop, Cardinal Ildefonso Schuster, in "Operation Sunrise," the surrender of Italy, which Allen Dulles, then with the OSS, was negotiating with the Nazis.

When peace arrived, the notoriety of Rauff's war crimes caused the U.S. occupation authorities to ignore his connections and slap him into San Vittore prison. The report of an American interrogator declared that Rauff had sharpened "political gangsterism to stream-lined perfection and is proud of that fact"; he would be "a menace if ever set free." Rauff did not have long to wait. The very next day a priest arrived and arranged his transfer to an American army hospital. Rauff had fallen into the hands of a different brand of Americans, enthusiastic anti-Communists who did not consider him a gangster but an asset. This was "Unit Z," an OSS counterintelligence unit headed by Lieutenant James Jesus Angleton, whose feats and defeats as a worldwide paranoid chief of mole hunters would be legend for forty years.

Angleton and his agents debriefed Rauff on his extensive knowledge of regional Communist activity, and when the Italians wanted to prosecute the SS criminal he wound up in a prisoner-of-war camp where security was so poor that he simply strolled away.

"I went to Naples," Rauff testified decades later before a Chilean immigration court. "There a Catholic priest helped me to go to Rome, where I stayed more or less for a year and a half, always in convents of

---

[1]Ironically, Rauff almost didn't make it into the SS because his wife-to-be had been married to a Jewish lawyer. Himmler eventually forgave this "oversight," which Mrs. Rauff attributed to her failure to study "racial biology."

the Holy See." He laundered money with a Nazi forger to help keep afloat the Vatican "ratline," the escape route supplied with clients, usually by way of Austria, through a network of old SS men and agents of the U.S. Army Counter-Intelligence Corps. The CIC paid $1,000 each for most such escapes, somewhat more for customers over sixty; children traveled at half price. For prominent fugitives requiring "VIP treatment," the fee ran as high as $1,400.

The prestige and power of the church, especially in Italy, kept the movement of war criminals immune. Typically, a well-placed monsignor would certify as real the fake identity of an escapee, and this enabled a laundered Nazi to receive an emergency passport from a field office of the International Red Cross.

No question: the Vatican was "the largest single organization involved in the illegal movement of emigrants." So reported a State Department intelligence officer, Vincent La Vista, himself a Catholic, in a top secret dispatch sent to Washington on May 15, 1947, but not declassified until 1984. The Holy See's justification was simply "the propagation of the Faith."

So when Rauff heard that the Syrian government was looking for help with the training of its military, his Vatican connections procured his passport for Damascus and his eventual emigration to Chile. He became the affluent representative of a German company and lived in a large villa at Santiago.

There he enjoyed congenial company, since many of the most prominent Nazi refugees lived well if not lavishly, and made no attempt to keep their identities secret, at least to the Nazi community, which knew how to take care of its own. The governments of Argentina, Bolivia, Chile, Ecuador, and Paraguay generally managed to politely but firmly fend off all extradition requests. At some social occasions it was just like old times. Sometimes Adolf Eichmann showed up, and in May 1984 Rauff spent an agreeable week of partying with Dr. Josef Mengele, the Auschwitz "angel of death," and General Hans Ulrich Rudel, the most highly decorated Luftwaffe pilot, later an activist for right-wing political causes.

In his memoirs, Rudel kept the faith and thanked the church for its "unforgettable" contribution to keeping alive "valuable members of our people."

Rauff kept faith with his reputation for brutality. Shortly before his death of lung cancer in 1987, he wrote a friend that he was renouncing Catholicism. "Himmler was my God," he explained. "The SS was my religion."

His friends knew. "Heil Hitler! Heil Rauff!" they cried at the funeral in Santiago's main cemetery. Several wreaths arrived with flowers braided into swastikas.

In his eulogy, the Lutheran bishop Ricardo Wagner spoke of Rauff feelingly. "His love was for the sea," he preached. The bishop's allusions to the atrocities committed by the deceased were, at best, ambiguous: "Nobody can know with final certainty what another man did or didn't do," he intoned.

### Eichmann's Deputy Finds Work with the CIA

And then there was the case of Alois Brunner, Adolf Eichmann's deputy. Brunner was no run-of-the-mill war criminal either. Eichmann referred to him as "my best man." This small, bowlegged SS *Obersturmbannführer,* who never weighed more than 130 pounds, was a utility killer. Dashing to extermination sites all over Europe, he was directly responsible for the slaughter of at least 100,000 Jews.

As Eichmann's successor in Vienna, he swept Vienna *judenrein* with astonishing rapidity by applying an administrative device that Eichmann later called "the very cornerstone" of the Final Solution. "Brunner invented Jewish collaboration," Simon Wiesenthal explained. Through a variety of schemes, Brunner compelled Jews to turn into collaborators, to actually help with their own destruction.

He also relished killing personally. Eyewitnesses saw him kick to the floor and casually shoot to death the banker Siegmund Bosel on a frigid deportation train eastward; the ailing old man had irked him with pleas for mercy. Sometimes Brunner fired at random into crowds of prisoners. Administering hour-long beatings with his horsewhip seemed to energize him.

From Vienna he was called by Eichmann to round up the Jews of Berlin, where his reign would become notorious as "the Brunner time." Next he mopped up in Salonika, Greece; then in the French concentration camp at Drancy; and finally he saw to the liquidation of the Jews in Slovakia. He did not spare children. He called them "future terrorists."

After the war he was interned, with the name and false papers of one Alois Schmaldienst that showed him with a lower army rank. He was soon released, and his cover served him until 1954, when things suddenly got a trifle hot: France sentenced him to death in absentia, after which Brunner decided that Europe was no longer safe for him. SS friends directed him to one of the *Anlaufstellen* (starting points) of the ratline southward, probably Innsbruck, Austria. From there a train took him to Nauders, the last stop on the German side of the Alps, where Franz Lechner, a former SS security guard at Hitler's *Wolfs-schanze* (Wolf's Lair) headquarters, was waiting.

Lechner was accustomed to high-level fugitives. Among his many clients had been Richard Glücks, whose post in the concentration camp inspectorate made him boss of all the KZ (*Konzentrationslager*, concentration camp) commandants.

The following day, Brunner and Lechner hiked to Italy along the Brenner Pass, at 4,500 feet the lowest of the classic Alp crossings since Roman times, to the nearest sizable town: bilingual Brixen, now called Bressanone, since the Austrians had had to give it up following World War I.

There was more to Brixen than mountain resort charm and a thirteenth-century cathedral. Lechner took Brunner to the Papal Prefecture, an office of the Vatican, where a passport under the name of George Fischer was waiting, along with a driver's license and other paperwork needed by "Dr. Fischer" to travel on to Damascus, Syria. Brunner was pleased to see how smoothly the many steps of the system meshed to protect him and convey him to his well-chosen destination.

In Damascus, he slipped quickly back into undercover work. The intelligence organization of General Reinhard Gehlen, flush with financing from the CIA, needed a "resident" in Damascus, a local bureau chief. Brunner/Fischer fit the role. Soon he also worked out of Cairo, Egypt, on a CIA-sponsored scheme to train the Egyptian military. But 7 rue Haddad, Damascus, became home and the Syrian government his last employer. He was an adviser on "Jewish affairs." Twice he was injured by bombs that came in his mail.

Brunner's hatred for Jews had still not abated twenty years later: In the mid-1970s, reporters for the German magazine *Bunte* found and interviewed him. He had "no bad conscience," he said, for getting rid "of that Jewish garbage." In 1987, two more writers, Charles Ashman and Robert J. Wagman, interviewed him by telephone and his message about the Jews remained the same. Said Brunner, "They deserved to die and I would do it all over again because they were human garbage."

For other journalists who talked to him when he was in his eighties, he had a word about his future. "Israel will never get me, I won't be another Eichmann," he declared to a West German periodical in 1985. Apparently Brunner is still alive in Syria, though the local authorities deny it. France, Austria, and Germany have requested his extradition, the latter country's prosecuting authorities having offered 500,000 deutsche marks (over $224,000 in December 2000) bounty. Thanks to the insistence of Serge Klarsfeld, president and founder of the Sons and Daughters of the Deported French Jews Association, in the year 2001 there will be a trial in absentia against Brunner in Paris.


*"I Remember with Deep Gratitude . . ."*


Adolf Eichmann, as everyone knows, was kidnapped in Argentina and hanged in Israel — though not until he had enjoyed fifteen years of peaceful civilian life, thanks to the very secular (and illegal) help of the Catholic church.

At the war's end, Eichmann had retreated to the fallback headquarters of the SS at Bad Aussee, a resort in the pretty Austrian lake country southeast of Salzburg. The town was in an uproar. He reported to Ernst Kaltenbrunner, the chief of the SS directorate, his friend since their grade school days, who ordered him to take charge of about a hundred youngsters and old men, many lacking any military training; Eichmann was to organize them for a final defense in the hills.

But when Kaltenbrunner was captured by an American advance patrol (he was later hanged at Nuremberg), Eichmann, uniformed as a Luftwaffe corporal with papers identifying him as Adolf Barth, took off for Germany, where he worked until 1950 as a truck driver, logger, and chicken farmer in various obscure rural towns, identified as Otto Eckmann, then as Otto Heninger.

His final pseudonym, Ricardo Klement, was assigned to him en route to hospitable Argentina. Old SS associates arranged for his passage, as usual, via the ratline from Austria to Rome, where, according to his instructions, he reported to his key rescuer, an Austrian priest, Father Anton Weber.

The harried father was overrun with requests for phony passports, and often his supplicants were phony, too — non-Catholics who were not entitled to Vatican protection like war criminals who were church members. So when Weber was the least bit in doubt, he had the applicant recite the Lord's Prayer and the Ave Maria. Eichmann was so eloquent in his denunciation of Bolshevism, however, that Father Weber swallowed all skepticism and issued the papers without insisting on his test.

Once he clutched his passport, Eichmann/Klement confessed: he was a Lutheran. But he was a most grateful one. Later he said, "I remember with deep gratitude the help that I received from Catholic priests and decided to honor the Catholic faith."

Father Weber had once again performed his life's task. He had won a convert — tainted but loyal to the church.


*The Enemy of My Enemy Is My Friend: Eichmann's Collaborator and the CIA*


Baron Otto von Bolschwing joined the Nationalsozialistische Deutsche Arbeiterpartei (NSDAP) — National Socialist German Workers' Party, or Nazi Party — in 1932 when he was only twenty-three years old and immediately became a member of the SD (*Sicherheitsdienst*), the party security service. By 1939 he was the leading expert on, and intelligence officer for, the Middle East, organizing agreements with militant Zionist Feivel Polkes for the training and emigration of German Jews to Palestine. In return, Polkes and his organization, the Haganah, kept the Nazis informed about British activities in Palestine. At the time, Adolf Eichmann was specializing in Freemasonry and Jewish affairs, and soon came into contact with von Bolschwing, who arranged meetings between Eichmann and Polkes, which helped establish Eichmann's later reputation as an expert on "Jewish affairs." In the 1960s, while under interrogation, Eichmann revealed, "The first time I was occupied with Jewish matters was when Mildenstein [a Nazi officer] visited me at my workplace together with von Bolschwing — never before that." He also recalled that "Herr von Bolschwing would often drop in at our office and talk about Palestine. . . . He spoke so knowledgeably of the aims and situation of Zionism in Palestine and elsewhere that I gradually became an authority on Zionism. . . . I kept in touch with Herr von Bolschwing . . . because no one else could give me firsthand information about the country I was most interested in for my work."

Eichmann and von Bolschwing worked as a team in 1936–37, making the first program for the systematic confiscation of Jewish property, with the ultimate aim of "purging Germany of its Jews." In an SS policy study, von Bolschwing explained that "the Jews in the entire world represent a nation which is not bound by a country or by a people but [rather] by money. Therefore they are and must always be an enemy of National Socialism . . . [and they] are among the most dangerous enemies."

On June 20, 1941, von Bolschwing, who was chief SS officer in Bucharest, Romania, organized a pogrom night with the Iron Guard. Hundreds of Jews, including many children, were murdered. Some were hung on meat hooks with their throats slit and their bodies branded as "kosher meat" with red-hot irons. At the end of the war, the SS files in Bucharest were discovered by the Americans, practically intact — a prize trophy for the U.S. intelligence service. One would think that, in possession of such records, the Americans would have hunted down a man like von Bolschwing and brought him to trial. Wrong. As the saying goes, "The enemy of my enemy is my friend," and in 1945 von Bolschwing was hired by the OSS.

The baron was initially assigned to the Gehlen Organization, a group of former Nazi spies hired by the CIA under the leadership of Hitler's intelligence chief for the Eastern Front, General Reinhard Gehlen. The general had surrendered to the Americans in 1945, and, using his Russian files as a bargaining chip, he came to a gentleman's agreement with the CIA. He and his fellow spies were to work for the U.S. government until Germany set up its own intelligence agency.

For nine years von Bolschwing worked with Gehlen in Europe, and in 1954 he was brought to the United States, where the CIA needed him for his expertise in interrogating, his methods including the use of bullwhips, drugs, and electrodes. Since Nazi criminals were not conceded American citizenship, the CIA officially declared that they had investigated the baron's past and that he was clean. In 1959, Eichmann's collaborator became a U.S. citizen.

In the U.S., von Bolschwing worked for Alfred Discoll, former governor of New Jersey and president of Warner-Lambert Pharmaceutical, and became associated with fellow employee Elmer Bobst, who was a mentor to Richard Nixon, and was thus involved in the latter's 1960 presidential campaign. In 1969 he was working in Silicon Valley for a high-tech firm called Transinternational Computer Investment Corporation (TCI), which held classified Defense Department contracts, an organization of which he eventually became vice president. Finally, in the 1970s the Justice Department started proceedings to deport the baron, who agreed in 1981 to a consent judgment denaturalizing him. Stripped of his U.S. citizenship, von Bolschwing was allowed to remain in the country because of his poor health — the baron was suffering from a degenerative brain disease and died a free man in a California nursing home.

# 9

## ADENAUER WAS NO DEMOCRAT

Almost forty years after leaving office and more than thirty years after his death, Chancellor Konrad Adenauer remains far and away Germany's most admired personality, according to all the polls.

Nevertheless, the voters of Lower Saxony were entitled to rub their eyes in puzzlement during the regional elections of March 1994. Had something happened to set back the calendar by decades? Why was Adenauer's stern and grizzled visage shown in huge close-up on the new election billboards? Had the master been resurrected for yet another run at public office?

Not quite. Looking closely at a bottom corner of the poster, voters spotted a modest picture of a young current candidate of the conservative ruling party, the CDU. Today's political operators could think of no contemporary backing more effective than the coattails of *der Alte,* the old one, gone these many years.

More was at stake than met the eye. A vote for the memory of Adenauer was also a vote for enshrining Hitler. To be sure, Adenauer was no Nazi, but his reputation during the war was at best mixed. On the one hand, during the Third Reich he was arrested and sent to a concentration camp from which he escaped; after which he was caught and arrested again. On the other hand, though he was approached by Catholics, conservatives, and Communists to join one of the resistance movements, he steadfastly refused. His image as a trustworthy democrat was based largely on myth. What is not myth is that as Hitler's aged, durable successor, *der Alte* forgave Nazis en masse, protected war criminals, and operated a government so loaded with Hitler holdover officials that the Führer would have felt quite at home. Adenauer ruled in the name of stability, anti-Communism, the revival of nationalism, and continuity. The voters felt comfortable with all of these achievements, even though "continuity" meant Nazi faces and business as of old. Or possibly they felt comfortable *because* not too much was changing.


"I can't run the country without him," said Chancellor Adenauer, when John McCloy questioned the old gentleman about his most infamous aide, unquestionably the second most powerful personage in the country.

For fourteen years, Dr. Hans Maria Globke, monosyllabic, unobtrusive despite his bulk, held total sway over the chancellor's executive office and exercised his vast powers for the benefit of colleagues from his own "brown past." Under his expressionless, bespectacled eyes, two-thirds of the Foreign Office personnel came to consist of former Nazis. It was Globke who oversaw another nest of Hitler henchmen, General Gehlen's intelligence service. And it was he who ran interference when, as so often, the chancellor's other incriminated ministers came under fire from outraged political opponents.

Again and again, Globke's resignation was demanded. Again and again, he offered politely to step aside. Again and again, Adenauer declared him indispensable.

A lawyer with a magna cum laude mind and an impeccable memory, Globke was considered the best-informed functionary in the land. It was known that personal spies operated for him in the government departments, and the ministers were frustrated because they could not ferret out the underlings who were ratting on them.

"They are all scared of him," said Adenauer of Globke, chuckling. For hours, the pair would exchange confidences while walking in the park behind the chancellor's office. Globke's desk was chronically littered by an ocean of buck slips, many of which he passed to his master as prompters during conferences. Theirs was a seamless partnership.

Globke was long accustomed to high-level approval. In 1938, during his Nazi incarnation, his previous chief, Interior Minister Wilhelm Frick, later executed at Nuremberg, declared in a letter to Hitler's deputy, Rudolf Hess, "*Oberregierungsrat* Dr. Globke is undoubtedly one of the most competent officials in my ministry. To an outstanding degree he participated in the realization of the laws named below."

Those "laws named below" were the so-called Nuremberg Laws, which Globke had turned into more than the degradation of Jewish citizens. He composed the official 300-page compendium of regulations that interpreted how the laws' discriminatory provisions were to be implemented. In principle, he articulated the forerunners of the fit-versus-unfit "selections" that later determined life or death in concentration camps.

Globke's first goal was to earmark all Jews generically, to set them officially apart from the rest of the population. It was he who decreed the infamous ruling that all Jewish men would have to adopt "Israel" as their middle name and all Jewish women would have to call themselves "Sarah." From there, Globke's laws descended into a maze of further humiliations.

"House rules for the brothel" was the phrase flung by one of Globke's opponents. Another said, "He served the spirit that had millions of victims." A third declared him guilty of "judicial prostitution."

The pedantry that would serve Adenauer so worthily was first displayed in Globke's clinical elucidation of what constituted not just a "one-quarter Jew" but also a "three-eighth Jew," and these evaluations were not statistical footnotes. They could become death sentences because they pinpointed exactly what constituted the crime of *Rassenschande,* or racial despoliation.

As the Interior Ministry's "co-director for Jewish questions," it was Globke who directed all judicial and police authorities to note that, in addition to intercourse, "coitus-like acts" also constituted *Rassenschande.* To make himself clear, Globke cited the case of a man named Katzenberger who rendered himself culpable with a gentile woman named Seiler "by pulling her to him, kissing her and petting her thighs."

In special cases, Globke was called in to render a judicial verdict. Thus he refused marriage permission between one Richard Hofman, citizen of "German blood," and a "first degree mongrel," Melitta Bussien from Klein-Machnow near Berlin. His written decision requested that the relevant Gestapo office be notified for further action.

Only upon his retirement was Globke held responsible for his record. Sort of. When he wanted to move into a villa above Vevey in Switzerland, the politically sensitive authorities checked his dossier and refused him residence in their hygienic country.

Globke had many high-ranking compatriots of old in the postwar Adenauer government. Among them were the following:

**President of the Federal Republic: Heinrich Lübke.** In 1944, he supervised the design and construction of two concentration camps. He recruited 2,000 Buchenwald inmates to work twelve-hour shifts 1,300 feet underground so that armaments factories could escape serial Allied bombings. Lübke was responsible for inhuman working conditions that caused a dysentery epidemic and the deaths of at least 267 slave laborers.

**Minister of transportation: Hans Christoph Seebohm.** He "aryanized" Jewish businesses in Czechoslovakia for the Nazis. As the postwar leader of the right-wing German Party, Seebohm was described by *Der Spiegel* magazine as the "prototype of the eternal Nazi" and made rabble-rousing speeches attacking Allied vengeance — the "monstrous crime the victors committed against Germany, Europe, and the whole world."

**Minister for refugees: Theodor Oberländer.** During the war he campaigned for the extermination of Slavic peoples. In 1960, he was forced to resign when it was discovered — or made public — that he had participated in the liquidation of 7,000 Jews and Polish intellectuals in Lvov. He was then political officer of an SS terror unit. For years Adenauer had defended him, although he conceded that Oberländer's past had been "deep brown."

**Personal assistant to the chancellor: Herbert Blankenhorn.** A member of the Nazi Party since 1936, this diplomat had been a ranking official in the Ribbentrop Foreign Ministry. Adenauer entrusted him with the organization of a new diplomatic service. When Blankenhorn received 140 files of unencumbered job applicants, he ordered them to be mixed alphabetically with the papers on 10,000 old Nazi functionaries so that the innocent received much less attention than the guilty. More than sixty ambassadors and ranking officials of the Adenauer Foreign Ministry were Nazi Party members, and many had been instrumental in carrying out the Final Solution.

These and like-minded top-echelon officials, in turn, routinely channeled old Nazi colleagues into the new ministries. Adenauer's ex-Nazi intelligence chief, General Reinhard Gehlen, placed cronies throughout the new Defense Ministry. Hundreds of Hitler's judges and prosecutors were reemployed in their former functions, and not only at rank-and-file levels.

Heinrich Ebersberg, a fairly typical example, had served as the personal assistant to two successive Nazi ministers of justice. In 1949 he was made a judge, and in 1954 he was recruited as a *Ministerialrat* into the Bonn Ministry of Justice.

One of the ministers he served, Franz Schlegelberger, ordered many executions of Jewish prisoners and co-authored the notorious *Nacht und Nebel* (Night and Fog) decree authorizing the arrest of anyone without the slightest formality. The postwar judiciary rewarded him with a pension of 1,450 marks a month, paid until his death at ninety-three, and pensions were likewise handed out wholesale to other judges, SS leaders, generals, and former officeholders of party organizations.

Among those who rated consideration was Heinrich Haffner, the last chief judge of the *Volksgericht* (People's Court). As successor to the most bloodthirsty executioner of all, Chief Judge Roland Freisler, who was killed on the bench in an air raid, Haffner presided over a tribunal that handed out death sentences like traffic tickets. During the final battle for Berlin, Haffner piled all the members of his court into cars in a futile escape attempt. Then he changed his name; lived unmolested as a manufacturer of buttons; and, in 1954, after several investigations, was pensioned with the rank of chief prosecutor.

Forgiveness was also extended to Dr. Herta Oberhäuser, a physician at Ravensbrück concentration camp. She had administered injections of tetanus or gangrene to young female Polish inmates. "Oberhäuser can be described as little better than a sadist," said a British pathology professor who studied her record. She actually rubbed ground glass or sawdust into post-operative wounds in search of treatments for infections. At the Nuremberg trials, where she referred to her subjects as her "guinea pigs," she was given a twenty-year sentence. Soon this was commuted, whereupon she was readmitted to practice as a returning prisoner of war and rewarded with a cash grant and an interest-free loan by the state and medical authorities of Schleswig-Holstein.

At times, Adenauer's Germany recalled the 1930s all too vividly. Even Sepp Dietrich was still in vogue, and there was no throwback more redolent than old Sepp. Joseph "Sepp" Dietrich was scarcely literate, had little knowledge or understanding of strategy, and though he was much loved by his men, he was not very well respected by his fellow Nazi commanders. After the war, Field Marshal von Rundstedt described him as "decent but stupid."

A hero of World War I, Dietrich joined the Nazi Party and the SS early in 1928, rising quickly in the latter's ranks even though he was not very bright. In 1933, on Hitler's personal request, Sepp formed the SS *Leibstandarte* (which later developed into the Waffen-SS), a unit for the protection of the Reich Chancellery. He was one of the leaders in the Night of the Long Knives (the Röhm putsch), and his reputation grew steadily in spite of frequent disagreements with Himmler. During the war Sepp headed the *Leibstandarte* in several campaigns up to 1943, when he took over the SS Panzer Korps, which he led in the final battles in Russia, Belgium, France, and Hungary.

Sepp surrendered to the Americans in 1944, was tried, found guilty of complicity in the Malmédy massacre, and sentenced to life imprisonment in 1946. In 1950 this sentence was reduced to twenty-five years, and in 1955 he was released. However, in 1957 a German court sentenced Sepp to eighteen months in jail for the shooting of SA (*Sturmabteilung*) leaders during the Night of the Long Knives. Released in 1959 for medical reasons, he continued to live in Germany up to his death in 1966. At his funeral, 6,000 ex–Waffen-SS men were present to pay homage to their cherished leader.

# 10

## "HITLER TODAY" — THE HISTORIANS'

## ANGRY DEBATE

$G$uido Knopp — *Doctor* Knopp — is overwhelming, a one-man tumult. Even years ago, walking with him through the monumental and intimidating headquarters building for the 6,000 staffers of ZDF, the Second German Television Network, on the cornfields way outside of Mainz, I felt I was tagging along with a candidate for high public office.

A lanky Goliath with a seven-league stride, Knopp grinned and boomed at all who passed in the corridors and slapped them on the back, throwing out pleasant familiarities. He was a breaker of barriers. I was working on a very small film for him, yet when he introduced me to a roomful of his associates, he had shouted, "An important new contributor, if grossly underpaid!"

Knopp himself *is* important. As the ZDF network's multi-awarded chief of the Department for Contemporary History, he controls the spigot for much of the television diet that all Germans consume about their past. Knopp's staff manufactures documentaries wholesale. In America, documentary makers are often lonely eccentrics tucked into artists' lofts. In Mainz they were very mainstream, grinding out history like sausages, mostly about the Germans and their wars, their leaders, their crises, and, especially, about Hitler, Hitler, Hitler.[1]

---

[1]When I visited him, Knopp was preparing for late 1995 release a new six-part series to examine Hitler, successively, as a criminal, seducer, dictator, aggressor, private citizen, and spoiler. Knopp wrote the companion book to the TV series,

A Ph.D. in history, Knopp came to ZDF in 1978 from the conservative national daily *Die Welt,* where he had been foreign editor. He was twenty-nine and bored. The mayor of Aschaffenburg, the picturesque middle-sized town southwest of Frankfurt that Knopp called home, was also restless. "He wanted to bring a little life to the place," the TV impresario recalled.

The mayor had turned to the right "impresario" for a headline event, and the topic was obvious. The Hitler wave, by then several years running, was still rolling on. "Whether we like it or not, the world of today is the work of Hitler," the historian Sebastian Haffner had recently proclaimed, and it was not lost on Knopp that Haffner's *The Meaning of Hitler* was number one on the country's best-seller lists.

Haffner's record had bestowed a certain immunity on him, especially his having quit Hitler's Germany in disgust in 1938 with his Jewish fiancée, Erika Hirsch. He functioned with distinction as a journalist in London and did not return to Germany until 1954 when he started writing for *Die Welt* and *Stern.* Though he sympathized with the student revolts in 1968, Haffner was a political conservative and an ardent Cold Warrior. Two years before the Wall came down, he caused a stir by writing that the reunification of Germany was neither conceivable nor desirable. Haffner died in 1999.

Germans — at least the intellectuals — liked to defer to historians as impartial arbiters and elder wise men. And something else kept these sages in vogue. As more and more Germans were becoming preoccupied with their nation's past, a specialized vocabulary developed to deal with events dimly remembered from the time of one's parents and grandparents. It became fashionable to ruminate about "repressing" (*verdrängen*) what had transpired; about "working it off" (*aufarbeiten*); "mastering" (*bewältigen*); "working it through" (*durcharbeiten*); "reeducating the young" (*umerziehen*), and other such locutions. Who was more qualified to wrestle with the past than the specialists, the historians, reliable scouts, to shed true light at last?

They were perceived as the totems of clarification and defogging, the ultimate cryptographers.

---

which was published as *Hitler: Eine Bilanz* — *Hitler: A Summary.* His new book, *Hitler's Henchmen,* was published late in 2000 by Alfred A. Knopf.

Haffner was not the only brand name available. Knopp decided to bring together a prestigious group for a public discussion in Aschaffenburg on the weekend of July 1 and 2, 1978. He named the event *Hitler Heute,* "Hitler Today," and loaded the program in advance, somewhat mischievously, so that the proceedings were more or less guaranteed to turn out lively.

Perhaps too lively, or so some of the invited dignitaries decided. Thus, the Institute for Contemporary History in Munich declined to dispatch a representative, fearing Knopp's inexperience and the possibility of excessive controversy.

Haffner agreed to attend, but the potentially hottest drawing card, Joachim C. Fest, begged off because his own best-selling Hitler biography and especially the follow-up that had made him famous left him overexposed on the subject. Or so he hinted. Robert Kempner, the Nuremberg prosecutor, bowed out, pleading last-minute illness. Professor Gerald Fleming, the feisty Hitler scholar from the University of Sussex, England, did not wish to appear in the company of some of the invited guests. And Professor Eberhard Jäckel, of the University of Stuttgart, possibly the most respected "Hitler scholar" within his profession, was also reluctant but finally yielded to the blandishments of Knopp's persuasive salesmanship.

One of the other deterrents was Professor Werner Maser, author of a 669-page Hitler biography that some critics had labeled "sloppy" when it appeared in 1971. Worse, Maser, who is the self-appointed *Verwalter des Hitler Nachlasses* — administrator of the Hitler estate — had turned to pushing a questionable new hobbyhorse, a Frenchman named Jean-Marie Loret, who alleged he was Hitler's illegitimate son. The darkest cloud over Aschaffenburg, however, was also Guido Knopp's fondest joy (his "stink bomb," as he conceded years later with a broad smile): the most embattled Hitler chronicler of all, David Irving, the London author and Hitler fan, notorious for egomania, bizarre viewpoints, and impressive worldwide book sales.

A consummate showman, Irving shook Aschaffenburg from the moment he made his entrance in his Rolls-Royce, and, throughout, all of Knopp's verbal skills and decibel level were needed to manage his cast of twelve stars so they would not feel like extras in The David Irving Show. Further spice was added by right-wing bomb threats, which caused police to search all participants, a rare precaution at that time. The media descended on Mainz: there were observers from some fifty newspapers, four television networks, and twelve radio stations. One correspondent arrived from Brazil, the scene of a best-selling post-Nazi thriller, The Boys from Brazil, which had just been turned into a hit movie starring Gregory Peck as Dr. Mengele and Sir Laurence Olivier as the Nazi hunter Ezra Lieberman.

Suspecting that his notions about Hitler would come under expert assault, Irving jumped in to defend himself with a classic maneuver: he attacked, viciously, plunging the meeting into a series of rancorous confrontations.

"Do you want the total truth?" he shouted at his startled peers. This question would merely have sounded quaint to non-Germans, but his colleagues immediately understood Irving's mean-spirited allusion. Back when World War II was moving into its final, most mortal phase, propaganda minister Joseph Goebbels had screamed into a mob of the faithful a battle cry that became famous overnight: "Do you want total war?" And the faithful bawled back, "Ja, ja, ja!" Now Irving used a parallel challenge to declare total war on his colleagues.

Plagiarism was his first charge. "German historians only work from memoirs," he asserted. "They buy twenty books, read them, and then write the twenty-first. Then comes another one, buys the twenty-one books, and writes number twenty-two. And so the legends grow and the faking becomes ever worse."

The reaction among the audience of several hundred laymen and academics was mixed. The applause was vigorous, but so were the catcalls of "Pfui! Pfui!"

Next, Irving taxed his fellow researchers with acute laziness. While they kept copying each other, he said, he sought out the keepers of original documents, letters, and diaries. His peers squatted behind their desks. "They can't go into the field," he charged. "They can't sit for hours with old widows."

This was heavy artillery, for even scholars who detested Irving did respect his excavations in the homes of widows and in other obscure repositories of forgotten papers. Thanks to this diligence he had turned out volumes about the firebombing of Dresden; on the secret German project to make an atomic bomb for Hitler; and other spectacular work. His then recent biography, *The Trail of the Fox* (1977), a life of Field Marshal Erwin Rommel, was a Main Selection of the Book-of-the-Month Club in the United States and was acclaimed as authoritative all over the world.

Hitler was Irving's Achilles' heel and his vulnerability became evident during the ten years during which he wrote *Hitler's War*, also published in 1977. He admitted that he "identified" with his subject and referred to him by first name. Since he adored Hitler and could not locate any secret documents to link his hero with the Holocaust, he simply declared that Hitler was completely ignorant of the destruction of the Jews. If historians like Fest and Maser kept writing history otherwise, so he told the Aschaffenburg gathering, they were copycats and "should be ashamed of themselves."

This outburst set off applause, calls of "boo!" and a counterattack from the less creative historians. Sebastian Haffner weighed in with a list of quotations from some of the Hitler speeches in which the Führer pledged to stamp out all Jewish "vermin." Haffner demanded, "Do you think this is all idle prattle, *Herr* Irving?"

Eberhard Jäckel scoffed: "The structure of the Third Reich made this totally absurd. In that Reich, nothing of such scope could happen without Hitler knowing about it."

"That's hair-splitting," countered Irving. "I ask for only one detailed line. In America and now in England, too, I have made the following offer: if one shows me a single line from a war document — and it doesn't necessarily have to be a direct order from the Führer — or any proof that Hitler knew about the destruction of the Jews, I will pay that person $1,000. So far nobody has come forward."

Guido Knopp thereupon read a document sent in from England by Professor Fleming. In February of that same year (1978), Fleming had obtained a sworn statement from a respectable citizen, a former Wehrmacht sergeant in a communications center of German-occupied Russia. It disclosed a radio order he had decoded in July 1942. The order was signed by Hitler and was directed to his commissioner for

Ukraine, Erich Koch. It called for the elimination of the 70,000 Jews still subsisting in ghettos in the area of Rovno, Koch's headquarters.

Irving, the authority on documents, jeered. Fleming's source, he judged, lacked the rank necessary to decode such a document. The sergeant's declaration had to be fake and "was not to be taken seriously."

The assembled historians found Professor Maser an easier target. With Irving having shown the way to incivility, they turned to attacking Maser about Hitler's alleged illegitimate son.

"Why is this historically relevant?" wondered Professor Albrecht Tyrell.

"I sometimes feel that Maser digs for too many earthworms," said Haffner.

"Maser doesn't see the forest for all the trees," insisted Tyrell.

"Maser's attempt at documentation doesn't yield a shadow of proof that such a Hitler son actually exists," bristled Professor Jäckel. "I consider the entire story pure sensation-mongering."

The distant — yet not so far-off — past continued to hang heavily over the gathering, and David Irving, in particular, was not about to let it go. When the remark was heard among the discussants that Hitler had been "no charlatan," Irving offered his view on the Führer's popular appeal.

"In 1938, Hitler received 49 million *Ja* votes," he said, "99.97 percent of German voters."

"Those weren't free elections," countered Haffner mildly.

Irving: "There were 49 million *Ja* votes. One talks of fake election returns, but there is no proof."

That was too much for Professor Iring Fetscher from Frankfurt University. Pounding his fist on the table, he shouted, "How can you talk such nonsense? How can you claim that civil liberties existed in a totalitarian state? Listen, my father was shot by the Nazis! . . . It simply isn't true that a 99 percent majority agreed with Hitler in 1938."

Irving: "I ask you to stay calm . . ."

Professor Jäckel: "Free elections are only possible in a pluralistic system. The National Socialist state was nothing of the kind."

With time beginning to run out on Guido Knopp's "Hitler Today" weekend, he asked his congress to move on from what had in effect been preoccupying the experts so far: the traumas of "Hitler Yester-day."

"In Frankfurt," began Professor Fetscher, "we have for years seen a strange indicator: constantly rising prices for Nazi symbols in the flea markets. A World War II belt buckle without swastika costs 10 marks, a buckle with a swastika costs 20 marks, an SS buckle is 30 marks."

"In Munich," said Knopp, "Hitler's driver's license lately brought 4,500 marks."

"Above all," said Fetscher, "one phenomenon disturbs me very much: a great many very young people are involved. It's not just the eternal enthusiasts from yesterday. . . . One would have to examine more precisely the impact of a Hitler film like Fest's. . . . Do people leave the theater and say, 'That was one terrific fellow'?"

The historians, accustomed to limiting their attention to bygone times, left it to the one professional filmmaker in the group, Hans-Jürgen Syberberg, to attempt an exploration of Hitler as a contemporary happening. The previous year, 1977, Syberberg had finished his seven-hour art film *Hitler: A Film from Germany,* an internationally controversial amalgam of fantasies. This artist found the realities of his Aschaffenburg environment meaningful and unsettling.

"We are sitting here in a hall that is filled to overflowing," he said. "Outside stand dozens of policemen, heavily armed and equipped with all the technology there is. And everyone in the public suddenly is talking about being part of a *movement,* even left-wingers, constantly about a *movement.* This language is a true heritage of National Socialism.[2] No one talks about that. It is part of a vast repression that is going on currently. We live in an aggressive nation where groups are locked in devilish combat. That is Hitler's heritage. . . . The danger of Hitler lay in the fact that he was eminently modern."

Knopp, still steeled for combat, asked Irving whether the British biographer's "heroization" of Hitler was not "dangerous."

"What's dangerous is a trivialization of the Hitler wave," Irving responded. "People pretend that there is very little interest in Hitler

---

[2]"The National Socialist movement" was a hallowed cliché of the Hitlerian vocab-ulary. Thus, Munich was "the capital of the movement."

among Germans. But the interest exists. One can't track it by some public opinion institute going around and asking people on the street, 'How do you feel about Hitler?' That won't yield anything. Most Germans share my opinion: Hitler was a man of format."

Dr. Helm Stierlin, the one psychiatrist among the panelists, had been saying little thus far. A professor at the University of Heidelberg, he was author of such books as *Separating Parents and Adolescents* and *Adolf Hitler: Family Perspectives*. For seventeen years he had been on the staff of the National Institutes of Mental Health in Washington.

"The stronger we are all emotionally affected," he said, "the stronger shame and guilt come into play and the harder it is to gain perspective, and the more necessary it is. Many parallels exist in the psychotherapeutic work with families. The stronger the entanglement, the more difficult it is to cope with the conflicts. And the more necessary. Otherwise the past remains an open wound."

Professor Jäckel reminded his peers that a forbidding generation gap aggravated the difficulty of dealing with the Hitler memory. "Again and again I hear from my students who now teach history that the destruction of the Jews is particularly difficult to convey to young people. They simply cannot conceive how a bureaucracy can murder such an enormous number of people."

Professor Fetscher added, "They are ashamed to an enormous degree because their parents and grandparents were unable to prevent Hitler."

It was agreed that only further long and laborious education would wean the people from their Führer and that the prognosis was not bright. Said filmmaker Syberberg, "When I see what information students do receive, I am overcome by nausea."

He was an exception.

# BOOK 3

## THE HITLER WAVE

# 11

## REMEMBERING HITLER AS

## A SUCCESS STORY

Professor Eberhard Jäckel of Stuttgart University and retired Frank-furt newspaper publisher Joachim C. Fest are no longer on speaking terms. More than thirty years after Hitler's bodily exit, their conflict over his memory grew too intense for these suave, best-selling authors, both distinguished historians, both highly visible in the media.

It is a reliable measure of Hitler's contemporary standing with the Germans — and of the deeply rooted nostalgia he still arouses by re-membrance of his accomplishments, yes, his accomplishments — that Fest rose to become by far the more celebrated and affluent of the two. Their difference: Jäckel branded Hitler a mass murderer, while Fest wrote a famous biography in which, one way or another, explicitly *and* implicitly, he termed Hitler "great."

Intellectually, the Hitler wave was anchored in Fest's *Hitler,* inter-nationally accepted as the stellar entry among several "standard' works on the subject. Published in 1973, when the author was forty-seven, it sold 300,000 hardcover copies in Germany alone, and it is easy to see why. Fest's version was thoughtfully composed by a master of narrative. It offered scope, sophistication, even elegance. But its appeal as a popular hit radiated from a deeper well.

Fest's *Hitler* was more than a book of 844 printed pages. It was an act of patriotism. This lofty biographer did not indulge in crudities like his colleague, Professor Werner Maser, who was fascinated because the Führer's eyes were so "startlingly blue" and "he knew cars and motors as thoroughly as the experts." Nor did Fest trivialize the Holocaust.

His treatment of the Jews was, as the Germans like to pronounce, "correct." It was an exercise in minimalism: a terse summary here, a couple of descriptive pages there, and no attempt to minimize the horrors. Only the index suggests what is operative in Fest's concept of Hitler and what is not. There is no entry for Adolf Eichmann. The planner and executor of the Final Solution was ignored, even though Fest was writing more than ten years after Eichmann's trial, with its massive trail of revelations, preceded by months of interrogations, all published.

Instead, Fest gratified his readers with evidence of Hitler's "greatness" (Webster: "markedly superior in quality; noble of soul").

The preoccupation with the Führer's nobility began with the first line of the book's prologue, a good example of the Festian sweep: "History records no phenomenon like him. Ought we to call him 'great'? No one evoked so much rejoicing, hysteria, and expectation of salvation as he; no one so much hate. No one else produced, in a solitary course lasting only a few years, such incredible accelerations in the pace of history. No one else so changed the state of the world."

Having asked, rhetorically, in his first paragraph whether Hitler "ought" to be called great, thereby seeming to shift the responsibility for such a judgment to his readers, Fest rushed to take his seat as judge and jury in the first few words of the next paragraph, where Hitler's cup runneth over and his greatness becomes fact. "Hitler's peculiar greatness," we are told, "is essentially linked to . . . a tremendous eruption of energy that shattered all existing standards. Granted, gigantic scale is not necessarily equivalent to historic greatness . . . but he was not only gigantic . . . The eruption he unleashed was stamped throughout . . . by his guiding will."

Triumph of the will! Consciously or not, Fest was summoning the splendor of Leni Riefenstahl's film of that name, a title that the Führer was said to have personally coined for the propaganda masterpiece that his favorite filmmaker created of the 1936 Olympics.

In case any reader needed further documentation for the diversity of Hitler's powers, Fest ran down the details: "To a virtually unprecedented degree, he created everything out of himself and was himself everything at once: his own teacher, organizer of a party and author of its ideology, tactician, and demagogic savior, leader, statesman, and for a decade the 'axis' of the world."

The word "demagogic," like much of Fest's other pained criticisms, hardly registered. Readers were entitled to receive the volume as mostly heartwarming. Indeed, the biographer's admiration for his subject was expressed explicitly.

"If Hitler had succumbed to an assassination or an accident at the end of 1938," he wrote about midway through his text, "few would hesitate to call him one of the greatest of German statesmen, the consummator of Germany's history."

Great . . . greatness . . . greatest . . . The theme ran like a leitmotif through page after uplifting page; the apocalyptic years after 1939 melted away into an embarrassing afterword.

Thus, on page 434 of the American edition, "reclaiming swamps and wetlands, reforestation, building autobahns and regulating streams became visible and inspiring signs of accomplishment and faith in the future."

Further down the same page: "Employment was indeed the key factor for the success of the Third Reich's rigorous social policies."

Still along the same page: "What really mattered was the feeling of restored social security after traumatic years of anxiety and gloom."

And at the bottom of the page: "By granting everyone opportunity to rise, the regime in fact demonstrated class neutrality."

Moving on in Fest's story, we find that "Hitler accomplished an amazing amount" while demonstrating exemplary control: "He was good at portraying feelings; he took pains not to show them. No wonder that he was long regarded as the really progressive, modern figure of the age." At least Fest found this to be the view of most of his contemporaries.

True to its basic premise, the book's last page again paid respects to the "towering leader," the "great demagogue" who was, overall, such a "great" figure of history.

More revelatory even than the book's vast success was Fest's person. He was no contemplative academic, removed from controversy and deadlines. Born in Berlin, he was a city councilman for the conservative

Christian Democratic Union, then, successively, political editor at the RIAS radio, editor in chief for contemporary history at the NDR network, and chief of *Panorama,* a leading TV public affairs show. After taking nearly five years for his writing, including *Hitler,* Fest joined the leading conservative daily *Frankfurter Allgemeine Zeitung* as co-publisher and held that post until 1994. In 1999, he published a biography of Albert Speer, Hitler's architect and later minister of armaments and ammunition. Speer had joined the NSDAP in 1931, where he became famous for his organizational skills, initially in the promotion of rallies and party days and later in maintaining the war economy at an all-time high in spite of Allied bombardment.

In 1945 Speer refused to follow Hitler's *Nero-Befehl* — Nero-Order, according to which the retreating Nazi army was to burn everything behind them in order to hold up the Allies. At the Nuremberg trials in 1946 Speer was sentenced to twenty years in prison (rather than hanging) because he admitted his role in the Third Reich but claimed he had no direct knowledge of the Final Solution.

Once he was released, Speer published a 1,200-page memoir, *Erinnerungen (Recollections;* the translation is entitled *Inside the Third Reich),* which was extraordinarily successful, making him a wealthy man. Up to his death in 1981, Speer presented himself as a penitent man who "didn't know but should have known." Because of the apparent complexity of his relationship with Hitler, his charismatic character, and his influence in so many aspects of the Nazi rule, he has — in addition to his voluminous writing — been the subject of no fewer than five biographies.

Fest met Speer in 1966 and describes him as "somewhat humble, unassuming, almost demure." Of the meeting, he recalls, "I could hardly believe that this friendly gentleman should be identical to the NS-minister, who was one of the most powerful men of the Third Reich." His book *Albert Speer: Eine Biographie* has received excellent reviews on Amazon.de and in *Der Spiegel* magazine.

Fest's assessment of Speer is that of a striver marching archly down his undeviating mainstream groove, surely not someone out of sync with popular opinion. Fest knows where his readers live.

\*    \*    \*

Eberhard Jäckel, the historian who took issue with Fest, saw the Hitler legacy in infinitely darker hues. Thus, there was nothing stiffly "correct" about Jäckel's perception of the Holocaust. He reviewed only stark horror.

"In the end this wasn't even a gigantic pogrom any more," he wrote in the 1980s. "The bureaucratic process of cold-bloodedly organized, mechanized mass murder without precedent in history reached a point . . . where language ceases to function."

Nor did Jäckel shrug off, as did Fest, the collective feelings of the Germans for their Führer as wholesome admiration. "The attitude of the Germans to Hitler appeared to have been primarily determined not by admiration, respect or fear," Jäckel analyzed. "Especially during the war, there was a downright infantile dependency upon a beloved father and it could escalate to pity." To the bitter end, citizens felt protective toward him. They would sigh over bad news and say, "The Führer is truly spared nothing," or in matters provoking particular outrage, "If only the Führer knew!"

A number one best-seller of 1978 in Germany, *The Meaning of Hitler* seemed to encourage a somewhat ambivalent view of the Hitler inheritance, at least at first glance. The author, Sebastian Haffner, a small, mild, friendly Berliner then in his early seventies, was once described as "the Prussian with the British passport."

His numerous fans respected Haffner — born Raimund Pretzel — for his judicious books about such figures as Churchill and Bismarck, as well as for his anti-Nazi past. A lawyer and not Jewish, Haffner had wanted to become a judge. Unable to marry his Jewish fiancée, he left with her for Great Britain in 1938, wrote his first book, *Germany: Jekyll and Hyde,* and served with distinction as a correspondent for the *Observer,* initially in London, then in Berlin after the war.

Haffner's appraisal set out much like Fest's apologia. It applauded Hitler's "resolution, boldness, courage, perseverance," and his ability to energize followers with his "mass hypnotism." The next twenty-four-page section, labeled "Achievements," rang with praise for Hitler's "organizing talent" and the "uncanny dynamism" of the party that was his creation and became the vehicle for the success of this "miracle worker."

"Among the positive achievements of Hitler, the one outshining all others was his economic miracle," Haffner wrote. "At least as sensational, and just as unexpected, was the re-militarism and re-armament of Germany. . . . By 1938 it was the strongest military and air power in Europe. An incredible achievement!"

Postwar hindsight was helping nobody, Haffner argued. "Today the 'How could we?' of the old people and the 'How could you?' of the young trip easily off the tongue. At the time, however, it required quite exceptional perception and farsightedness to recognize in Hitler's achievements and successes the hidden seeds of future disaster."

The list of glory was truly formidable: "The unemployed had again been given work. . . . The Treaty of Versailles had really become a scrap of paper. A colossal achievement, to have united virtually the entire nation behind him — and accomplished in less than ten years! . . . Never before had women moved into so many male occupations."

Haffner sounded breathless. "As a star performer," he concluded, "Hitler probably ranks even higher than Napoleon."

In an interview later, Haffner explained that by giving Hitler credit for positive deeds he hoped to achieve credibility and balance. "If people only hear abuse," he said, "it's human nature that one day they'll raise the question: was everything really all that bad? It's important to prevent that."

And so Haffner composed twenty-four devastating pages entitled "Crimes."

"Hitler had countless harmless people put to death, for no military or political purpose, but merely for his personal gratification. He was, among other things, quite simply a mass murderer. Here we are using the term in its precise criminological meaning."


Of the three leading German authorities on the Hitler legacy — Fest, Haffner, and Jäckel — only Jäckel issued a prognosis a generation ago that still proved valid in the 1990s.

Haffner declared the Führer dead and forgotten. "The people really felt betrayed by their Führer and justly so," he concluded in *The Mean-*

*ing of Hitler.* "Germany cut loose from him in the end — more quickly than expected and also more thoroughly. . . . Thirty-three years after Hitler's suicide, no one in Germany professing Hitler and wishing to take up his heritage has even the slightest political outsider's chance."

Fest's writing also was funereal. "He did not last beyond his time," this silky prophet preached. "Hitler had no secret that extended beyond his immediate presence . . . [the] effects [of his life] were vast, the terror it spread was enormous; but when it was over there was little left for memory to hold."

Jäckel, pessimist and realist, called it right: "The Germans were liberated from Hitler, but they will never rid themselves of him."

# 12

## HOW THE OLD GUARD KEEPS
## THE LEGEND ALIVE

Polls document that a sizable minority of Germans, more than one third, has been consistently unwilling over the decades to brand Hitler as a criminal. Instead, perhaps reflecting the stated opinions of several best-selling German historians, they see him as "one of the greatest statesmen."

These romantics — plus undoubtedly many others who for obvious reasons refuse to respond candidly to pollsters — saw the world not in conventional configuration. For them, the political clock had stood still. The past endured. Hitler was in their bones, a living symbol. And their permissiveness was of a piece with the laissez-faire that was accorded to venerable Hitler loyalists. The public was not greatly exercised over the misguided fidelity or the crimes of these oldsters during the Third Reich; indeed, the postwar activities of this claque were noted mostly with understanding or tacit approval. These old-timers had been on intimate terms with the deity, touched by greatness, which made them interesting.

The old ones, in turn, knew that they held sway over a large, appreciative audience and found satisfying ways to use their fans to provide a comfortable living and, in the cases of genocidal war criminals, a protective atmosphere for continuing political activity. Culpability varied, the goal did not: the perpetuation of Nazism.

*Anton Joachimsthaler: the Keeper of the Flame*

Anton Joachimsthaler would be surprised if someone called him a Nazi. He thought of himself as a lay historian, a tinkerer with a preoccupation named Adolf Hitler. Well over six feet tall, Joachimsthaler was a hearty Bavarian, once a railroad engineer, indefatigable and guileless. Since he was a bit lonely himself, it came naturally to him in his sixties to empathize with the aging folk from the mountain, the Führer's inner circle, living mostly alone and in the past, especially the half dozen secretaries. Hitler had invariably behaved in a courtly manner toward these totally committed workers, but since their lives belonged to him they never married.

Joachimsthaler was a repository of such internal data because, over the years of researching, he constantly met more and more Hitler courtiers: the valets, drivers, guards, and the lonely women.

"They're all in touch with one another," he said, "and word got out about me, 'He's OK.'"

Shouldering his responsibilities as a guardian of the Hitler legacy, he was frequently enraged at presumptive competitors whose efforts he found mistaken or inferior. One of these scholars was the history professor Werner Maser, whose hefty Hitler biography Joachimsthaler deplored as being full of "erroneous information." Furthermore, "Maser's trafficking with his sources was more than careless," he accused.

Thus challenged, Joachimsthaler produced a volume of his own, slender but stern, 252 pages with 888 footnotes, called *Adolf Hitler: Correction of a Biography*. Since Hitler footnotes are a booming cottage industry, this correction sold respectably, even though it tackled only a modest early slice of Hitler's life, the twelve years from 1908 to 1920, thirteen years before he rose to power.[1]

I was calling on the agreeable Herr Joachimsthaler at his apartment in the northern suburbs of Munich, pursuing the suggestion of a knowledgeable contact at the Institute for Contemporary History.

---

[1]Joachimsthaler had earlier produced a book about a Hitler hobbyhorse so specialized that few ever heard of it: a transcontinental superrailroad with ten-foot gauge to help unify the economics of the future-and-forever Reich to come.

His diligent labors enjoyed respect there. My interest centered on the 1985 autobiography *He Was My Chief* by Christa Schroeder, which Joachimsthaler had spent four years editing and augmenting with 134 pages of his own notes.

His longtime fraternal feelings for what he called Hitler's *Hofstaat* (Court State) had brought him in contact with Frau Schroeder years earlier. A Berlin friend of his, once attached to Führer headquarters as a cameraman, knew that Joachimsthaler was planning to drive from Munich to Berlin and asked him to take Frau Schroeder along.

Chatting during the trip, the historian learned that his passenger, trim and shrewd, had once been a legal secretary and had joined Hitler when he seized power in 1933. Until the end in the bunker, she had taken his dictation, literally and figuratively. It also turned out that she was working on her memoirs, having been asked to write up a sizable batch of notes during her internment by the Allies in 1945 and resuming work, off and on, in the 1970s.

Inspecting her partial manuscript, Joachimsthaler was encouraged. True, he told her, it was getting a bit late for memoirs of Hitler. The market was so receptive, everybody had been remembering their time with the Führer: August Kubizek, his boyhood playmate; Hanna Reitsch, his pilot; Heinz Linge, his valet; Wolf Hess, the son of Hitler deputy Rudolf Hess; Emmy Göring, Hermann's widow; the many surviving generals; and of course, the writing star of stars, Albert Speer.

Still, Joachimsthaler thought that Frau Schroeder's work might be salable. She could grovel like the most abject sycophant, gushing on about her Führer's delicate hands ("beautiful, in movement or at rest"); the generosity of his tipping; the "amazement" voiced by noted architects over Hitler's mastery of their profession.

Yet she was also able to muster a professional biographer's prisms for masses of detail, and at times she could interpose some distance between her boss and herself. Shuttling between dependency and independence, Schroeder was no full-time drone. Although she never dropped her reverence, not even when she worked alone with Hitler or he asked her to stay for tea, she took it upon herself to speak up and champion certain of his eligible and largely unknown female admirers while turning scathingly against others.

Appreciatively, Joachimsthaler read in Schroeder's manuscript that she once urged her chief outright to get rid of his longtime mistress Eva Braun. Christa judged her superficial and silly.

"Eva is nothing for you, *mein Führer,*" she told him.

The Führer didn't blink.

"Instead of holding this impertinent remark against me," Schroeder wrote, "he looked at me in amusement and said verbatim: 'But she suffices for me!'"

The insolent secretary was pleased; her assessment of Eva had been vindicated.

"'She suffices!'" So she mimicked Hitler. "Nothing about the great love that some scriveners claimed to know about after 1945."

Assuredly, Frau Schroeder was no scrivener. She worshiped, but she worshiped at the source, the Führer's mouth, and attentively so. Was she jealous of Eva Braun? I couldn't put the question to Frau Schroeder because she had died a decade earlier at the age of seventy-six. I'm inclined to doubt it. Her editorial collaborator, Herr Joachimsthaler, almost certainly appraised the relationship correctly.

"She saw him as a father," he told me. "Hitler never had a family. His inner circle was his ersatz family. He was sentimental about them."

Sentimental and dictatorial. When Schroeder became engaged to a Yugoslav diplomat, she astutely omitted telling her chief about it. Hitler found out and was quite upset. He didn't care for foreigners and soon the engagement was dissolved.

His favors were reserved for native folk of racially pure blood — the "Prinzesserl," for instance, the "little princess." When she was little, her father owned a Munich inn where the first of the Nazis gathered in the early 1920s. Hitler liked the little princess, and ever after — for decades — kept her name on his list of people to whom he dutifully sent Christmas presents.

Joachimsthaler told me the story because he said he wanted me to know what a kindly fellow Hitler was at Christmas and on other family occasions. As my host led me out of his apartment, where Nazi files all but created gridlock, we stopped at one room where the walls were lined to the ceiling with nothing but file folders. With a sure hand, the guardian of Hitler's benevolence fished out and showed me the denazification file of the little princess.

German thoroughness back then, German thoroughness now.

I suggested to Joachimsthaler, without a trace of noticeable sarcasm, or so I hoped, that he might find it commercial to market a warm article called "Christmas with the Führer." The idea seemed to appeal to him.

Frau Schroeder would certainly have realized that I was making a macabre joke; she knew that the picture of Hitler as the kindly uncle was preposterous, and this awareness troubled her greatly.

"For years everybody has been drilling into me that I must write what I know about Adolf Hitler," she noted in 1979. "But instead of giving myself the assignment to work diligently for at least two or three hours a day, I was always overwhelmed by my awareness of the many levels of Hitler's personality. It plunged me into depression."

Her ambivalence had already begun three decades earlier, shortly after the war's end. On a transport to a war crimes trial of Nazi doctors, she found herself sitting next to Dr. Karl Brandt, Hitler's personal physician and major general Reich commissioner for health and sanitation. Brandt was charged with special responsibility for, and participation in, medical experiments on concentration camp inmates including freezing, euthanasia, epidemic jaundice, bone, muscle, and nerve regeneration, and bone transplantation. The doctor was a defendant, Schroeder a witness.

"Was the boss a good or an evil person?" she asked Brandt, posing the dilemma she would never lay to rest for the next four decades.

Brandt had barely survived the war, having been sentenced to death by Hitler for alleged "betrayal." He offered Schroeder a firm diagnosis.

"He was a devil."

Not long afterward, Brandt was hanged by the American occupiers, "rightly or wrongly," Anton Joachimsthaler observed to me, shrugging. On the scaffold, Brandt made his final speech, in which he declared that his sentence was "nothing but political revenge. . . . It is no shame to stand on this scaffold. I served my fatherland as others before me."

Joachimsthaler was his ever cheery self. At the elevator, I asked him if the Schroeder book had been published. "Oh yes," he responded. It had gone through six printings, with a paperback yet to come, and his publisher was urging him to make further use of his wide network of Hitler contacts. "It doesn't matter what I write," he said, "they'll take everything."

### General Remer's Five-Decade War

Loyalty to Hitler thrust Major General Otto Ernst Remer into a pivotal role in history at the age of thirty-two. By 1993, Remer was a retired general of eighty-one, but the Führer — "basically a democrat" was the way Remer recalled him — remained enshrined in his mind as his leader, the idol of his life's cause and that of the general's many followers.

Still tall, lean, and perfectly erect, Remer wore his leather-trimmed jacket like a uniform. The white shirt was stiffly starched, and over the decades his voice of command had dimmed little more than his defiant and very public ideology.

"What is this?" he once rhetorically asked of a magazine writer as he poured lighter fluid from a cigarette lighter, then sniffed the fumes. When his interviewer shook his head, unable to solve the puzzle, Remer replied, "That's a Jew who is homesick for Auschwitz."

Without this loyalist, Hitler might have been overthrown on July 20, 1944, at the height of World War II.

Still a mere major in the army, Remer was already a hero before he became the key to that celebrated occasion (which Germans glorify as proof that some of them did oppose the Hitler regime). Eight times he had been wounded in forty-eight days of close combat. Hitler personally had decorated him with the Knight's Cross and Oak Leaf Cluster. As a further honor, the major had been given command of the elite *Grossdeutschland* battalion guarding the heart of the government command complex in Berlin's Wilhelmstrasse district.

Toward 5 P.M. on the fateful twentieth of July, Remer's commanding general, the commandant of Berlin, told him that Hitler had been "accidentally" killed at Führer headquarters in East Prussia. Remer's men were to surround the government complex and permit no movement in or out. They rushed to do so, setting up machine guns in the streets.

Unknown to Remer, his commanding officer was a co-conspirator of *Walküre,* a high-level but sloppily planned bomb plot to assassinate their commander-in-chief. In fact, Hitler had only been slightly injured. Since the generals had picked out a complete new government but had not troubled to cut telephone lines, Joseph Goebbels, the little propaganda minister who had taken charge of the crisis in Berlin, had confirmed Hitler's survival by talking to the leader himself.

Nevertheless, control of the capital stood uncertain. Goebbels was seen to retrieve some poison pills from a closet ("Just in case," he said). Then he had Remer summoned to his office, not knowing that the major had just been instructed to arrest him.

When the major, strapping and bronzed, entered at 6:40 P.M. with a brisk "Heil Hitler!" and his pistol drawn, the situation was ripe for a hero.

Remer later related, "The minister asked me whether I was a confirmed National Socialist. I said that of course I stood 100 percent behind the Führer." He added, however, that the Führer was dead and that he had to follow the orders of his commanding general. He was suspicious, thinking that perhaps Goebbels was involved in a fight to succeed Hitler.

Whereupon Goebbels called out triumphantly, "The Führer lives!" Remer stared uncertainly, so Goebbels shouted again, "He lives!"

He explained that a "tiny clique of ambitious generals" had tried to stage a cowardly putsch and that he had just spoken with Hitler. Since Remer looked pleased but incredulous, Goebbels made a little speech about "this historic hour" and the "enormous responsibility" resting on the major's shoulders. Then he offered to call Hitler on the spot.

"After all," he told Remer with a slightly sarcastic tone, "can't the Führer give you orders that cancel the orders of your general?"

Remer agreed, but inwardly he remained uncertain. He wondered whether somebody might try to imitate Hitler's voice. Then he remembered having been summoned by Hitler the year before for a soldier-to-soldier talk about combat tactics. He knew Hitler's voice.

The phone connection was made, and as Remer later reported, "The Führer said he was uninjured and asked whether I recognized his voice. I replied in the affirmative." Goebbels and his entourage only heard the major repeating, "Jawohl, mein Führer . . . jawohl. . . ."

The generals' plot had collapsed. Remer had saved the government. The grateful Hitler rewarded him handsomely: Remer was leap-frogged to the rank of major general and given command of an infantry division. Encircled near Berlin in the final days of the war, Remer was ordered to break out toward the south. Instead, he put on civilian clothes and retreated west across the Elbe into American-held territory, leaving his troops to fend for themselves.

His attack of cowardice proved no handicap in 1950, when Remer activated his political credits as the Führer's 1944 rescuer and formed the neo-Nazi Socialist Reichs Party. He proved an effective drawing card, winning 300,000 votes in Lower Saxony before his party was declared unconstitutional. An unfavorable libel ruling drove him to Egypt and Syria, where he set up an arms importing business and worked with another famous Nazi refugee, the aforementioned Alois Brunner.

Nostalgia brought him back to Germany in 1981 to organize the "Remer Brigade," later known as the "German Liberty movement." In Bad Kissingen, a cozy spa, the general next established his own news-paper, *Justice and Truth,* and a mail-order business for literature denying the Holocaust and railing against refugees ("Assimilation is Geno-cide"), an activity for which he was repeatedly imprisoned for breaking Germany's anti-Nazi laws. His wife, Ameliese, was his partner.

The company's mid-1990s list offered Remer's memoirs about the drama of July 20, 1944, entitled *Verschwörung und Verrat um Hitler* (*Conspiracy and Treason around Hitler*); his 516-page exposé of the international "hate campaign" that drove Germany into both world wars; and blasts denouncing Zionism and complimenting deniers of the Holocaust.

*Conspiracy and Treason around Hitler* was aptly titled, since it covered considerably more than the bomb plot. In spare, seemingly factual prose, it was a bizarre, wrong-way accounting of several World War II landmark events: the Allied landings in Normandy, Hitler's defeat at Stalingrad, the German failure to build an atomic bomb. All these disasters, and many more, he claimed, were rooted in sabotage, trea-son hatched by Hitler's enemies. And, of course, the generals of the July 20, 1944, plot, now celebrated as darlings of the anti-Hitler resistance, are Remer's most despicable traitors.

Ridiculous? Not to many German readers. My edition of the work (1993) was the fifth. The octogenarian war hero is still a voice of influence.

An honored guest at neo-Nazi assemblies, including rallies for the historian David Irving, Remer was long pessimistic about the outlook for his political kind. With reunification and the subsequent opinion shift in the direction of the new nationalism, Remer detected a revolutionary *Umschwung* — reversal — in the political atmosphere. His prospects improved "suddenly, overnight." Says he, "Perspectives have opened up that we cannot yet fully appreciate." Remer, faithful to the end, died in 1997.


*Hitler's Men Go Down Fighting: Colonel Peiper and François Genoud*

Joachim "Jochen" Peiper received a military education and was sworn into the SS in 1935 when he was only twenty. In 1940 he was assigned to war duty as Himmler's first military adjutant in Belgium, where he was quickly promoted and won several prestigious awards for bravery. Transferred back to the *Leibstandarte* in 1941, Peiper fought on the Eastern Front and later was commander of the unit at Malmédy in Belgium at the time of the notorious massacre where seventy-two American prisoners were shot in cold blood.

At his trial in Dachau in 1946, Peiper signed a confession in which he took responsibility for the massacre and was sentenced to death by hanging. Five years later the death sentence was commuted to life imprisonment, and in 1956 Peiper was released on parole through the intervention of Senator Joseph McCarthy. In 1958 he was released from parole, and in 1959 he purchased a plot of land near Traves, France, where he built a house with the blessing of the regional prefecture that, in full knowledge of his identity, granted him a five-year residential permit good for the entire European Community. In the early 1970s he moved to France with his wife, where he worked as a translator of military books for a German firm.

In June 1976, the French Communist newspaper *L'Humanité* published a sensational article that opened up a whole anti-Peiper campaign, pointing out the scandal that a high-ranking ex-SS officer had been given sanctuary in France. It was, the paper maintained, a provocation that soured diplomatic relations with Germany. Before long, leaflets, graffiti, and posters accusing Peiper covered Traves. His mailbox was broken into and he received several threats to his life by phone. In the light of the events, the prefecture decided not to renew Peiper's residence permit.

In July 1976, Peiper's wife went to stay with friends in the Black Forest. On the night of July 14, Peiper's house burned down. The torso of a man that fitted Peiper's measurements was found, and next to him was an American Smith & Wesson .38 revolver, together with thirteen boxes of exploded ammunition. There was no evidence of any self-inflicted wounds. Peiper, in his final act of violence, was using his American-made weapon to fight off his attackers.

François Genoud was a teenager when he met Hitler in a hotel near Bonn in 1932. They shook hands and the boy expressed his admiration for National Socialism. Sent by his Swiss parents to learn discipline in Germany at the age of sixteen, Genoud became engrossed with the Führer and joined the pro-Nazi National Front when he returned to Switzerland in 1934. In 1936 he traveled to Palestine, where he became the confidant of the grand mufti, Amin el-Husseini, an anti-Semite who spent most of the war years in Germany.

During the war, Genoud set up a covert operation for the German counterintelligence service in Switzerland and became friends with Karl Wolff and Paul Dickopf, who was an agent of the *Abwehr,* the German Intelligence Service. After Hitler's suicide, Genoud, who was working as the representative of the Red Cross in Brussels, acquired all posthumous rights to the writings of Hitler, Bormann, and Goebbels, increasing his fortune. Using his Swiss banking contacts, he helped many Nazis escape, an operation that led to a network called ODESSA (later *Die Spinne* — the spider). Genoud also paid for the defense of Eichmann and Klaus Barbie, the "butcher of Lyon." But this was not enough for Genoud. He wanted to continue his Führer's work because, as he said, "My views have not changed since I was a young man. Hitler was a great leader, and if he had won the war the world would be a better place today."

Genoud believed the true inheritors of Hitler's legacy were the Islamic fundamentalists. Accordingly, he financed terrorist groups, disseminated anti-Jewish and anti-Israeli material throughout the Middle East, and assisted the Palestinian hijackers of a Lufthansa plane in February 1972.

But this idyll could not last forever. In the 1980s, Genoud's misdeeds slowly came to light and judicial inquiries were started. In 1993, a bomb exploded in front of his house and he barely escaped injury. Genoud started to feel trapped. True to his Führer, in May 1996, after a pleasant meal with his friends and family in Lausanne, Genoud, as he had planned with his daughters the previous year, drank poison and died. He was eighty-one.

# 13

## MULTIPLE LIVES: OLD NAZIS MASKED

## AND UNMASKED

*The Double Life of Leni Riefenstahl*

"Hitler has so left his mark on my life that I can still remember every single word of my conversations with him."

So wrote Leni Riefenstahl in her memoirs, published in 1993 when she was ninety-one years old. And that was a lot of Hitler to remember, for he was already her admirer when she called on him in 1932 to volunteer her services to propagandize his then new cause. He was the sponsor and financier of her most spectacular documentaries, and when he began to think of life after World War II, so he told Leni, he wanted to spend it as her partner, making movies.

So much loving attention from Hitler should, in theory, have ruined Riefenstahl's postwar career, and yet she blossomed. "Genius" was one label awarded to her in five remarkable pages of acclaim for her 1993 recollections in the *New York Times Book Review*. The same appraisal also celebrated her as "the greatest woman filmmaker ever," "high striving," a creative force of "greatness" and "artistic integrity."

Riefenstahl had stage-managed an astonishing double life for herself. When suicide forced her Führer into his shadowy afterexistence, she simply retooled her skills. After minor entanglements with the denazification machinery, she switched from creating the Nazis' most effective advertising to a sedate new specialty: documentaries about primitive peoples and life underwater.

Her rebirth was not unique. Other achievers who flourished under Hitler also continued to prosper. They had been activists of influence, not small-time fellow-travelers (*Mitläufer*), some with very big names. Without tacit approval from the public, if not sympathy, such human engineering would have been impossible. It was a sign of the times. Hitler's times.

Riefenstahl, like some of these other reformed careerists, rose to high station within the fiercely competitive Nazi bureaucracy thanks to the Führer's own protective arm. She was a handful, and her immediate boss, Propaganda Minister Joseph Goebbels, was frequently furious at her. "There is no way of working with such a wild woman," he wrote in his diary for November 6, 1936, when Riefenstahl was producing her masterpiece about the Olympic Games in Berlin. "Now she wants another half a million marks for the film. I stayed ice cold. She cries."

But Hitler wanted her to have the money. She got it, and on November 26, 1937, Goebbels wrote, "I tell the Führer about Leni Riefenstahl's Olympic film. He is delighted that it came out so well. We want to do something to honor Leni, she has earned it."

On July 8, 1938, Goebbels waxed ecstatic: "This film is a smash hit. What a courageous female Riefenstahl is!" His sudden admiration was so overwhelming that she apparently had to fend off several attempts at seduction. But Goebbels and Hitler were not the only ones to want to honor her — that same year, French prime minister Edouard Daladier presented her with the gold medal at the Paris World's Fair for her documentary *Triumph of the Will*, and her *Olympia* won the golden lion at the Venice Film Festival.

In 1940, Riefenstahl started on her next work, *Tiefland* (*Deep-land*), for which she recruited sixty Sinti and Roma gypsies from the concentration camps. During the war, however, a serious illness hindered her from completing her work. After the war, she was arrested several times, escaped, put in prison, released, her property confiscated, and once she was put in a mental institution. In 1948, she was brought to trial for having failed to pay the gypsies she used for her filming of *Tiefland* and of having falsely promised them release from the concentration camp. Thanks to her lawyer, Dr. Gritschneder (who has since won fifty libel cases for her), she was found not guilty. In 1949 the Baden State Commissariat for Political Purging in Freiburg absolved her, for she had never been a member of the NSDAP and apparently did not have a "close relationship" with Hitler. She went back to work, and *Tiefland* was released in 1954.

As her fame as a Nazi propagandist made filming difficult for her, Riefenstahl developed a career as a photographer. In the 1972 Olympics in Munich, she used a pseudonym and was hired as an official photographer. She then went on to make documentaries about the Nuba tribe in Africa and the underwater world in the tropics.

But the world was to honor her again. In 1976, the International Olympic Committee invited her to the games in Montreal. That same year, the German Art Directors Club awarded her a gold medal for her work. In 1987 she published her memoir, *Memorien,* which was poorly received in Germany but nonetheless was translated into nine languages and went on to gain great success worldwide. *Time* magazine labeled her "one of cinema's greatest innovator artists," and *Variety* declared her memoir "immensely readable, providing valuable insight into the talent and tenacity of a gifted female artist."

*Die Macht der Bilder* (*The Power of Images*), an award-winning 1993 German television documentary on Riefenstahl — produced with her cooperation — was released under the title *The Wonderful, Horrible Life of Leni Riefenstahl* in the United States, where it reignited the ongoing debate about her. The U.S. film union Cinecon gave her a lifetime achievement award in 1997. Throughout the years she organized several much-acclaimed exhibitions of her work around the world. The most recent took place in Berlin in the spring of 2000. At age ninety-eight, she has just released a calendar of her photographs for the year 2001!

### Kurt Waldheim: From the Holocaust to the Top of the UN

The United Nations was created in 1945 in response to the horrors of World War II in order to maintain world peace and, hopefully, avoid the reoccurrence of events such as the Holocaust. In 1971, a candidate for the Austrian presidency, Kurt Waldheim was elected secretary-general of the United Nations. Waldheim had joined the Austrian diplomatic service in 1945, represented his country as an ambassador to Canada and in the General Assembly of the UN, and worked for the committee on peaceful uses of space. At the end of his four-year term as secretary-general, Waldheim was reelected to a second term, which ended in 1981. So far, so good. But there is an inherent contradiction in the purpose of the organization and the choice of secretary-general. During World War II, Kurt Waldheim had been a member of the Wehrmacht, served in the Nazi-occupied Balkans and Greece as an intelligence officer, and in Russia as a *Schwadronchef* (squadron chief), a post that gave him authority and responsibility for the acts of the German soldiers under his command.

These facts came to light only in 1986, when Waldheim again became a candidate for the Austrian presidency. Both as intelligence officer and *Schwadronchef,* he had to have been aware of what was happening around him, where his prisoners were being sent. At least in theory, he was in a position to decide their destiny. However, Waldheim, like many other Austrians and Germans, claimed that he had only "done his duty," and that he was unaware of what was happening. Despite these damning new revelations, Waldheim that year was elected president of Austria.

A year later, however, the United States declared Waldheim persona non grata and his entrance to the country was prohibited. In 1988, under pressure from the World Jewish Congress, an international commission of historians was set up to make an inquiry into the president's past and to ascertain whether he was in fact a war criminal. The result was negative to the more serious allegations, but concluded that Waldheim's personal actions did in fact facilitate Nazi atrocities, and the commission's reconstruction of Waldheim's role in World War II differed greatly from his own.

Waldheim's version of his wartime activities maintained that, after having been a volunteer in the Austrian army from 1936 to 1937, he began to train as a diplomat. He was later conscripted into the German army and sent to the Russian front, where in 1941 he was wounded. The rest of the war, he maintained, he spent studying law at the University of Vienna. The truth, as confirmed by the commission, is that during those crucial three years when he was supposedly studying law, he was actually serving as a German army staff officer in the Balkans, from 1942 to 1945. As interpreter and intelligence officer in the Balkans, Waldheim was part of a Wehrmacht unit that organized brutal reprisals against Yugoslav partisans and civilians, and in 1943 was responsible for deporting to concentration camps almost the entire Jewish population of Salonika in Greece.

Waldheim did not run for a second term. In his latest book, *Die Antwort (The Answer)*, published in 1996, he wrote the following about the commission: "I am satisfied with the main results of the inquiry by the commission. However, the more aggressive language of the conclusive remarks of the commission does not match with what they had previously wanted to render as indisputable historical truth."

In 1994, the pope honored Waldheim with the Pious Order decoration, which is the papal equivalent of knighthood. Evidently the church had fallen for his earlier self-portrait, later elaborated on in *The Answer,* as a man who is "profoundly misunderstood" and the victim of a hate campaign by the World Jewish Congress. Yet again, in that book, Waldheim does anything but clarify his role in the Wehrmacht. Rather, he contradicts himself, concluding, "Throughout my life I have stood for understanding and collaboration among people, and I profoundly regret that certain people did not behave in the same way toward me." In an interview with the German-language magazine *Profil,* Waldheim clarified that by "some people" he had meant the World Jewish Congress: "It is a worldwide net that operates here. That has a great power."

Waldheim still receives an annual pension from the UN of $102,000.


*The Erich Priebke Case*

In the Argentinean ski resort of Bariloche, former Nazi officer Erich Priebke was very well respected. He was head of a German-Argentinean association that ran a school with 1,500 students of different nationalities, among them some Jews. The fact that Priebke participated in the massacre of 335 Italian civilians at the Adreatine Caves in 1944 didn't seem to matter. American journalist Sam Donaldson and his TV news crew discovered Priebke in 1994. Following his interview, which was shown on ABC News's *Primetime,* Priebke was put under house arrest by the Argentinean authorities on request of the Italian government.

A member of the Gestapo, Priebke, thanks to his knowledge of Italian, was mainly used as an interpreter and translator. In 1940, while he was in Rome as Reinhard Heydrich's interpreter, Colonel Herbert Kappler, the head Nazi officer in the city, asked for an assistant, and Priebke was appointed. Though Priebke had till then always held desk jobs, in 1943 things began to change. The Gestapo became the leading Nazi presence in Rome, with Kappler at its head, and Priebke was assigned to deal with the public, the police, Italian authorities, and the Vatican.

On March 24, 1944, under Hitler's direct orders, 335 Italians were murdered to avenge the deaths of 33 German soldiers killed in an ambush by partisans. According to German martial law, ten lives were to be sacrificed for every German soldier killed. Kappler, with the collaboration of high-ranking German officials and the Italian police, wrote a list of names of the people who were to be killed. Among them were fourteen-year-old boys and men over the age of seventy. Of the 335 victims, 75 were Jews. All the members of Kappler's office who spoke German were ordered to participate in the shooting, and those who refused were threatened with death. Priebke admitted to shooting twice that night. He claims he had never killed anyone before and that he only shot because he had no choice.

After the war, Priebke was captured and remained in British prisons in Italy until he escaped on New Year's Eve in 1946. For two years he lived a free man with his wife in Italy and then immigrated to Argentina where, in 1952, he registered at the German consulate and obtained a passport under his real name. Priebke claims he was unaware that an order for his arrest had been issued in 1946, and that he was not included in the 1948 trial against Kappler only because the authorities didn't know where he was. Thus he lived freely without ever assuming a false name, traveling extensively, and returning to Italy twice as a tourist. In 1978, he had lunch in Rome with former

Gestapo chief Major Karl Hass, another war criminal the Italian authorities were supposedly looking for. Why nobody could find either man remains a mystery to this date.

In any event, the Italian request for Priebke's extradition suffered several delays, and only in November 1995 did the Argentinean government finally comply. The first trial, in Rome, ended in August 1996, fifty-two years after the crime. The court found Priebke guilty, but the aggravating circumstances, necessary to override Italy's thirty-year statute of limitations on murder, were not recognized and he was released. Before he could return to his wife in Argentina, however, this first court was accused of being biased. Apparently, the president of the tribunal, Agostino Quisitelli, had told Priebke's lawyer, long before the trial was over, that his client would be released. The highest appeals court, the Corte di Cassazione, declared that the original court had indeed been biased, and a new trial ensued.

This time Priebke was convicted and sentenced to fifteen years in prison. The court reduced the sentence to five years because of an amnesty on war crimes. Germany's request for the extradition of Priebke was refused on the grounds that a person who was extradited may not be tried for the same crime in another country.

In the meantime, SS Major Hass was arrested when, the day before his testimony at the Priebke trial, he attempted to escape from a hotel and fell from a balcony, severely injuring himself. He was sentenced to ten years and eight months for the same crime. His sentence, however, was immediately suspended and he was set free, for reasons that are as unclear as they are disturbing.

# 14

## HOW THE NAZI DUST VANISHED

## UNDER THE RUG

*Justice Rehse: The Verdict Is Death*

Very small and subdued, Hans-Joachim Rehse had served as associate justice of the People's Court in Berlin. The summit of Hitler's justice was his turf. From 1942 to 1945, Rehse handed down 231 of the court's more than 5,000 death sentences, which were routinely carried out by guillotine.

All told, Nazi courts signed 40,000 death sentences. "It was mass murder," said a historian. "Head off, head off! Imagine how many that is per week!"

No court ranked higher in the land, and Justice Rehse's *Volksgericht* did not restrict itself to trite criminality. It specialized in treason, and in the Third Reich this definition included defeatism, listening to enemy radio stations, telling anti-Nazi jokes, and bad-mouthing the Führer.

The chief judge, Roland Freisler, a Nazi Party member since 1925, was known as a "blood judge" and an "iridescent personality." He raged at defendants, tore them down by ridicule, insulted them, interrupted them, sometimes did not let them talk at all, and 90 percent of his verdicts resulted in the death penalty. The little Justice Rehse served this sadist loyally and quietly through most of the war.

Peace found Rehse at first in retirement in provincial Schleswig-Holstein, then reemployed as an auxiliary administrative judge. A rumor that he had been one of Justice Freisler's partners got him fired after two years, but in 1963 a Munich court declined to prosecute because Rehse had been helplessly "deluded" into following the law as mandated under Hitler.

In 1967, a Berlin court finally judged that Rehse had illegally exceeded his brief in seven of his death verdicts. These defendants included a Catholic priest who had told a sad joke about the hoped-for death of Hitler; a museum director who told a friend that Hitler started the war; and a mailman who said on the street that Göring was enriching himself with fancy properties abroad.

This time Rehse was given a five-year prison sentence — which he never served. On appeal, a higher court cited as applicable the following ruling of Hitler's Justice Ministry: "Basically, the following observations are punishable by death: that the war is lost; that Germany or the Führer started the war senselessly or frivolously and will lose it; that the Nazi Party should resign; that the Führer is sick, unfit, a butcher, etc."

"With a retrospective view of that time," as the court phrased it, Rehse was acquitted on December 6, 1968. As a result, indictments against sixty-two other members of the People's Court were likewise dropped.


In 1968, the place to be was in the streets. The eruption was world-wide. Just about everywhere, "the people," mostly the young, were marching against authority, primarily against the police.

On Telegraph Avenue in Berkeley, students were rioting to end the Vietnam War. In New York's Morningside Heights, they marched to "liberate" Columbia University. In Chicago's Lincoln Park, rioters against stone-faced Mayor Dick Daley threw some of the tear gas canisters back at the cops.

Europe was little different. In Paris, the New Left protested from makeshift barricades in the tradition of the 1789 revolution. In Prague, citizens threw themselves in front of invading Soviet tanks. Students were revolting all over Germany, and in Berlin the setting for almost daily protests was in front of the redbrick fortresslike city hall in the Schöneberg district. It was the well-remembered enormous square where in 1968 John F. Kennedy, that hero figure, had denounced the

Berlin Wall, thrust out his chin at Nikita Khrushchev, the Soviet bully, and shouted in defiance, "Ich bin ein Berliner!"

By 1968, being a Berliner had become a dubious privilege, at least to resentful pacifist intellectuals like Jörg Friedrich, a twenty-four-year-old historian-in-waiting. "The Americans said, 'Germans to the front' and the front was Berlin," he remembered. "We didn't want any part of that. We were against the Americans. And we were against our state because this state was a hiding place for the old Nazis."

As everywhere else, the fury of the young was focused on the *Bullen,* as they were called in Berlin: the police. "This was the Gestapo!" Friedrich grumbled, still furious years afterward. "They were protecting fascism!" Thus held in contempt, the cops were regularly taunted with such rhymes as, "In den Betten seid ihr Nullen, auf der Strasse seid ihr Bullen" ("In bed you're zeroes, on the street you're bulls"). Infuriated officers in battle dress fell on the demonstrators with their truncheons, usually targeting the heads.

Shortly before Christmas in that time of bloodshed — it was the year Martin Luther King and Robert F. Kennedy were assassinated — Jörg Friedrich put on his construction worker's hard hat, as usual, and trudged to Schöneberg for a demonstration, a *Demo,* as usual. "It was almost like a profession," he recalled, laughing. That December day he was going to protest the quasi-survival of Hitler for the umpteenth time, specifically the recent acquittal in court of Hans-Joachim Rehse.

Rehse was no household name and the *Demo* was nothing special. Friedrich suspected that most of his 2,000 or so fellow demonstrators had no idea who Rehse was. Even the normal banners naming the cause of the day were not in evidence. But Jörg Friedrich, student of causes, knew of Rehse's death sentences and that the judge was now going free because that was the government policy initiated by Chancellor Konrad Adenauer and upheld by the then current chancellor, Kurt Kiesinger.

"Adenauer said, 'I'm not going to prosecute my voters!'" That was the way Friedrich remembered it.

That day in Schöneberg the protesters were addressed, via bullhorn, by a petite brunette, Beate Klarsfeld, née Künzel, twenty-nine. A former Berliner living in Paris, she was married to a Jewish lawyer whose father had been murdered in Auschwitz.

"She was my Joan of Arc," said Friedrich.

The analogy was not unfounded. A onetime secretary, Klarsfeld had gone to Paris as an au pair girl, ignorant of the Holocaust. Enlightened by her husband, she turned herself into an original: the only full-time Nazi hunter who was female, gentile, and made so implacable by her zeal for justice that she would, over the years, bag Nazi big wheels rivaling those of the great Simon Wiesenthal.

A month before the *Demo* against Judge Rehse, Klarsfeld had achieved an enormous amount of publicity for an act of anti-Nazi defiance that made front-page headlines throughout the world. Flashing a French press pass, she had walked into a Berlin convention of the CDU, the ruling Christian Democratic Union. Kiesinger was signing autographs at the head table. Klarsfeld walked up as if to ask for an autograph too. Instead, she hit him in the face with the back of her hand, shouting, "Nazi! Nazi!"

Sustaining a blackened left eye, the chancellor had to camouflage his embarrassment with dark glasses. Klarsfeld was given a one-year jail sentence, later reduced to four months' probation. Encounters like those with Kiesinger left her jubilant. "There have to be Germans who don't simply let the grass grow and sweep everything under the rug." So ran her campaign theme.

Kiesinger had indeed been a Nazi, his party membership dating back to 1933. During the war he had been deputy chief for a propaganda section of 148 people in the Foreign Ministry. His functions were confined to his desk, but for approval across that desk came a steady flow of sensitive internal directives for Nazi propagandists throughout the Reich. These documents often dealt with what Kiesinger's chief, Dr. Franz Six, called "the physical elimination of Eastern Jews." Six, who later led a terrorist *Einsatzgruppen* unit, was sentenced to twenty years after the war because, in spite of the ingenuity applied by the deniers, the Holocaust refused to die.

# 15

## CASHING IN ON THE "HITLER WAVE"

The revival of the Hitler legend on a grand scale was the dubious achievement of two men. This is how they managed it.

The steady drift toward a populist Hitler renewal became noticeable in the early 1970s, first as a fad among the young, the generation that found in the Führer an appealing symbol, largely because he was taboo for parents and grandparents and therefore made to measure as a rallying cry for the traditional revolt of young against old.

Teachers in the Munich schools reported that more and more teenagers were sewing swastikas onto their jeans; telling demeaning jokes about Jews; greeting each other with a cheery "Heil Hitler!"; and generally adopting the Führer as their idol.

"Under Hitler we wouldn't be seeing any terrorists," they were heard to say, and when they began to join small neo-Nazi groups, they encouraged one another by remembering the early struggles of their role model: "Hitler started with seven men, too."

The Germans called this trend their "Hitler wave" (*Hitlerwelle*). It proved to be no fad. It was an engulfing surge of bittersweet nostalgia that spilled across the German border. In London, the *Sunday Telegraph* noted an "astonishing resurgence of the Hitler cult." In New York, *Time* magazine reported a "worldwide revival" and concluded, "Adolf Hitler's presence never vanishes. His career is still the fundamental trauma of the century."

And it might well overflow into the twenty-first as well, for fresh reminders keep surfacing in the daily flow of news events. When the neo-fascist Vladimir Zhirinovsky burst onto the Russian political

scene in 1994, television news shows and magazine covers throughout the world pointed up the danger by breaking out their old Hitler
pictures and flashing them in the background.

From the onset of the *Hitlerwelle* entrepreneurs stood ready not
only to cash in on the bandwagon but to create waves of their own:
products that served as both reflections and as further stimuli of the
trend, modifying and regenerating according to the dictates of supply
and demand.

Creations from outside the German market were imaginative but
marginal. In the interminable television sitcom *Hogan's Heroes,* the
American captain led his merry crew in making fools of the German
keepers in their prisoner-of-war camp, especially the memorable, over-
weight Sergeant Schulz, whose barked assent, "Jawohl, Herr Kom-
mandant!" became a byword.[1] In *The Boys from Brazil,* moviegoers
were asked to accept good old Gregory Peck as the evil fugitive, Dr.
Mengele, and the stately Sir Laurence Olivier as the cozy Jewish
crime-hunter hero, Lieberman. Meanwhile, droves of blank, blue-
eyed Hitler youths were everywhere reborn as blank, blue-eyed clones.

For German audiences, thrillers or slapstick would obviously never
do. What could possibly be funny or fantastic about Hitler? A deft
touch was required — reality heightened by romance — and the
Hamburg publisher John Jahr struck the appropriate chord in the
500,000 biweekly copies of his magazine-sized ninety-page booklets
*The Third Reich,* initiated in 1974 with a promotion budget of $1.2
million.

More than any other force or personality, Jahr was first to perceive
the commercial potential of the *Hitlerwelle* and take action. He pack-
aged it.

Jahr was a media wheeler-dealer in the mold of a Hearst or a Murdoch. When this fireman's son died in 1991 at the age of ninety-one,
his holdings included Gruner & Jahr, a publishing house with sales of

---

[1]Hitler as a comical (if frightening) target of black humor was pioneered as long
ago as 1940, when Charlie Chaplin wrote, directed, and starred (as "Adenoid
Hynkel") in *The Great Dictator.* That masterpiece drew mixed reviews, some accusing Chaplin of making Hitler, the embodiment of evil, simply buffoonish.

$2 billion a year; three banks; a television network; three women's magazines; several supermarkets; the Hamburg gambling casino; and extensive real estate properties in the U.S. and Canada.

Revolutions left Jahr practically untouched, regardless of their political colorations. Having begun as a sports reporter following World War I, he became advertising manager for two Communist magazines that the Third Reich promptly prohibited. In the Hitler years, Jahr started a women's magazine and a book mail-order house that published works about U-boat captains and ace fighter pilots.[2] As soon as World War II ended, the British occupation authorities granted him licenses to launch still more magazines; these became legendary successes, with circulation figures in the millions.

It is difficult for the printed word to do due justice to Jahr's *Third Reich* series. Its impact derived from the visual presentation. It was an ingenious fusion achieved by photographers, headline and caption writers, and makeup artists, a mix that transformed pictures into fiery propaganda and respectable contributors into inadvertent Nazi advocates. One of these involuntary converts, the historian Sebastian Haffner, was credited with the leading article in the first issue, a perfectly factual retrospective presented in large print on the cover as "*Volk,* Your Savior Is Here."

Inside the issue, a vibrant picture spread about aerial barnstorming was entitled "Hitler over Germany." It reported on the Führer's crucial election campaign of 1932: "While uncounted parties agitated against one another, Hitler rose above the conventional election turmoil aboard his plane to the sky, floating above the clouds from town to town."

Other articles celebrated Horst Wessel, author of the hate hymn bearing his name; the cleanliness of Hitler Youth leaving picnic grounds; the history of the swastika; and the orderliness of life in the Oranienburg concentration camp. A special issue entitled "The Truth

---

[2]Jahr enjoyed the protection of Bruno Streckenbach, his friend from the old sports scene, who had risen to head of the Hamburg Gestapo and later became one of the organizers of the mass-murder *Kommandos* in the Soviet Union. Said to be responsible for the deaths of one million people, Streckenbach died in Hamburg, unpunished, in 1977.

About the Holocaust" gave space to the British historian David Irving and his often-repeated charge that the *Diary of Anne Frank* was a forgery.

Bonus offerings included page after page of straight reprints without commentary, taken from such Nazi propaganda as the pornographic weekly *Der Stürmer*, published by *Gauleiter*[3] Julius Streicher, hanged as a war criminal at Nuremberg. Here he marched solemnly at the head of his brownshirts; the photo was headlined "The loyal comrade." A smiling Hitler chucked blonde little girls under the chin ("Beloved and engulfed by jubilation"). Wielding a shovel, he was "Friend of workers and roadbuilders." A heroic painting of the Führer with the collar of his greatcoat turned up was captioned "Liberator of the people, savior of the Reich, Führer of all who are good."

Almost inevitably, most issues included double-page spreads of naked young women, "Nazi playmates," by courtesy of "the great German art exhibits."

Editor in chief for the series was Christian Zentner, a Ph.D. in political science and onetime Harvard student, who in 1974 invented a device that came close to the lawful printing of money: a substitute for *Mein Kampf*. Hitler's seminal work having been banned in Germany, Zentner composed his own book and called it *Adolf Hitler's Mein Kampf: A Selection with Comments*. The cover is blood-red and extraordinarily flaglike: a large round black centerpiece dominates. The print is in white Gothic script. The book became a staple item; my 1992 edition was the eighth.

The exploitative aspects of Jahr's *Third Reich* series occasioned comment. Indeed, the criticism published by the Institute for Contemporary History in Munich of the "suggestive" content and makeup was so strongly worded that Jahr filed suit. Hitler lost. At the end of a lengthy proceeding, the Institute was authorized to continue distributing the following claims:

---

[3]A *Gauleiter* was the head of a Nazi administrative district. Streicher was responsible for the district of Franconia, but he was more than that. He was the founder of the German Socialist Party, which he then handed over to Hitler in 1922. A member of the Reichstag (1933–45), he held the title of *Obergruppenführer* in the SA.

The series is an "irresponsible publishing speculation"; "The Hitler period is presented as harmless and is sold as an entertaining sensation"; historical education is subordinated to the interests of the publisher; "above all," the publisher is interested in making use of ("borrowing") names with good reputations.

The exploited names were not only of writers — Haffner, the sainted chronicler William Shirer, and such guaranteed anti-Nazis as the prolific and popular Bernt Engelmann. Jahr's inventive crew also recruited reputable scholars for symposiums to air such newly fashionable issues as feminism, Nazi style.

From the mothballs of her retirement in an unnamed south German town, they produced as star panelist the long forgotten Frau Gertrud Scholtz-Klink, who was then seventy-three, the small, blue-eyed mother of eleven children, Nazi Party member since the 1920s, Reich Women's Leader since 1934. The six-page text of Jahr's panel mentioned she had been classified after the war as a "culpable principal," but not that she had hidden for three years under a false name and then served eighteen months in a French military jail.

The Hitlerian view of feminism, long documented, was largely unremembered except perhaps for the slogan "children, church, and kitchen" (*Kinder, Kirche, Küche*). The Führer had called the emancipation of women an invention of Jewish intellectuals. Goebbels had likened an upright German woman to "the female bird that preens herself for her mate and hatches eggs for him." The *Völkische Beobachter* denounced all makeup as "un-German." Women were declared ineligible as jurors, judges, or prosecutors because "they cannot think logically or reason objectively."

And at the 1937 Nuremberg party rally, Frau Scholtz-Klink rated her leadership and the significance of her female followers by calling out, "Even though our weapon is only the soup ladle, its impact should be as great as that of other weapons."

By the 1970s, under interrogation by specialists who included a former federal minister of health and a psychoanalyst from the Menninger Clinic at Topeka, Kansas, Scholtz-Klink's soup ladle had turned into an instrument of women's lib. Hitler had been the caring "father" who put Germany back on its feet — so she reminded forgetful contemporary readers. But even he was handicapped by the natural-born ignorance of all bachelors, "a typical male like hundreds of thousands of others in Germany and the rest of the world."

In the management of the "Jewish question," no doubt "things happened of which we had no knowledge," Scholtz-Klink conceded. "That was not my concern." For the status of women, however, she considered herself a model pioneer fighting the good fight against the male chauvinists, a premature Gloria Steinem. "We were a step ahead of our men," she declared, and the John Jahr editors splashed this sentence in large capital letters across two pages.

By 1979, the *Third Reich* series as originally conceived had run its course, to be supplanted by other creative minds with more sophisticated mainstream fare. But not for good. Demand persisted. The Jahr company revived the series, retitled *Pictures of History*. Again Hitler appeared as the humane private citizen, the Nazi soldier as the ultimate hero. For the equivalent of $12, mood-making recordings were available such as *Marching Music of the Third Reich* and *The History of the Waffen-SS*.

It was reported that the selling of the Hitler memory had provoked quarrels among John Jahr's four heirs, all of whom were active in the family business, and that distribution of such merchandise was to stop by 1989. Nevertheless, I was still offered a video celebrating Hitler's birthday in 1994, albeit at a reduced sale price of $50.

Alexander Jahr, the son responsible for the Hitler business, had no difficulty justifying its worthiness. Hitler should not be portrayed as "a crazy carpet-eater," he maintained. The Führer's fascination had to be shown. "Otherwise the victims will have died in vain."

Applying media history by way of context, a different contribution of the Jahr company comes to mind. The second series title, *Pictures of History,* was expertly chosen to emphasize the product's mighty visual dimension. But it fails to disclose a remarkable spin: the editors succeeded in making pictures lie. This had been done before, here and there, mostly in war reportage, but never on such an ambitious scale.

John Jahr galvanized the Hitler wave. Joachim C. Fest made it respectable. A new, improved vehicle did it: film — sound, fury, movement. Hitler lives!

Of course, Hitler had been a film star before, and not only as ridiculed by Charlie Chaplin. Sir Alec Guinness had had a go at the role in the eventful 1970s. The film, *The Last Ten Days,* was based on a ninety-one-page volume by the much-decorated *Rittmeister* Gerhard Boldt, who had been present in the final phase of the *Führerbunker* in 1945 and was chosen as one of three couriers to deliver Hitler's political testament to the world at large.

Boldt had been a daring intelligence officer, but as an authority on Hitler's last days, his book, first published in 1947, lately "completely revised," offered little fresh material except that it had been an "extraordinary moment" when he finally met the trembling Hitler, who gave him a "peculiarly piercing look."

Sir Alec did his best, studying and reexamining Hitler's gestures and facial mannerisms from newsreels and coming up with a generally sympathetic portrait of a fallen genius under unbearable siege. One critic called it a "costume festival."

Hitler, in person, as interpreted by Fest, did much better.

To think of his documentary, *Hitler: A Career,* as simply a movie would be like dismissing the Hiroshima bombing as a conventional explosion. *Hitler: A Career,* a relentless two-hour-and-thirty-five-minute wave of emotion produced in 1977, was a nuclear event. The topic guaranteed its appeal. The target was the home front, not some distant enemy. And, when all was said and done, it was also a true-life love story: the entwining of the Führer with his people.

The official ratings called the production "particularly valuable." Schools in liberal Hamburg banned it for classroom instruction; in conservative Bavaria and in schools of other regions it became mandatory viewing for students. No postwar film was a bigger box-office hit. In its first month, 400,000 Germans had already flocked to view it. And no political event ever triggered more intense discussion. It was like showing *Gone with the Wind* with the blood of the Civil War barely dry.

Befitting the first fully illustrated, fully orchestrated appreciation of Hitler and his times, no less, many reviewers reacted gingerly, as if commenting on a daring sex education film. Fest's subject matter was still not totally fit for polite society. It was, however, becoming unavoidable. The film pounded powerfully against taboos now clearly antiquated — indelicacies that parents and grandparents had kept in the closet, along with other family skeletons.

On the surface, Fest had done solid, professional work. And about time. Three decades after the horror of World War II, the curiosity of the no-longer-all-that-young was insistent. How do I tell my child? Better to let the facts of life get out via the upright Herr Fest than through ignorant peers or dirty books.

The ultra-right-wing *National-Zeitung* liked the film best. It welcomed "the first, still hesitant glimmer of the truth ... positive achievements of the regime that are still impressive today, indeed partly even worth duplicating."

On the "bright side," the reviewer registered the "fascination" of the huge Nazi demonstrations and "the wave of devotion and consent on which this man was carried to incontestable successes." The paper lauded the "remarkable reticence" with which Fest treated the "mass annihilations allegedly committed by the German side." And it approved his refusal to coddle the "lie of the six million" who were said to have been murdered.

The leading intellectual weekly, the liberal *Die Zeit,* seemed to have seen a different Fest.

"The film is dangerous," it declared without qualification. "The untrammeled, uncritical admiration of [Hitler's] personality and his works dominate to such a degree that the balancing vocabulary of illegalities, concentration camps, SS, war, death, and destruction cannot be heard. Criminal offenses are cited (though by no means all), but they don't get under the skin. In his dislike for viewing history together with its morality, author Fest indulges in negligent abstinence."

Some of the counts in this indictment:

• "Burning books are briefly shown, but not burning synagogues."

• Concentration camps make an appearance, "but we don't learn how many people were incarcerated there."

• "We witness one mass execution in the East, but nowhere are we told how many millions of victims the 'Führer' had on his conscience."

The conservative daily *Die Welt* admired Fest's "new" picture of Hitler as "masterful" but specified numerous factual flaws. Among the film's erroneous assertions:

• That Hitler annexed Austria only because he was bored;

• That only Hitler's iron will (*"Durchhaltewille"*) saved the front before Moscow in the winter of 1941;

• That "Hitler could not be bought and was not in league with big business."

A leading authority on the Nazi period, Hermann Graml of the Institute for Contemporary History in Munich, found the Fest production gross.

"No trick is scorned to attribute to the undifferentiated nation, entirely in the manner of Hitler, the alleged characteristics of females. In this film the viewer becomes a voyeur, watching how, by the ingenious seducer, the Lady Germania is made pliable through irresistible techniques. . . . Hitler appears as the engine of history."

Elsewhere, reactions were more elemental. In a Mainz movie house, two women and one man rose and sang along when the "Horst Wessel Song" was played in the film. A Molotov cocktail landed in the lobby of the Karlstor theater in Munich, and later some of Hitler's declarations elicited applause from a few spectators, while others shouted "Lies!" and "Insulting!" At the Urania theater in Hamburg, three masked men threw acid on rolls of the film. And in Stuttgart, a delegation of protesters picketed wearing uniforms of concentration camp inmates.

Viewing the film for the first time in the peaceful Connecticut countryside in the mid 1990s, I felt it overpowering me. The images hit like a hail of punches to the stomach, a drumfire, two relentless hours of "insults" — to use this medical term in the way doctors describe body blows.

The film was not about Hitler's career. It was about the glory of mutual enslavement, the Germans manacled to Hitler and he to them, partners wallowing in collective passion.

I was overwhelmed by masses, masses by the hour, masses without elbow space as far as the camera could sweep, congealed masses heiling, screaming, marching to orgasms of Valhalla hymns. Overhead, seas of flags and banners, bunched together and on the move, biblical swarms of locusts.

Front and center: the Führer in exhortation, the Führer glowering, grimacing, heiling, howling, tearing transfixed into his accursed enemies. Most often, he is shown alone, the exalted hero figure, strutting across infinite spaces of blood-red carpeting, or preening, taking in the adulation of rank upon rank parading by on horseback, in tanks, to the *clop-clop-clop* of jackboots hitting stone by the tens of thousands.

And always on the *move:* limitless energy, his and theirs.

A few negatives flipped by: chaotic street battles and alien Jews with long beards and huge hats, the hated days before the Führer brought blessed law and order. Only near the end came evil mud, godless freezing, valiant death, undeserved.

Whenever it emerged from the din, the commentary was calm, the message reasonable. "The individual was nothing" — so I could make out at one point. But the words were lost in the flickering images, almost a mockery. I remembered Charlie Chaplin in *The Great Dictator,* shrieking an unremitting guttural outburst over the radio. When he paused for breath at last, the interpreter was heard to murmur, "His excellency has just made a reference to the Jewish people."

Joachim Fest's spoken references to Hitler's career turned likewise into wisps of mist. "He gave sugar to the monkeys," Guido Knopp told me at his Second German Television Network, ZDF. "It was a propaganda film. The pictures overwhelmed the text and muddied up the rotten genius of Hitler."

The falsity of the production was all-inclusive. Overall, optimism energized much of it, a feeling of all-for-one gaiety. Some of the specifics bordered on the unbelievable. In Fest's only depiction of a concentration camp, newly liberated inmates appeared in surreal state. Official photos taken by the Allied military showed such victims as barely breathing skeletons or piles of bones. Fest's KZ victims were happy campers, smiling, shouting, waving energetically from flagpoles.

How did Fest find such survivors?

If his film were to have depicted reality, it would at the least have required an equally earnest Part II to lay out the brutality of the horrors, the injustices, the lies, the fabrications. Such candor would not have been in keeping with the demands of the marketplace, the prevailing mood that, in 1977, prompted the posthumous Hitler to be set to music in a rock opera.

Yes, literally. Its title was *Der Führer*. The producer was EMI-Electrola, the biggest record company in the world. Among the sixty musicians were players of the Hamburg State Opera. Just before the final curtain, the putative Hitler rocked and rolled:

> I still live
> And you will follow me
> Anytime, anytime
> Whenever I call you.

The first call came early and the outcome was not promising.

# 16

## THE HOLOCAUST AS SOAP OPERA

The programming chiefs at NBC television were under increasing pressure: their ratings were falling badly behind both CBS and ABC. NBC's creative team was in desperate need of a blockbuster, and in 1977 the herd instinct showed them the way.

ABC had lately shattered all records with *Roots*, Alex Haley's colorful popularization of the historic American tragedy, slavery. Its smash success led NBC to an eye-opening insight: if the rendition was lively enough, personal enough, human enough, even the most depressing calamity could be turned into a ratings bonanza. Never would lemons make lemonade more readily, and so the NBC programmers seized this inviting commercial solution to their dilemma.

Violence sells, as everyone knows, and only one case of mass murder offered horror on a scale to rival — or maybe surpass — slavery: the Holocaust. Eureka! NBC would follow up on Haley's *Roots* story, the oppression of blacks, with a Jewish *Roots* — Hitler's more recent, far better remembered attempt to wipe out another detested minority.

*Kristallnacht!* Auschwitz! Gas chambers! The rise and fall of that bastard Hitler! This was at least as big as *Roots*. It was also reasonably safe. If massive death meant massive ratings, how could such a spectacular production misfire, even at a cost of $6 million? It couldn't, and it didn't, and more. The four-part series, *Holocaust*, shown on NBC in April 1978, in Germany in January 1979, and also in thirty-one other countries, actually made a dent in world public opinion. In Germany, indeed, the seemingly impossible occurred: an American television commercialization of the Holocaust, of all things, became an emotional, even hysterical counterpoint to the Hitler wave. At least for a moment or two.

In New York, the world's largest Jewish city, it was easy to find sympathetic talent. The two Jewish NBC vice presidents who were placed in charge of the project, Paul Klein and Irwin Siglstein, considered the assignment something of a family obligation. So did the writer they called in to assemble the screenplay, Gerald Green, once Greenberg, a son of immigrants whose mother's entire family had been murdered in Vilnius, Lithuania.

Green, fifty-seven, was the perfect pick: an old-fashioned storyteller of irrepressible energy who combined respect for his assigned topic with a knack for satisfying huge audiences. Originally a journalist, he had been managing editor of NBC's *Today* show and a facile writer of news and documentaries for the network. Moving on to become a prolific and successful novelist, he had also shown sensitivity for the Holocaust in his nonfiction book on the artists of the Terezin (Theresienstadt) concentration camp.

For the TV Holocaust series, Green drew on the enormous historical literature to create a panorama sweeping enough to intimidate Tolstoy, the storyteller's patron saint. Green reconstructed every major horror that typified the Final Solution over the years. Then he personalized the authentic events through the interwoven life stories of the fictitious Jewish Weiss family and the Nazi Dorf family. The product, a galvanizing cocktail of history and Hollywood, with 150 speaking parts, raised an instant and furious controversy.

Primed by Green's novelization — the paperback had already sold one and a half million copies before his docudrama aired — the film was viewed by 70 million or more Americans, but it was savaged by the most illustrious of the Holocaust survivors, Elie Wiesel, and with rare passion. He all but denied Green's right to call himself a Jew. "Untrue, hurtful, cheap," Wiesel began, "shocking," "a soap opera," "an insult for those who died and those who survived." He was "horrified" that the Holocaust might be thus remembered.

The entire production, so Wiesel bristled, was rendered incredible because members of the two protagonist families materialized ubiquitously at all the most dreadful crimes. The story struck him as artificial, too all-inclusive ("hardly a name is left out, hardly an episode remains unmentioned"). Pictures of naked women and children moving into the gas chambers, and their moaning after the doors closed, were morally objectionable.

"Worse," Wiesel wrote in the *New York Times,* "it is obscene. The last moments of the lost victims belong only to them."

Green replied in the same newspaper, "Mr. Wiesel objects that we attempt to show everything," he wrote. "Why not?" And why not allow fictional characters to dramatize history? The revered Tolstoy did exactly that, he pointed out. "Mr. Wiesel need be neither horrified nor fearful. The '*Holocaust*' telecast will whip up new interest in the subject."

Most American critics also disagreed with Wiesel. "The most overpowering drama ever shown on the screen" was the verdict of Tom Shales, the *Washington Post*'s respected reviewer. *Time* said Green had "shaken awake" more people on the subject of Nazi crimes than any work since the *Diary of Anne Frank*. Others praised the opportunity to let viewers identify with "living, suffering and loving" human beings.

Wiesel had enlisted articulate allies in Germany, however. Long before the series could be shown on their turf, German critics took his side and sent reports to this effect from New York to their readers back home. "A soap opera," they echoed. "Too brazenly," said the commentator for the influential *Frankfurter Allgemeine*, Sabina Lietzmann, "authentic and invented elements are mingled in a way that robs actual happenings of their historical character and relegates them to the realm of fantasy." To this critic, the line between "story" and "history" had become disastrously blurred. She blamed the fiasco on the project's origin as a creation of the commercial American ratings wars.

The German network chiefs now became terrified. Although they had paid $700,000 for their rights to the series and had to invest another $120,000 to make it accessible in German, they withdrew it from the planned major scheduling and relegated it to the "third program," the ghetto for cultural offerings with less than mass appeal to be shown at the (for Germany) relatively late hour of 9 P.M.

And then the skies caved in. The fate of the film that had been denigrated as mere soap opera began itself to resemble the vicissitudes of soap opera.

Some advance intimations had come to light. Moved by the overwhelmingly receptive audience feedback in America, Sabina Lietzmann confessed to grudging second thoughts. Nearly half a year after her damning first review, she conceded that *Holocaust,* told in terms of people, possessed the power to "force" mass audiences to view and empathize in a way that a documentary could not.

Now she wrote, "When we are faced with the alternative either to let no information come out or else a 'story' tailored according to entertainment recipes, then, resigned to the realities, we choose the story."

And a week before the German airtime, Gerald Green's blending of fact and fiction received a crucial boost from Eugen Kogon, a well-known commentator with persuasive credentials. Born in 1903, Kogon had become a journalist increasingly famous for his anti-Nazi opinions. Arrested in March 1938, he was sent to various prisons before landing in Buchenwald in September 1939, just as war broke out. An economist as well as a journalist, he was plucked from the inmates by the camp doctor, Erwin Ding Schuler, as his clerk, a privileged position that enabled him to survive. Because of his intimate knowledge of the horrific medical experiments carried out at Buchenwald, Kogon's name was on the list of "forty anti-fascists" who were to be executed in April 1945, before the camp was evacuated. But the Nazis' best-laid plans went badly awry during those last hectic weeks of the war and the order was never carried out. Kogon went on to have a distinguished career as an author and journalist, writing several books on Nazism and the concentration camps. Thus when he pronounced Gerald Green's work not only worthy but a necessity, something all Germans should see, the battle was all but won. When the miniseries was shown in the latter half of 1979, the reaction was extraordinary: the critics crawled all over one another trying to outdo their journalistic brethren with higher and higher praise. Millions of Germans sat glued to their TV sets as they followed the trials and tribulations of the Weiss and Dorf families. Was it therapeutic? Did it touch the hearts and minds of the German viewers? From all reports it did. The question is: How long and how profound was the impact?

One German who definitely and roundly disliked Green's depiction of his native land in those turbulent years was Edgar Reitz. A television producer and director who was forty-seven years old when *Holocaust* was shown, Reitz had a number of reasonably successful TV films to his credit, but nothing to suggest the scope and ambition of his next enterprise, prompted by, and in reaction to, Gerald Green's "soap opera."

# 17

## WHAT THE GREAT *HEIMAT*

## SERIES HUSHED UP

Edgar Reitz's *Heimat* is a cinematic event," pronounced the then chief arbiter of American film critics, Vincent Canby, in the *New York Times*. Usually difficult to please, he raved: "*Heimat* is immensely, easily watchable, an extraordinary succession of mostly ordinary events and characters — history seen from ground level."

First shown in Germany in the spring of 1984 as a two-part movie, at $30 per ticket, nearly sixteen hours (!) long, *Heimat* chronicled life from 1919 to 1982 among the fictitious locals in the fictitious village of Schabbach, tucked into the rural Hunsrück mountains of the northern Rhineland. The insular region had once been home to Reitz, who conceived, wrote, and directed this marathon.

Each segment of this eleven-part television version was seen, discussed, laughed at, wept over, often with nostalgic recognition, by a powerfully touched audience of nine million Germans.[1] *Heimat* was truly huge: seventeen miles of film, a shooting script of 2,000 pages, five years in the making, 32 little-known but professional principals, 159 other speaking roles for amateur actors, 3,863 extras.

Appropriately, *Heimat* is a big word — at one and the same time weighty, yet also heady, a match for Reitz's canvas. The dictionary's

---

[1] All of *Heimat* was screened in America, only as a theatrical film in art houses, during the spring of 1985. In Britain, the BBC showed all 11 segments on TV with English subtitles.

terse definition, "home, native place or country," is as descriptive as saying champagne is a drink. *Heimat* also bubbles. It's not a place but a feeling. I've always thought that the term evoked one's roots, one's parental domicile, one's intimacy with first cronies. But even this is too narrow a vision.

The philosopher Ernst Bloch interpreted the concept sweepingly as "an abundance of desires and longings, wishes and yearnings," no less. Reitz, the filmmaker, defined it as "the distant and yet familiar world in which memories and their images in the mind's eye are one."

Yes, and not to forget geography and people.

Fittingly, the forests of the Hunsrück — its highest mountain measures only 2,700 feet — are heartland, a hilly version, perhaps, of Indiana. And they are a placid, jolly bunch, the Rhinelanders. I know because my father was one of them. Reitz, however, left his native soil at eighteen to perpetrate films as disturbances of the public equilibrium.

By 1979, at forty-seven, he had done well with a number of productions. His most recent films had not enjoyed overwhelming success, however, and Reitz, depressed, entered a period of critical self-appraisal. Should he, the son of a minor craftsman, a watchmaker in the village of Morbach (population 2,000), continue to strive for importance as a filmmaker?

It was midwinter and he sought isolation at the home of friends on the island of Sylt, off the German-Danish border in the North Sea. The solitude there turned out to be more than expected. It snowed for two weeks. "We were virtually under house arrest," Reitz recalled. As it happened, *Holocaust* was shown on the TV set constantly. "It was our only contact with the outside world and there was no way to get rid of it."

Nature had provided Reitz with a turning point in his life, because *Holocaust* left him furious as well as motivated. The nerve of it, the insult against Germany! And what a disgusting display of his most detested bugaboos! He composed an intemperate essay to at least make a start at settling his accounts with them all.

First he attacked the "commercial aesthetics" and uniformity of the "entertainment merchandise" drummed up by American television.

The industry was simply too rich, too intent on world domination; otherwise it couldn't finance the ultra-expensive American-made miniseries that Reitz so detested.

The *Holocaust* series, he charged, was "advertising" for such staple goods; little wonder that it yielded only crocodile tears among the Germans, including himself. It was all of a piece. "When the American race problem and the massacres of blacks were treated in *Bonanza,* it was mere 'commercial hypocrisy.'"

The "language of the international entertainment business" seemed to Reitz to rest on unreality. "The difference between a true scene and a calculated scene à la *Holocaust,* from commercial dramatists, is much like the difference between 'experience' and 'judgment.'" Judgments could be manipulated, shoved across desks, huckstered. Experience comes from within authentic people.

And people were never like the "cardboard comrades" of Gerald Green's *Holocaust,* the Weiss family and the rest of that cast. "Not a single situation could have happened in precisely that way in the lives of these many people," Reitz railed. "I don't believe in tear-jerking the 'heart'; that can't open the floodgates of perception in a people. On the contrary, this is how one becomes conditioned to no longer perceive individual misfortune."

So much for the Americans. The German critics, "merchants of guilt," were no better. It should have been their job to pinpoint for Germans the "untruth" of such a commercial product. But that was not for these satraps of market interests. How Reitz hated the "refined intellectuals" who "fell to their knees" when they heard *Holocaust* being praised as the most successful program in German TV history!

"Here comes the uncle from America," he mocked, "He pulls the Holocaust from his pocket, millions perch in front of the tube, thousands call up, umpteen thousand cry, how can one possibly raise critical reservations and look like a naysayer? One has to be with it!"

These go-along critics, wrote Reitz, were frightened of getting trapped among the unsuccessful. "Just in time, they head for the neighborhoods with the villas of the affluent, hoping that the rich will go pissing with them. Their yearning cry for a 'breakthrough' is like the longing of the *petit bourgeois* for a '*Führer,*' still, even today."

It troubled Reitz deeply that supposedly perceptive people also saw a breakthrough in *Holocaust,* a coming to terms with the ugly past. Even the Drs. Mitscherlich spoke of a "breakthrough." Reitz thought that the famous psychiatrists went along with this notion because they had been "incapable" of making headway with their complaint about the German inability to mourn. Now they seemed to have surrendered to Gerald Green's phony Americanized Holocaust sufferers.

"That pained me," wrote Reitz. He determined that he would re-create the true modern Germany on film, all of it, as it was and is, capturing only authentic emotions but not making judgments. He would do justice to the sweep of the enterprise by blessing it with the sainted title *Heimat.* This inspiration entailed some risk despite its honorable roots. A low-cost category called *Heimatfilme* had become synonymous with kitschy soap opera under the Nazis. Reitz was unworried. He was an artist with a lofty dream.

On paper, it seemed a good deal less. Tolstoy would not have had to worry about competition from its plot. Dense with detail after detail, all but drowning in trivia, the saga of Schabbach's Simon family meanders through the decades, beginning with the return from the World War I army of Paul, who marries the heroine, Maria, the younger daughter of Katharina, whom the critics would crown as the godmother of all German grandmothers. Paul's brother, Eduard, becomes a Nazi, then mayor, and marries Lucie, who used to run a brothel in Berlin. . . .

The first radio is a hero in this tale. So is the first car, the first telephone, the first real highway. In the beginning, the Nazis do well by Schabbach, then not so well, and once the Americans arrive, Lucie, the ex-madam, switches allegiance with lifelong aplomb.

*Heimat* accused or excused nobody. It did not analyze or moralize, examine or explain. Everything simply happened. The Nazis? "A national tragedy," Reitz had said in an early interview. And so Hitler, too, simply happened, a tragedy.

In fairness, *Heimat* did not picture the Nazis as Boy Scouts, although their doings remain somewhat shadowy. A couple of relatives move to a larger apartment that had been vacated, with no explanation given in the film, by Jews. Another relative watches shootings in the East — on film, at a neutral sanitary distance. A boy tracks new telephone poles to what the audience recognizes faintly as the outside of a concentration camp (the boy doesn't, so presumably he doesn't pass the word). Maria's brother, Wilfried, an SS man, tells the guests at a 1943 wedding about something called "the final solution," but small heed is paid.

The fascination of *Heimat* was in the superb acting, the brilliant photography, and the slow, comforting everydayness of the action — the so-human behavior of characters who in their countless vicissitudes did come across like real people with lifelike emotions — and in Reitz's artistry, how he achieved effects that moved onlookers and made them captives. Some of the footage was in black and white, so when Reitz wanted a Nazi spectacle, the sudden blood-red of swastika banners exploded to make his case.

The doughty, quiet optimism of the Simon clan helped. "We'll make it, all right," was the stoic underlying message as they lurched from crisis to crisis. It was a neutral, reassuring picture made for pleased, even smug, approval. The audience identified with the actors. This was the rank and file. They had all been there themselves. Give or take a little wishful thinking, this was how they wanted their history to have been. Thankfully, the film thumbed its romantic nose at Gerald Green's cataclysmic *Holocaust*. It cleansed the concept of *Heimat* and all it stood for, making it respectable, making Germany respectable.

Was *Heimat* also an honest representation of the Nazi era? Or did it bypass essentials? Vincent Canby in the *New York Times* accepted the banalities of the film as valid, rightful art. As a movie critic, he was willing to leave troublesome questions unconsidered. "It's not about guilt," he wrote, and that was that.

Or was it? For me, warning signs were hoisted by a remarkably unified statement released by a group of German filmmakers when Reitz's work won a major prize at the Venice Film Festival. These professionals were individualists, not made to agree on anything, and yet they adored *Heimat,* this version of their Germany, and wanted to say so. They praised it as "the requiem for the little people."

That pained me. "*Heimat* is about memory," as another critic said, and one of my abiding memories of the Nazi period was a scene I and my colleagues of our World War II psychological warfare outfit experienced with monotonous regularity when we interrogated German prisoners of war. Over and over, when we asked these men about uncivilized events during the Third Reich, no matter how gently the matter was put, they reeled back and fended off the question, invariably in the same language, as if by script and under instruction.

"But I was only a little man," said the sergeants and colonels and even generals. Some bristled, some yammered, some offered the words as a sad self-recognition that had only occurred to them at that moment. Regardless: every one of our prisoners declared himself to be a helpless pygmy. All issued blanket denials of responsibility for any uncivilized or even any unethical occurrences. They were able to do so, in protest and relief, because they thought of themselves as helpless and insignificant — only little men.

More than half a century away from our interrogation tents in Normandy it finally occurred to me that no American, and no Briton, would ever label himself in such a self-deprecating — and exonerating — way. And it was only then that Germans learned — from Steven Spielberg, another American Jew like Gerald Green — about Oskar Schindler, in every respect a very big man indeed.

Unlike Vincent Canby, the critic of the artistic, a young English historian took *Heimat* under closer scrutiny in the *New York Review of Books*. Timothy Garton Ash knew *Heimat*'s country and its people. He had lived in East Berlin as a British newspaper correspondent during the 1970s when Erich Honecker's country was terra incognita.

Viewed as a movie, Ash pronounced Reitz's work "superb." As history, it was a trick.

Granted, said Ash, *Heimat* was a film about what Germans remembered, a key stipulation, and that memory is selective, partial, and amoral.

"With this simple trick," wrote Ash, "Reitz manages to escape from the chains. . . . Not for him the agonizing directorial evenhanded, the earnest formulation of guilt, responsibility or shame. . . . Just memory and forgetting." Yes, forgetting.

Ash took Reitz to task for failing to pay history its taxes, yet even this shrewd analyst ultimately pronounced *Heimat* innocent of historical forgery. "In historical truth," he asked, "did the Hunsrück villagers see more than these glimpses of Nazi barbarism? I think not."

How wrong! Didn't the citizens of Schabbach know even one deeply evil *Kreisleiter* or other local Nazi bigwig? Didn't they listen to Hitler's harangues on the radio? Didn't they hear broadcasts from the BBC that laid out Nazi atrocities meticulously all during the war, and didn't they match these reports against some of the more transparent lies in Dr. Goebbels's propaganda sheets?

The little men of Schabbach knew plenty. They were not all that isolated. Reitz simply let them off the hook in his requiem.

In Reitz's Munich film production office, a one-man uproar reigned. While his assistants, clearly accustomed to the habits of their chief, went calmly about their business, Reitz, who was in his early sixties at the time of our meeting, was in shirtsleeves, towering tall and thin, his black hair boyishly tousled. As if pursued by insatiable demons, he was on the run, arranging chairs, issuing instructions, scheduling appointments, clucking over the state of the lunchroom, and prowling unsuccessfully for somewhere we might sit down and talk — the director looking for the spot to place the cameras.

The location was finally determined: a conference table taking up the center of the entrance hall. Traffic flowed past us at a steady rate. Ruddy-faced, bearded, ever frowning, intense to a point that might trigger an explosion in others, Reitz discoursed, lectured, spluttered, oblivious to the surroundings, his words racing around curve after curve. I had read that he credited his father, the watchmaker, for his own unusual capacity to maintain his concentration. The report must have been true.

*Heimat* had been succeeded in 1992 by its next and even longer chapter, *The Second Heimat,* thirteen installments totaling twenty-five hours and fifteen minutes, another enormous success in Germany, but a mere further stepping-stone in Reitz's own saga. The turbulence I was witnessing in his office concerned the ongoing work toward *Heimat 2000.* Reitz said it would be shown around the turn of the century. Never having met anybody for whom the 1900s had already expired, I felt like Scarlett O'Hara in *Gone with the Wind Meets Star Trek.*

The title *Heimat* had been kept secret by him until the initial film was finished and the production paid, Reitz disclosed. He knew, of course, that the Nazi *Heimatfilme* had made the word controversial. So for working purposes, he named his epic *Made in Germany.* That was a little slap at the American-made *Holocaust,* and there was no point in giving the jittery German television network executives a case of apoplexy by reminding them of Hitler. That was no longer politically correct in their politically correct industry.

"Hitler lived in their heads," Reitz recalled. "He *owned Heimat!*" Reitz felt that German life "must be taken out of Hitler's hands." He was concerned that the *Heimat* title might stamp him as a neo-Nazi in some minds. Still, the word was a tradition that preceded Hitler by centuries and would help the film to be received as authentic.

"Das ist die Wahrheit!," Reitz called out at me. "This is the truth!" Truth, not only actual but also as perceived, was still in the forefront of his mind a decade after the furor.

And a tempest did hit him when the film with its real title went before the television decision-makers. "They thought I had tricked them," he said, and his relationship with them remained bitter until the moment the film became a hit. It was only aired, he confided, when one of his friends, a major producer of theatrical movies, said he'd be delighted to show it and scoop television.


The Nazis affected Reitz's life very little when he was a boy, and he remembers that such distance was typical for his generation. The key question — "How does a normal person become a Nazi?" — is therefore only "touched" by his film, he agreed. It simply was no issue in the Reitz household.

His father, the watchmaker, was disinterested in politics, and a physical handicap kept him out of more than marginal army service. Nazis? Edgar Reitz remembered only "the SS uncle." He was a relative who was held in low regard because he had never learned a trade: "My father said, 'Such people can become big shots only under people like the Nazis.'" There seemed to have been no mention of other Nazi sins. Nazis were other people . . . or so the sheltered Reitz seemed to believe when he made the first *Heimat.* Since then, more of the world had crowded in on him. Reitz had been traveling a great deal in recent years and his horizons had widened.

"I see how easy it is to get along if you're not German," he reflected. "I saw the Holocaust Museum [in Washington] and came out asking myself why Germany still doesn't have such a memorial." He sounded exasperated. "The Germans still don't understand themselves," he said. "We still have that problem today. It must be a very difficult question. Hitler still lives with a lot of people."

He seemed to be speaking from a distance away, like an anthropologist exploring a remote tribe, and also like a filmmaker who might make revisions if he had to shoot the first *Heimat* over again. Hitler and his inheritance — not central in the original film — preoccupied him as he struggled with *Heimat 2000,* which is still in the works.

"How can Germany return to normalcy," he asked fifty years after normalcy had supposedly returned to his nation, "so that Hitler stops being the censor of our lives?" If German life had to be "taken out of Hitler's hands," as he had vowed a generation ago, the liberation was still pending.

And then came *Schindler's List.*

My friend Jörg Friedrich, the unabashed young Berlin historian, was unimpressed. We were talking about the likely impact of the film on German attitudes about Jews generally and the Holocaust specifically.

"It's a ritual," he scoffed. "Everybody runs to these things and acts as if they knew nothing. Every ten years or so they go and cry their eyes out." He mentioned the *Diary of Anne Frank* and the TV series *Holocaust* — warmly received years before *Schindler* but with no discernible lasting aftereffect.

My friend Rafael Seligmann, the Jewish historian and author in Munich, wrote a scathing article in *Der Spiegel* magazine called "Republic of the Shocked" (or "Republic of the Stricken"). Schindler, synagogue arson, murder of refugee children, he wrote —

it was all the same: the country was invariably "shocked" and reportedly felt "collective shame."

"What is the consequence of shame?" he demanded. "The same as shock, namely nothing. A child is ashamed because he wet his pants. The next day, he'll wet his pants again and will again be ashamed."

One of my distinguished new acquaintances, Hermann Graml, senior historian at Munich's Institute for Contemporary History, was also disgusted with the public's professions of ignorance whenever new treatments of the Holocaust such as *Schindler's List* appear. "They run there and act as if they'd never heard of it," he said. "It's grotesque!" However, he thought that the shock over *Schindler* struck deeper than usual. It seemed unique.

Graml's twenty-five-year-old daughter phoned him and for the first time interrogated him about specific crimes shown in the film. "Did that really happen?" she wanted to know.

The public reaction was extraordinary. Within two months of the film's release, four million Germans had flocked to see it in two hundred theaters; more than half were young people. The critics couldn't have been more enthusiastic. "Everybody should see this film," said the normally reserved *Frankfurter Allgemeine Zeitung* on its front page. It also posed the question of questions: "The viewer is forced to ask why others didn't try to do what Oskar Schindler managed."

Rank-and-file moviegoers displayed great emotion. In Cologne, half a dozen young women collapsed sobbing. "I have never seen an audience behave like this," said Wolfgang Röhrig, a twenty-six-year-old student. "It was as if they were in church." At the end, audiences everywhere filed out in stunned silence.

At the German premiere in Frankfurt, with director Steven Spielberg and the president of the Federal Republic in the audience, one viewer had special reason to feel affected. He was Michel Friedmann, a thirty-eight-year-old lawyer in Frankfurt, born in Paris, the son of two surviving "Schindler Jews." The parents hailed from Kraków, where Schindler did his great deeds and the film was made.

I spoke with Friedmann, who came to the premiere with his mother, Evgenia. The Schindler story had been well-known to him. His parents had often spoken of their strange German rescuer. The son thought he knew all there was to be known about Schindler and "his" Jews before he saw the picture, but he was wrong. The film authenticated the feeling of the Holocaust experience for him for the first time.

"I saw my parents and I was crying," he told Craig Whitney of the *New York Times*. "I saw the millions who didn't survive, and I was crying, and I saw the Germans who murdered, and I was crying, too."

Will the film help change German attitudes in the long run? Friedmann took a cautious view. "It's an impulse," he said, "it will open the door for some to know more. People were shaken up, but it's only an opening for long-term further work."

More than just another ritual? Perhaps, perhaps not.

# BOOK 4

## SPREADING EVIL

# 18

## SELLING DENIAL

**denial**: a defense mechanism that simply
disavows or denies thoughts, feelings or needs
that cause anxiety.

— *The Penguine Dictionary of Psychology*

Calmly considered, it has to be the ultimate absurdity, the grisliest
sick joke ever. Who could conceivably deny that some six million
Jews perished in the Holocaust? And who could possibly believe a lie
of this dimension?

Yet such liars, and such believers, exist in abundance. And their
ranks are growing.

First, a sampling of the liars and what they want the world to
believe about the Holocaust.

"It's just a myth and at last the myth is being eroded," says David
Irving, the British historian and the most effective of the "revision-
ists" (their term). What happened to the murdered millions? "A shell
game," claims Irving. The victims were "whisked into new homes,
lives, and identities in the Middle East, leaving their old, discarded
identities behind as 'missing persons.'" And Hitler himself had nothing to do with the killings. If he had known about them, he would
have stopped them.

"No execution gas chambers" — no such things existed in the
extermination camps, according to Fred A. Leuchter, Jr. The self-

appointed Boston "engineer" conducted spurious "forensic research" at the principal death sites in 1988.

"Hoax" was the word for the Holocaust from Bradley F. Smith, media project director of the Institute for Historical Review in Los Angeles, the primary force in the worldwide denial movement. "Something was wrong with the story of the six million, and what was wrong was being covered up."

Who swallows such nonsense? The polls turn up plenty of believers. Many of the respondents are the same defensive justifiers who decline all responsibility for the wartime treatment of Jews (42 percent of German voters, according to a 1992 poll) and Germans who believe that "the Jews are guilty of complicity when they are hated and persecuted" (32 percent).

Attitudes in the United States were similar. A Roper poll taken after President Reagan's visit to the Bitburg cemetery in 1985 showed that 40 percent of the American interviewees wanted Jews to stop calling attention to Nazi atrocities.

By no means all deniers are inspired by anti–Semitism. Many are guilty of nothing but unconsciously censoring memories or feelings too painful to be dealt with consciously — a defense mechanism long understood by psychologists. Also, the postwar revelations of the truth were simply too gross, too terrible, to be accepted as credible by many respectable people; there were even Jews who refused to believe the facts when the horrors first leaked out from the East while the killings were still in progress.

The palpable evidence can therefore be ignored: not merely the photos of the dead and those who barely survived in the newly liberated death camps, but the contemporaneous accounts from war correspondents. Some of these eyewitnesses vented their rage by attempting fragmentary body counts. "All that was mortal of 500 men and boys lay there in two neat piles," reported Edward R. Murrow in 1945 of one small corner in Buchenwald.

"Beyond the imagination of mankind," wrote R. W. Thompson of the London *Sunday Times* from Bergen-Belsen. The photographer Margaret Bourke-White told her editors at *Life* magazine that she would not believe what she saw until she could view her finished pictures.

My own family having been small, we lost "only" my aunt Marie, deported to Theresienstadt and never heard from again; and my uncle Max and his wife, Mathilde, among the last to be gassed at Auschwitz, a mere breath before the camp was liberated by the Russians. I have written elsewhere of my cousin Martha, her husband, and her daughter, who barely survived Bergen-Belsen and almost perished, just as the war ended, on a death train that wandered, without food and almost no water, all across Germany for thirteen days. It was nearly fifty years before I was able to persuade Martha to talk about her experiences.

Quixotically, the denials still mount half a century later. "As you're getting more right-wing groups, it is going to get even worse," predicted Deborah Lipstadt, an Emory University historian and author of *Denying the Holocaust: The Growing Assault on Truth and Memory*. "You'll have more and more groups looking for someone to blame as the economy gets worse. So you blame the foreigners, you blame the Turks, eventually you're going to get to the Jews. And eventually you're going to have to deal with the Holocaust."

The techniques of denial are ingenious. In recent years, denial spokesmen sponsored advertising campaigns in U.S. university newspapers to encourage campus discussion about "the other side of the Holocaust" — as if there were "another side." This reach for respectability did spark protests — at Duke University all members of the history faculty signed counter-ads — but the appeal for debate in the name of academic freedom, along with the challenge flung at conventional wisdom, that favorite target of students, undoubtedly influenced some tender and rebellious young minds.

Plain ignorance of history plays into the hands of the apologists. Repeatedly, throughout the 1980s and 1990s, polls disclosed astonishing American innocence. In one survey, 22 percent admitted not knowing what the Holocaust was, and another 10 percent identified the event incorrectly.

The proliferation of the denial lie does not depend on bad times; it is a function of a generalized malaise, the disaffection with reason and liberal politics. "Holocaust denial is one of the major tools of the far right," said Michael Whine, executive director for the Board of Deputies of British Jews, the English roof organization. "The Holocaust is too big a crime, it's a barrier to electoral victory, it must be answered with denial."

Professor Lipstadt noted a wider context. "There is an increasing fascination with, and acceptance of, the irrational," she wrote: the conspiracy theories still being spun around the assassination of President John F. Kennedy; the hate-mongering of "Afro-centrists" who declared blacks to be "sun people"; the credence given to visits from outer space.

"Any fact can be recast," Lipstadt pointed out. "There is no historical reality." Thus Holocaust denial transcends the deniers and their followers. "Denial of the Holocaust is not a threat just to Jewish history," Lipstadt argued, "but a threat to all who believe in the ultimate power of reason. It repudiates discussion the way the Holocaust repudiated civilized values."


And so attention must be paid to the likes of David Irving, arguably the most controversial historian of influence produced by the age of Hitler, his abiding idol. Fittingly, most everything about Irving is outsize, beginning with his giant physique. At six feet two inches, he weighs 238 pounds of massive muscle, with wide, angular shoulders, a boxer's arms and an iron hand grip. His large, square face is craggy, lived-in. He doesn't seem to walk, he rumbles like a tank. His talk is razor-sharp and hyperintense.

Outsize, too, are the successes of his numerous huge histories, many of them international best-sellers; the volatility of the controversies and lawsuits that trail him on his incessant research and speaking missions crisscrossing Europe and America; the spread of the cavernous apartment on Duke Street in London's fashionable Mayfair, where he has lived and worked for nearly thirty-five of his sixty-one years; and his intimacy with Germany, Hitler's Germany.

"Where are you from originally?" he inquired when I called him in the summer of 1994.

"Berlin-Charlottenburg," I said, identifying the borough of my birth.

"Karl Hanke was your *Kreisleiter*," Irving shot back.

I was stunned. I'd never heard of my district's party leader. Intimidation was one of Irving's arts.

Hitler has been the center of this strange Britisher's universe since his German teacher was struck by this affinity during his school days. Irving's "fascination" with the Führer, so he told me, was initially "prurient," growing "more obsessive" later. To "de-demonize" Hitler became his passion.

Wasn't Hitler evil? "He was as evil as Churchill, as evil as Roosevelt, as evil as Truman," Irving once told a BBC audience, and he is not embarrassed by other unconventional inclinations. Five times since 1959 he has made the pilgrimage to the shrine of shrines, the Eagle's Nest at Berchtesgaden, to revel in Hitler's personal environment. Initially Irving told me, "I look at the voyeurs," but then he didn't deny the spell upon himself. "It's a bit of a thrill," he allowed.

When I asked what he wanted etched onto his gravestone, his response was too quick and effusive for me to catch it all in my notebook. Together, we agreed on a stone condensation: "He instituted the campaign for real history." And according to a cornerstone of real history, the Irving version, Hitler never ordered the execution of the "final solution to the Jewish problem"; indeed, until late during World War II, he had no inkling of the Holocaust. It was Himmler's doing.

This is no place to reiterate why Irving's assertions are untrue. The libraries are full of thorough refutations by all the reputable historians of the era, without exception. But the obvious nature of this lie, like the obvious lie of Holocaust denial, is symptomatic of the rotten needles embedded in haystacks of exhaustive and largely accurate research that make up the bulk of Irving's vividly written volumes beginning in the late 1970s, when he set out to mine his Hitler lode.

His main work, *Hitler's War*, published in 1977 by the prestigious Viking Press, survived powerful critical artillery. Irving's interpretation of Hitler as a "weak" leader prompted the British historian Alan Bullock to bristle in the *New York Review of Books*, "There is so great a volume of evidence against such a view that it is astonishing anyone can seriously suggest it."

Historian John Lukacs said that the book's "appalling" errors were "not the result of inadequate research; they are not technical mistakes or oversights; they are the result of the dominant tendency of the author's mind."

Historian Walter Laqueur found the book "of value to a few dozen military historians capable of separating new facts from old fiction, of differentiating between fresh documentary material and unsupported claims, distortions and sheer fantasy."

Nevertheless, Irving's career blossomed. As we have seen at the 1978 Aschaffenburg conference on "Hitler Today," he starred as the enfant terrible, and yet the establishment historians listened defensively to the outbursts from this producer of best-sellers. They even cringed a bit when he attacked them scornfully as lap dogs who never left their desks because they were too lazy to hunt, as he did, for original documents and knowledgeable eyewitnesses. *Hitler's War,* moreover, enjoyed a remarkably long life. Repackaged in 1989 as *Führer und Reichskanzler* (Munich: Herbig, 816 pages), it detailed inaccuracies such as these:

Page 159: Hitler is surprised to hear the news of the 1938 *Kristallnacht* pogrom and reacts with "indignation and concern." In fact, according to Joseph Goebbels's diaries, Hitler gave the order to set off the violence.

Page 437: "To what extent Hitler dealt with the liquidation of the Jews in the East cannot be determined." Actually, the Führer's involvement has long been extensively documented.

Page 699: "Hitler refused to see the films" showing leaders of the abortive attempt on his life on July 20, 1944, being hanged by piano wire suspended from meat hooks. But according to armaments minister Albert Speer, Hitler viewed the films repeatedly and with considerable enjoyment.

Combined with other writings and condensed to 794 pages, *Hitler's War* was republished in 1990 by Avon (paperback) publishing house (New York). It reported (page 706) that Hitler, with Irving evidently agreeing, dismissed photos of liquidations at the Majdanek concentration camp as "pure enemy propaganda"; also (page 460) that in 1945 "the world's newspapers were full of unsubstantiated rumors about factories of death."

\* \* \*

Irving's first and typically explosive splash into print came at London's Imperial College, in its *Carnival Times* magazine. The contents of a particular issue in 1959 smacked of fascism to some, but Irving, the student editor and already a passionate right-winger, passed it off as satire. It called Hitler "the greatest unifying force Europe has known since Charlemagne." The college authorities were not amused and Irving hastily resigned his editorship.

Failure branded his formative years. He was unable to attain a college degree, which troubled him deeply, and he further failed by not measuring up for the military, which rankled in a service-oriented family. His father was a commander in the Royal Navy, his older brother a wing commander in the Royal Air Force; young David could not satisfy the physical requirements for the RAF.

The implication of his incomplete education hurt the most. "Imperial College told me I was a failure," he said to a writer from the London *Sunday Times* for an unusually long and revealing article in 1970. "That's what leaves a mark." Convinced that he was destined for a life of manual labor, he signed on for menial toil at a Thyssen steel mill in the Ruhr. There he perfected his German and, to his delight, found his spiritual home and his true calling as a writer and propagandist.

At the mill was a fellow worker from Saxony who imparted firsthand accounts about the catastrophic firebombing of Dresden in which 135,000 died in the spring of 1945. While the strategic significance of the city, then still intact, was not marginal, it contained no sizable military targets.

"I was very shocked," Irving said to me. "It was something they never told us."

Of course, despite Irving's declaration, the bombing was extensively reported by the BBC and other media throughout the world. In fact, public controversy about the legitimacy of Dresden as a bombing target erupted immediately after the event and continued for years. Irving, moreover, had identified his own collective target. It was "they," meaning Winston Churchill and his allies, those war criminals guilty of terror attacks upon Hitler's civilian populations.

Out of Irving's anger emerged his first book, published in 1963, *The Destruction of Dresden,* a major best-seller that marked him as a writer of vigorous style and with obvious doggedness and skill for research into the most minute detail.

His debut in historical writing turned out largely fair-minded and deserving of its success. The book recalled Hitler having said, "If they threaten to attack our cities, then we shall rub out theirs." It accused "Nazism" of having "committed the greatest crimes against humanity in recorded history." Its worst slip into prejudice was the hyperbole, also shared by less radical critics, that Churchill had perpetrated a "massacre" upon defenseless citizens.

In 1967, Irving followed up with another dazzling research spectacular, *The German Atomic Bomb*. In recent years I had occasion to look into Hitler's botched attempt to beat the Allies at developing the first nuclear weapon. I found Irving's work reliable and by far the best source for this complex topic.

In 1970, however, at thirty-one, Irving became Britain's "best known historian" (the *Sunday Times*) by libeling a Royal Navy captain in his account of a World War II caper, *The Destruction of Convoy PQ17*. The money verdict was punishing by British standards, almost $80,000; the judge's assault on Irving's integrity cut deeper.

Irving had referred to a figure in the controversy as "a sly, slippery character." The judge told the jury, "If there is anybody who is a slippery and sly character, you might think it is Mr. Irving."

It was the start of Irving's descent into his permanent role. He saw himself as a "difficult author" whom the "establishment" wanted to destroy. "I've been hated by professionals," he told me with a touch of pride. His critics scorned him as an "evil" falsifier who slickly camouflaged his lies by tucking them away in masses of first-rate reporting. For certain, he was becoming an exceptionally stormy, exceptionally public figure, constantly enmeshed in fiery disputes, which he relished. His notoriety generated publicity that sold his books and paid for his Rolls-Royce and his apartment in Florida. Meanwhile, his identification with things German grew ever more visible, especially his preoccupation with Hitler, Hitler, Hitler.

"On greeting me, he clicked his heels and with a light, perfunctory bow, lifted my hand halfway to his lips," reported Susan Barnes, the *Sunday Times* writer who talked with him in 1970. By the time he worked on *Hitler's War*, so he confided with his characteristic openness to the author Robert Harris, he had hung a self-portrait of Hitler from the wall above his desk; a little mustache and a lock of black hair slanting across his forehead made him resemble his Führer; and he would volunteer why he abhorred alcohol.

"I don't drink," he said. "Adolf didn't drink, you know."

The German and British media markets, rich and feverishly competitive, reciprocated by blessing Irving with the status of a leading authority on Hitler, and in the spring of 1983, with the discovery of the Führer's "diaries," his big chance arrived. He needed it, being broke from an acrimonious divorce and harassment by the tax authorities.

He had known about the forgeries and had acquired pages from them as well as some related documents. Now, on April 22, he pronounced himself "shocked" at the interest shown by *Stern* and the *Sunday Times* and moved to cash in fast on his reputation as an expert for German documents. The *Observer* paid him $2,500 just for helping with an article denouncing the authenticity of the diaries. The *Mail on Sunday* paid him $8,000 for his papers and a statement calling the diaries forged. And the BBC made time for his showmanship. Waving his documents at the camera, he said, "I have smelled them . . . They certainly smelled."

By Friday, April 29, Irving was bored being on the same side as conventional historians, who also proclaimed the diaries a hoax. He was also having genuine reservations about his position and indicated this to the BBC. And on the following Sunday, eager to remain a player in the running feast of headlines, he phoned the *Daily Express*. "Hold on to your hat," he said, and announced that he now considered the diaries genuine.

This public relations mishap failed to damage Irving's good name in useful quarters. In 1985, the Deutsche Volksunion, the vehicle of Dr. Gerhard Frey, awarded him the $12,000 Hans Ulrich Rudel Prize. Rudel was the Luftwaffe ace fighter pilot who had returned from exile in Argentina for a career in neo-Nazi politics.

Publicity opportunities kept coming for Irving. In 1988, he testified in a Canadian trial of the Holocaust denier Ernst Zündel that he had found "no document whatsoever indicating the Holocaust occurred." Zündel had called Hitler "the Abraham Lincoln of Germany" and vowed, "We still love him."

In 1989, Irving distributed the *Leuchter Report,* which claimed that no gassings could have occurred at Auschwitz, and in his commentary he wrote, "The lid cannot be kept on the facts much longer."[1] A motion in the House of Commons declared itself "appalled by the allegations by Nazi propagandist and longtime Hitler apologist David Irving."

Irving countered with a challenge: "I will go into the 'gas chambers' of Auschwitz and you and your friends may release Zyclon B according to the well-known procedures. I guarantee you that you will not be satisfied with the result."

On the November 9 anniversary of *Kristallnacht,* in 1991, Irving, still combed and mustachioed like Hitler and wrapped in a trenchcoat, appeared on a public square in Halle before five hundred neo-Nazis and shouted into a loudspeaker for "the new German youth" to create "a new Germany." Dr. Frey was paying him 1,000 marks per appearance for such interventions in partisan politics.

In 1991 he was back touring Canada. In Regina, he told fans, "There were no gas chambers, they were fakes and frauds."

In 1992 Irving enjoyed a particularly productive spell. Invited to the "Adler" Inn at Pforzheim in the Black Forest by the local honorary chairman of the ruling Christian Democratic Union (CDU), Irving called Auschwitz a "tourist sideshow." The middle-class crowd cried, "Bravo!" and "Jawohl!"

That same year, Irving elicited further shouts of approval in Passau at a mass demonstration of Dr. Frey's DVU. It was the fiftieth anniversary of the Wannsee Conference that sealed the go-ahead for the Final Solution. Irving shouted, "In ten years there will be no more Israel!"

---

[1]Before forfeiting bail following his arrest in Germany for spreading illegal propaganda in late 1993, Leuchter was still starring on a major German TV talk show. His gospel also laid the groundwork for the documentary *Occupation: Neonazi.* The film's young protagonist was shown in the remnants of the Auschwitz gas chambers, shouting, "Where did the smoke go? Where did the smoke go?"

In his old haunt, Dresden, a crowd of 1,000 rose for a standing ovation when Irving stepped into the spotlight. Then, in the Moscow archives, he scooped up ninety-two dusty yellow boxes with the complete Goebbels diaries, preserved in glass plates. They had been unearthed by the Munich Institute for Contemporary History, but it was Irving who scooped the world by quickly deciphering the ancient German script and persuading his onetime adversary, the London *Times,* to pay him $125,000 to make them available.

But reverses began to dog him. A Munich court fined him $6,000 for claiming that the Auschwitz gas chambers were built after the war for tourists. Also, his movements were severely restricted: one by one, he was banned from travel in Germany, Austria, Italy, Canada, and Australia. In turn, he charged he was being victimized by censorship.

"It reminds me of the period in which I'm an expert," he told me darkly, and said he was mounting a counteroffensive. Since he had been effectively denied access to the German federal archives in Koblenz and thereby to the stacks of documents he had donated to them, he was demanding the return of the papers.

Left-wing demonstrators had caused disturbances in front of his London apartment house and Irving said he feared for his family's safety. He had given a personal fire drill to his new wife. A son-in-law, he reported, had "forbidden" one of his married daughters to speak to him. The young husband was of Polish origin.

To make up for lost speaking territory, Irving was branching out to the United States, where he could spread his word under the protection of the First Amendment. He had just returned from a two-week tour of conservative enclaves in the Deep South. His audience at the University of Alabama in Huntsville had numbered about 500. He was very pleased.

Banishment from his German fans clearly troubled him. Even his old patron Dr. Gerhard Frey, he reported, was keeping his distance. In return, Irving was punishing him with wisecracks. Frey, he muttered, was too interested in making money. "Almost Jewish" ("*beinahe jüdisch*") I was told with a wink by the great Holocaust denier, who also always denies that he is anti-Semitic.

No matter. His writings would advance his fortunes. He had finished his new opus, a biography of Dr. Joseph Goebbels, more than

900 pages long, the "real history" of the little man with the limp who spent his life managing Hitler's lies. David Irving would publish it himself. He could do without publishers or other middlemen such as pollsters.

However, at the start of the new millennium, Irving's luck changed. In her aforementioned book, *Denying the Holocaust,* published by Penguin Books Limited, Professor Deborah Lipstadt mentions Irving, describing him as a denier and revisionist, and recounts his theories using references and direct quotations.

In January 2000, Irving brought Lipstadt and Penguin to court for libel, complaining that he was a victim of an international defamation campaign. He claimed that Lipstadt's book accuses him of falsifying historical facts in order to support his theory that the Holocaust never happened. This of course discredited his reputation as a historian and he sought damages. At the trial, Irving did not hire a lawyer but chose to represent himself. In his opening speech, he explained that the defendants had to prove not only that his portrayal of facts was distorted but also that this distortion was intentional.

On April 11, High Court judge Charles Gray ruled against Irving, concluding that he indeed qualified as a Holocaust denier and anti-Semite and that as such he has distorted history in order to defend his hero, Adolf Hitler. Thus Irving, who had previously told reporters that his supporters had raised a £300,000 ($500,000) fighting fund, was ordered to pay £150,000 ($300,000) interim costs. Risking bankruptcy and the loss of his house in case of default, Irving set out on a three-month fund-raising tour of the United States while seeking permission to appeal against the verdict. His appeal was refused on December 18, 2000.

# 19

## WHY THE "HITLER DIARIES"

## WERE BELIEVED

The acclaimed British historian H. R. Trevor-Roper called it "the greatest scoop since Watergate," and on April 23, 1983, this world-class sensation was bannered across the front page of the London *Times*.

## 38 YEARS AFTER BUNKER SUICIDE HITLER'S SECRET DIARIES TO BE PUBLISHED

A 3,000-word article by Trevor-Roper led the paper, in which the author of *The Last Days of Hitler* put his considerable reputation on the line. He reported that he had examined the fifty handwritten volumes in Zurich and that they were legitimate.

He brought suspense to his own dramatic role as chief judge: "When I had entered the back room of the Swiss bank, and turned the pages of those volumes, my doubts gradually dissolved. I am now satisfied they are authentic."

The international media were gripped by a collective run for their checkbooks. An angry bidding battle between the British press lord Rupert Murdoch and Katharine Graham, the president of *Newsweek*, drove up the price for newspaper and magazine publishing rights to $3.75 million. The German magazine *Stern*, launch site and owner of the diaries, would pay out $12 million in the course of the enterprise.

The exorbitant costs notwithstanding, the publishing executives were elated. Among themselves, they referred to the diaries as "the publishing event of the century." Sidney Mayer, the veteran London publisher of Hitleriana, was proved right once again: "Hitler sells." And sells. And sells. Curiosity about the personal notations of the long-departed dictator remained so compelling that the daily circulation of the London *Times* jumped by 60,000 copies the moment the first diary pages came out. *Stern's* distribution shot up by 400,000, to 2.1 million.

Hitler intimates joined Trevor-Roper and some fellow historians in certifying the legitimacy of the diaries. Hans Baur, Hitler's gruff personal pilot, allowed, "It was Hitler's writing." Wolf Hess, Rudolf Hess's son, pronounced that he had no doubt the volumes were genuine.

The real insider in the case (and highest-ranking survivor of Hitler's inner circle), SS General Karl Wolff, the chief of Himmler's personal staff, had been the project's consulting authority all along. He treasured the diaries, and upon their publication he was ready with his view of their contemporary meaning — the interpretation of an incorrigible Nazi eager to keep alive the public's memory of the Führer.

"Here is confirmation," he told reporters from the London *Sunday People,* "for what my friends and I have said for years: Hitler never ordered the annihilation of the Jews. The picture of Hitler was blackened by these accusations and the reputation of the German people was damaged. The diaries cleanse this reputation, and my own. We are idealists and nationalists, not criminals."

The general was engaging in his favorite sport, hyperbole; the cleansing of his reputation would have required vastly more than a set of diaries, even if they had been genuine, which of course these were not. Wolff, then eighty-four, could look back on a rollicking career as an advertising man, convicted war criminal, betrayer of Hitler, and respected friend of Allen Dulles, the American spymaster.

His last years, so said Wolff's biographer, were devoted to constructing "a correction of the history of the Third Reich." A daunting task to say the least. Wolff died in July 1984.

"He was the ultimate chameleon," said Himmler's biographer.[1] This

---

[1]Much of the background presented here was drawn from two unusually thorough biographies, *Der Adjutant* by a German author, Jochen von Lang (1985), and *Himmler* by Peter Padfield (1991), a British military historian.

historian viewed Wolff as Himmler's sophisticated "public relations face," which was true. But it was also a colossal understatement. Tall, ruler-straight, well-spoken, elegantly tailored, with vast forehead and hawk nose, Wolff was a con man out of Münchhausen. Unfailing charm enhanced his negotiating skills. Charm and curiosity. Around the rigidly formal Führer headquarters, where he spent much of the war, he was nicknamed "General What's-New?"

Despite his frustrated hankering for fame — or, more likely, because of his overriding determination to survive the Third Reich — he kept his name out of the headlines during the Hitler days as well as afterward. His relative obscurity was misleading, however. Hitler and Himmler (who called him "Wölfchen," little wolf) considered him an indispensable confidant on matters of the greatest delicacy because, Münchhausen or not, Karl Wolff was anything but a fool. There is much to be gleaned from the life and machinations of this character, who really should have become an actor or a novelist.

Instead, Wolff became an *Altkämpfer*, a Nazi warhorse. He checked into the party early, two years before Hitler seized power, but he was different. He lacked the low breeding of most Nazi newcomers. His father was a judge, and Karl attended the best schools. As a teenaged lieutenant in World War I, he won the Iron Cross, first and second class, fighting with an exclusive regiment of Hessian Guards. Later he ran his own advertising agency, which he lost in the depression. Among the party's young primitives he advanced swiftly, taking a seat in the Reichstag in 1936, becoming SS *Gruppenführer* in 1937, and general of the Waffen-SS in 1940, when he was barely forty.

The aristocratic general and the vicious but mousy, semi-literate Himmler had grown close. Following literally in Hitler's footsteps, they rode in triumphant tandem into the freshly conquered capitals: Vienna, Prague, Warsaw. When Himmler took Wolff along for conferences in Finland, the SS *Reichsführer* reminded his alter ego not to forget heavy underwear.

Wolff, in turn, composed a letter in 1939, to be delivered to his chief in case of his death in the war. It thanked Himmler for "all that you have meant to me," and went on, "You personify all that is good and beautiful and manly." The letter was signed, "Your faithful and very devoted Wölfchen."

By the time war began, Wolff was all too undeniably indebted to his patron saint, the SS. Socially adept and ambitious, he lived convivially beyond his salary, and not in paltry style. He rented a large villa in the exclusive Dahlem district of Berlin and built himself another villa, ten rooms with beach and boathouse, in the Bavarian Alps on Tegernsee at the fashionable resort of Rottach-Egern. His pretty wife, Frieda, and their four children divided their time between the two residences. His mistress, the widowed Countess Ingeborg Bernstorff, was installed in a large apartment at Charlottenburg, Berlin, along with her three children, one of whom was fathered by Wölfchen.

When this captain's paradise had run up a debt totaling a staggering 150,000 marks, a party court intervened, though not too aggressively. SS negotiators wheedled the obligation down to 21,500 marks. Himmler gave his protégé 20,000 marks from an SS fund and persuaded the party treasurer to advance the remaining 1,500 to the classy compatriot who considered himself the *Reichsführer's* potential successor.

The mighty duo also shared the management of annoying repercussions from their sex lives. Wolff's countess wanted her general to get a divorce, and the general, a devotee of Himmler's racial theory of pure blood, was eager to acquire a blonde wife who had already given birth to model offspring: Nordic, blue-eyed. Wolff's legal spouse, the brunette Frieda with her brown-eyed children, wouldn't hear of a separation, and Himmler, wanting only peace in his official family, supported her. After a stalemate lasting five years, the countess burst into Himmler's private office, banged her fist on his desk, and very audibly demanded justice. The *Reichsführer,* detesting noisy confrontations, promised to cooperate. His consent was so long delayed, however, that Wolff asked Hitler to intervene, which he did, and Wolff married his blonde.

Himmler forgave him, probably because he too had to deal with a chronically jealous wife. Frau Marga Himmler, seven years older than the *Reichsführer* and grown corpulent, had been replaced in Himmler's bed by his secretary. When a son was born to them, Wölfchen became godfather and, often, his chief's father confessor. Finding Himmler looking emotionally and physically crushed at his desk one afternoon, Wolff assumed that the chief's double life was the cause, and he said so.

The response, as Wolff remembered it, delved into new and unexpected territory.

"No, dear Wölfchen," Himmler allegedly said with a wan smile. "I can cope with that. But you cannot imagine what I must take silently off the Führer's hands so that he, as the Messiah for the next two thousand years, can remain free of sin . . . It will be better for you and Germany if you have nothing to do with these things that depress me and that you don't know anything about them."

Only after the war, so Wolff claimed forty-five years later, did the reason for Himmler's depression dawn on him: "It concerned the Jewish problem" — the one problem he claimed to know nothing about.

Wolff's enlightenment concerning the Final Solution could not have come to him so veiled and so long after the fact. Barring an amnesia of record length and depth, the general was lying, as he often did. Even if Himmler wanted to spare him early knowledge, General "What's-New" Wolff witnessed the impact of the horrors upon a trusted participant: his friend SS general Erich von dem Bach Zelewski, whom he visited in the SS hospital Hohenlychen in the fall of 1941.

The two generals had long been close. They addressed each other with the familiar "Du," and von dem Bach's letters to his friend began with "Dear Wölfchen." Having commanded some of the bloodiest early massacres in Russia, Bach had landed in the hospital writhing in a nervous breakdown. "No wonder I'm done in," he told the chief physician of the SS. "Don't you know what's happening in Russia? The entire Jewish people is being annihilated there!"

No record exists of the bedside confidences exchanged between Bach and Wolff, but as soon as Wolff reported back to Himmler, the *Reichsführer,* alarmed at possible additional leaks, had guards posted outside the room of the talkative Bach. Surely he had not kept the cause of his agitation from an intimate like Wölfchen.

At that, even in this early stage of the Holocaust, the bloodshed was nothing new to Wolff. Some weeks earlier, in midsummer, he

had witnessed its effect on his revered boss. The pair had flown in
Himmler's personal J-52 to Minsk. The toll of executions there stood
at over 37,000; Himmler wanted to see how his men handled the
killings.

With arms folded across his chest and Wolff beside him, he stood
at the foot of a ditch twenty-five feet long, six feet wide, and six feet
deep, jammed with live bodies lying on their stomachs. The twelve-
man execution squad fired. Himmler turned green, jerked convul-
sively, staggered, vomited, supported by Wolff, who was neither
staggering nor vomiting.

Documents confirm that Wolff monitored further progress of the
killings and welcomed them. Following a phone conversation with
Wolff, who urged faster action, a letter to him dated July 28, 1942,
from the head of the eastern railway directorate, reported dutifully,
"Since July 22, a daily train with 5,000 Jews goes from Warsaw via
Malkinia to [the concentration camp at] Treblinka. In addition, a
train with 5,000 Jews goes twice a week from Przemysl to [the camp
at] Belzec."

On August 13, Wolff replied, "I noted with particular pleasure
that for two weeks a daily train with 5,000 members of the chosen
people has been going to Treblinka, because in this way we are in a
position to execute this population movement more speedily."

By February 1945, Wolff was commander of all SS forces in Italy.
The German troops were in a desperate state on all fronts, and the
long-promised "wonder weapons" that were supposed to turn the
war around were becoming a mirage. Wolff decided to risk the great
gamble of his life. If the war was lost, so, in all probability, was his
neck. It was time for a grand slam. Driven by desperation and egomania, he came up with an escape plan for all of the Third Reich in
which he would star as the savior.

Calling on the increasingly confounded and ailing Hitler in Berlin,
he said, "My Führer, if it's not possible for you to give me a date for
the wonder weapons, we must approach the Anglo-Americans and
seek peace."

He paused. Hitler said nothing. He tapped his fingers, cocked his head, and shortly indicated with a smile that the interview was over. Wolff, jubilant that the suggestion had not resulted in his arrest or execution — many heads were rolling around the Führer — interpreted the absence of a veto as consent to continue, without informing Himmler, the explorations that he had already set in motion. He would begin to close down the war by arranging the surrender of all German armies still fighting stubbornly in Italy.

This decision to play God set in motion a sequence of conspiracies worthy of a bustling Italian opera. Middlemen of Italian, Nazi, anti-Nazi, Vatican, and American loyalties ducked in and out of secret huddles in Berlin, Zurich, Rome, and assorted military headquarters. Eventually, Wolff plotted directly with Allen Dulles, head of the Swiss spy headquarters for the Office of Strategic Services.

It was a lovefest at a "safe house" on Lake Zürich, two con men in three-quarter time. Wolff offered up Italy "on a silver platter." Dulles chuckled, puffed on his pipe, and gained the impression that this urbane SS man could deliver. Optimistic reports were rushed to General Eisenhower in Paris.

Wolff's co-conspirators were already talking of him as the interior minister of a post-Hitler cabinet, but Wolff was less than certain that he could deliver German consent to surrender. Himmler, having gotten wind of his partner's freelancing, was furious and seized Wölfchen's family as hostages. The *Reichsführer* was running his own surrender negotiations with Swedish emissaries.

On April 18, shortly after 3 A.M., with the war's end little more than a week away, Wolff played his trump card: Hitler in his Berlin bunker, almost surrounded by Russian troops. Wolff hoped he was entering friendly territory; the bunker's last commandant was also a friend of his, ruffian SS general Wilhelm Mohnke. But the tottering Hitler, undoubtedly prodded by Himmler, could be a death trap.

Wolff broached another of his hat tricks. Triumphantly he announced, "I am happy to be able to report to my Führer that I can succeed through Mr. Dulles to open the doors for talks with the presidential palace [*sic!*] in Washington and the prime minister's office in London. My Führer, I request instructions for the future."

This was a fraud designed to feed Hitler's fantasies of survival. Wolff knew that nobody would negotiate with Hitler. And there were further complications he was lucky enough not to have heard about. In Moscow, Stalin had learned of Wolff's adventures and was pressuring the American ambassador with questions. Was the West selling him out? The Soviet dictator demanded to be represented in the Swiss negotiations.

Hitler felt he could not afford to alienate General Wolff and his connections abroad. Drained, the Führer went to sleep around 4 A.M. and the following afternoon took Wolff for a walk through the garden of the Chancellery; it was a rare pause in the Russian bombings. Leaning on a cane and moving in halting steps, Hitler predicted that a paralyzing stalemate between his enemies would allow him to hold out for favorable peace terms. Wolff should continue talking with Dulles and stall him.

Wolff did continue talking but did not stall, so at 4:30 on the morning of May 2 all Germans in Italy surrendered. Dulles and his people had been calling Wolff's project "Operation Sunrise." Fittingly, some lives were saved as of dawn that day, for the German armies elsewhere did not quit until May 7.

Having accumulated credits with the Americans, Wolff boosted his standing with them by testifying for the prosecution at the Nuremberg war crimes trials, as did his friend von dem Bach Zelewski. Appearing in full SS regalia, Wolff snitched on his comrades, including some of his own former subordinates. But he lived, while most of his closest associates were hanged or committed suicide.

Indeed, he lived fairly well. When a German denazification court sentenced him to four years in a work camp, Wolff cashed in his chips. Kindly angels made certain that he served only a week. And not too long afterward the angel-in-chief, Ambassador Robert D. Murphy, sent a top-secret cable to Washington: "Some U.S. intelligence authorities are of the definite opinion that military honor requires pardon and immunity for Wolff."

Allen Dulles's deputy told the State Department that Wolff and his associates "rendered services to the Allies, therefore the Allies were morally obligated to weigh the good along with the bad . . ." State recommended that "definite consideration should be given to those favorable aspects when weighing any war crimes with which they are charged."

Case closed. Wolff was back in the advertising business, at least until 1962. That year, a German court sentenced him to fifteen years for expediting Jewish transports during the war, and he did serve six of these. It was the merest interlude, for soon after incarceration that slapped his wrist for crimes inspired by Hitler, Wolff fell under the spell of another personality who, like Himmler, was a creature of the Führer. This new acquaintance had been a child when Wolff was dispatching Jews to concentration camps. Now they became another odd couple. Wölfchen's partner for his old age was a *Stern* magazine reporter named Gerd Heidemann, whose creativity made up for his lack of experience.

Heidemann was forty-one when the two men met in 1974, and he was another Münchhausen character: a short, fat chatterbox exuding enormous greed and energy, more salesman and conspirator than journalist. He was obsessed with the glamour and adventure of the Hitler era. It possessed him, and its grandiosity kept him broke. Mortgaging his house, he had purchased the decrepit *Carin II,* the yacht Hermann Göring had named for his wife, and the required repairs kept him hustling for money.

The yacht became the center of Heidemann's life in fantasy and fact. He charmed Edda Göring, pretty, not married, and devoted to the memory of her father, the *Reichsmarschall,* and started an affair with her. Together, they ran social events aboard the ship. Much of the talk was of Hitler and the Nazis, and the guests of honor were weathered eyewitnesses of the hallowed time, two generals who were brought by another *Stern* reporter, Jochen von Lang:[2] Himmler's

---

[2]This was the same capable reporter who became Wolff's biographer. He too was fascinated by Nazis, but he kept his distance and his professional head. In 1962 he had produced a fine book summarizing the Adolf Eichmann trial.

man, Karl Wolff, and General Wilhelm Mohnke, the last commander of the Hitler bunker.

"We started to have long drinking evenings aboard," recalled Heidemann. "I had always been a passionate reader of thrillers. Suddenly I was living a thriller."

So were they all, rousingly tipsy on champagne: Wolff, Mohnke, and some dozen others. Eventually, the old-timers' round was joined by former SS major Otto Guensche, another rare survivor of the *Führerbunker* command. He had supervised the burning of their leader's corpse. Ever since, he had been a close friend of Mohnke, having talked the general out of shooting himself when both were captured by the Russians after the fall of Berlin.

If Heidemann had not recruited such a congenial circle, the taciturn Mohnke would probably not have come aboard the *Carin II*. The general was a loner. He had endured ten harsh years in Soviet prison camps, and an early war crime charge hung over him unpunished. No explanation was known for this immunity,[3] but insiders were aware that Mohnke, then a captain, had ordered the shooting of forty-five helpless British prisoners of war at a barn in Wormhoudt, France, during the disastrous Allied retreat to Dunkirk in 1940.

Three mutual needs kept the bond solid for a decade between Wolff and Heidemann. Both were hungry for cash, both craved adventure, both wanted to mobilize new audiences to appreciate Hitler and his works. Crazed as they were, their proselytizing was so obviously sincere that it turned off at least one colleague. Shortly before his defection from the group on *Carin II,* one of Heidemann's more liberal writer friends from *Stern,* fed up with Nazi claptrap, entered a meaningful entry in the ship's guest book.

"On this silent sea, if one can so describe our Elbe River," he wrote with more than a touch of sarcasm, "we resurrected the glorious Third Reich with General Wolff."

To raise money, Wolff (unsuccessfully) sued the German government for an increase in his military pension. He auctioned off his size

---

[3]A secret deal must have been responsible for his freedom. The *London Sunday Times* finally publicized the massacre on April 24, 1988, but relevant documents were sealed until the year 2011.

58 SS cap and pieces of his uniforms, including a tunic of a type supposedly worn only by him, Göring, and the star pilot Ernst Udet. He
gave nostalgic lectures wherever he could. And when Wolff failed in
his efforts to find a ghostwriter for his planned memoirs — at one
point he claimed that an American publisher had offered him $1.2
million — he kept after Heidemann to take on the job.

Unfortunately, the bouncy little journalist was not up to a major
writing project. He was only a researcher and a scatterbrained hobby-
ist. He did make tapes of some of Wolff's reminiscences and also
recorded some of the drunken talk aboard the *Carin II*. He hoped to
shape them into a book, to appear first in *Stern* and to be titled *Ship-
board Conversations*.

No book ever materialized. What did work out was Heidemann's
adroit use of the still high-ranking and impressive-looking Wolff as
an introducer, the passport to contacts in the Nazi afterworld and the
open-sesame to stories for which *Stern* had eager audiences waiting
and for which the magazine was therefore willing to pay with largesse.

The magazine even financed Heidemann's honeymoon. When he
married for the fourth time in December 1978, his two prestigious
courtiers, the generals Wolff and Mohnke, appeared as the official
witnesses. Wolff then joined the newlyweds for a honeymoon trip to
South America, which also served the cause of research in old Nazi
lairs for news of lost Nazi celebrities who intrigued Heidemann,
especially Martin Bormann and Dr. Josef Mengele.

Bormann, Hitler's ubiquitous principal assistant, had in fact been
confirmed a suicide in Berlin when his remains were found in 1972.
This did not deter the little reporter who was known at *Stern* as the
staff's "bloodhound." And Heidemann certainly could not divine
that Mengele would drown off a beach in Brazil, four months after
the bloodhound began to track him.

Heidemann and Wolff did mingle with a lot of Nazi brass at German clubs all over Latin America, and Wolff gave lectures. After the
honeymoon trip, two more years of junkets through Latin America
ensued, and ultimately Wolff procured for Heidemann a long interview in Bolivia with Klaus Barbie, the "butcher of Lyon."

Heidemann's sinking patient, the *Carin II,* had meanwhile left
the little reporter increasingly desperate for large infusions of cash. In

January 1981, at last, providence intervened. General Mohnke led Heidemann to a Dr. Fischer, an antique dealer in the Stuttgart area, who had sold some extraordinary items to one of Mohnke's rich friends: watercolors from the Führer's hand, Hitler's top hat, and the swastika flag that flew over the 1923 Beer Hall Putsch and was trotted out as a holy keepsake on subsequent anniversaries of the Party's birth.

Later, all these treasures turned out to be fake, as did the pistol that Heidemann acquired, the weapon with which Hitler was supposed to have shot himself. But these revelations were still some time in coming. For the present, Heidemann had picked up a rumor that Dr. Fischer possessed long-lost Hitler diaries. Diaries! Intimate thoughts from the Führer's hand! The report left Heidemann quivering before the antique dealer, who turned out to be Konrad Kujau, only in his mid-forties at the time but certainly one of the most gifted and industrious forgers of all time.

Mohnke and Guensche were skeptical about the diaries when Heidemann first mentioned them. So was Richard Schulze Kossens, a Hitler adjutant who also survived the Berlin bunker. The four men talked at a party Mohnke gave following the funeral of Grand Admiral Karl Dönitz, Hitler's successor. It had been a heady occasion at Aumühle, outside Hamburg: 5,000 veterans, some in decorated uniforms, joined right-wingers to sing the combative first stanza of the national anthem ("Deutschland über alles") and listen to speeches evoking old glories.

Mohnke thought that the existence of diaries was "impossible." Schulze Kossens said Hitler would never have found time to make extensive notes. Christa Schroeder, Hitler's most worshipful secretary, later pointed out that the Führer never wrote more than a handful of words by hand. But Heidemann, and a bit later Wolff, were enchanted, and Kujau had no trouble unloading the enormous hoard of fakes that he had scribbled with so much diligence. The *Stern* reporter ingested this harvest like so much champagne, and his editors could hardly contain their exuberance when they pored over the riches that burst out of those homey-looking notebooks.

Hugh Trevor-Roper, the sage of Oxford, could all but see Hitler sneaking to work on the diaries: "We must envisage him, every night after he had apparently gone to bed . . . sitting down to write his daily record." And the professor had no difficulty visualizing Hitler as a practicing "compulsive diarist." Trevor-Roper well knew that Hitler hated writing by hand, and now he thought he was learning why: "That may be not so much because he was out of practice as because he already suffered from writer's cramp."

Rupert Murdoch was convinced. So was *Newsweek*. *Stern* lectured that the diaries would force the world "to deal, once again, with the fact of Hitler himself. Germans will have to wonder anew about their collective, inherited guilt. Jews will have to face their fears again. All of us will have to ask once more whether Hitler's evil was unique, or whether it lurks somewhere in everyone."

By the time handwriting experts had unmasked the diaries as fantasies by Konrad Kujau, so much attention had been lavished on the putative diarist that *Newsweek* claimed it "almost doesn't matter" whether the epic work was genuine.

The *New York Times* was apoplectic. Its editorial, titled "Heil History," scolded, "Almost doesn't matter? Almost doesn't matter what really drove the century's most diabolical tyranny?" Of course it mattered. And when Heidemann was sentenced to four years and eight months in prison, and Kujau to four years and six months, the world still lacked a final answer to what really drove the century's most diabolical tyranny. Once released, Kujau became famous for his fake paintings and opened a restaurant in Stuttgart that specializes in Mediterranean cuisine. Heidemann is on welfare.

Only the verity of Hitler's everlasting fascination was a certainty, as measured by the substantial circulation boosts of the London *Times* and *Stern* and the $50,000 collected by Kujau from the newspaper *Bild* for his story of how he tricked the world into believing that he was Hitler's pen. What is also sure is that the wellspring of public opinion was never tapped more spectacularly than by the infamous Hitler "diaries."

Did Himmler's General Wölfchen profit from the swindle? Nobody could ever be certain. Heidemann showed Wolff the diaries early and Wolff enthusiastically backed them as genuine. Indeed, the general claimed to have heard of their existence way back when he served at the Führer's headquarters. He boosted their standing further by staking his expertise behind Heidemann and by embracing the exculpation that he saw expressed in the contents.

Certainly Wolff was financially involved in Heidemann's con games. It is known, for example, that Heidemann on one occasion handed the general 30,000 marks in 500-mark notes, allegedly for a Himmler dagger that was not worth nearly so much. Other transactions could easily have taken place. Wolff was scheduled to testify under oath at the Heidemann/Kujau trial that began in Hamburg in August 1984. However, he died on July 15.

Given all the operators who had done well, at least up to a point, by selling Hitler, Robert Harris, then twenty-six, thought it would be fun and profitable to compile a book about the tragedy and comedy of the diary swindle. He called it *Selling Hitler*. Harris was precocious, a writer of uncommon dazzle and great charm, columnist for the *Sunday Times* of London, previously reporter for the BBC and political editor of the London *Observer*. He also was a Hitler fan, albeit of the insightful and constructive kind, and so he did not lack background for the task.

Hitler was the big bogeyman of Harris's youth, the personal villain in the comic strips parading around in his head. One of the first books he ever bought and devoured, at fourteen, was William Shirer's *Rise and Fall of the Third Reich*. When Harris was in school at Cambridge, and the Hitlerite historian David Irving became another of his preoccupations, Harris decided to invite this curious character to speak at a luncheon.

"It was pandemonium," the young writer remembered. Not many in the audience swallowed Irving's favorite thesis that Hitler didn't know about the Holocaust. When Harris was working on his book about the fake diaries, he got in touch with Irving again and marveled at what he heard.

"Irving talked about them as if they had been the diaries of Albert Schweitzer," he said.

*Selling Hitler* received wonderful reviews and sold well, so Harris decided to sell Hitler some more. In 1992 he wrote his first novel,

*Fatherland,* a futuristic whodunit set in Germany and based on the supposition that Hitler had won the war and was remaking Europe in his image. It was a huge hit in Britain, rode the *New York Times* best-seller list for three months, and finally also did well in Germany, although German publishers, fearing a backlash, would not touch the book. It had to be published in Switzerland and shipped from there.

Do books like his encourage the Hitler wave that seems to have become a permanent institution? "I don't think my books feed it at all," said Harris. "It's important that books about the Holocaust penetrate heads today. Unless books like mine keep it there, it will disappear."

It is possible, then, to do justice to Hitler without glorifying him. Harris performed this task well and had the word of his old hero, the late William Shirer, to show for it. Shirer was still living when *Selling Hitler* appeared. The venerable historian appreciated the work even though his eyesight was waning, calling it "one of the most gripping books I have read in ages."

Hitler sells, in many incarnations.

# BOOK 5

VIRUS CARRIERS

# 20

## INTELLECTUALIZING THE NEW

## RIGHT WING

An audience of about eighty was waiting in the Catholic Student Center of Friedrichshain, a dilapidated section of central Berlin, on the dreary evening of February 2, 1994. A lecture was scheduled on "Nietzsche and the Present Times."

The event did not take place.

The speaker was to have been Ernst Nolte, professor of history emeritus at the Free University in the city's western section. A spare figure, sedately dressed in a gray suit, gray vest, gray overcoat, and gray felt hat, he did not seem likely to ignite a storm. He was accompanied by a handful of students.

Some thirty young demonstrators blocked Nolte and his students' way into the center.

"He's a Nazi," someone yelled.

"Have you read my books?" Nolte retorted.

"All of them!" came the response.

At which point the demonstrators started shoving Nolte. Next they spat at him and sprayed his face with tear gas. He left, followed by his disciples. By the time the police arrived, the attackers had scattered. The elderly scholar had his eyes treated at a nearby hospital and retired to his large, gloomy apartment off the Kurfürstendamm in the more comfortable west.

Most media were subdued in the treatment of the incident. They called the professor "controversial" and "conservative" and noted that he had been a principal in the noisy national *Historikerstreit* — Historians' Dispute — of 1986. At the time, so the news stories recalled, he had asserted that Auschwitz had been a mere reflex, a reaction to the crimes of Communism. According to Nolte, Auschwitz would never have happened without the horrors of the Stalinist gulag.

Perhaps because the assault on him had luckily blown over without serious consequences, perhaps because Nolte exudes so much middle-class reasonableness and respectability and dignity of old age, there was no mention that many fellow historians considered him the most dangerous person in Germany. He had not really been a Nazi. For the 1990s, he was a force infinitely more virulent than a pensioner with an old party membership card.

He was generally considered the leading post-Nazi prophet, a guru with many admirers. He was no apologist. Defensiveness was not his way. He was an artful hyperactive retoucher intent upon whitewashing Hitler forever.

Nolte was far too sophisticated to deny that the Holocaust mass murders had occurred. He invented exculpatory fictions to explain the crimes away or at least to deflate their enormity, always taking care to supply a kernel of fact in his mix.

"About 25 percent of what Nolte says is true," Walter Laqueur told me in Washington later, half jokingly. A distinguished American historian, born in Germany, Laqueur had been arguing with Nolte for thirty-five years. He saw the man as an oddball, a lost soul, and an unreconstructed anti–Semite.

In Germany, this was a minority view. On his home ground, Nolte was respected as a savant, even by his opponents, a wise man subjected to maltreatment. Indeed, in putting forth his version of history, Nolte had powerful defenders who saw him as a victim of left-wing persecution. So when the stately organ of the politically correct middle-of-the-road public, the *Frankfurter Allgemeine Zeitung,* examined the Friedrichshain assault under its editorial microscope, it saw red.

"Ideological terror" of the left was running amok in Berlin, according to the headline. The country was being threatened by the onset of "something resembling civil war." An "ideological dictatorship" loomed. All this was inferred from the claim of the one demonstrator who said he had actually exposed himself to the circumlocutious verbiage of Nolte's works.

To the newspaper defending Nolte, the motive of the professor's principal attacker seemed unequivocal.

"He decided, as an intellectual, to fight another intellectual not with words but with a weapon," the article said. "That was complete barbarism."

It was also how martyrs are made.

It happened that I had spent more than two hours in conversation with Nolte under the cavernous ceilings of his home, a few days before the attack on him in Friedrichshain. Fortunately, I had done what all of the professor's students, readers, and interviewers need to get done before facing the oracle in person. I had done my homework.

I therefore knew that the Historians' Dispute of 1986 had been no closed academic huddle but a public examination of a nation's soul, a dissection without precedent that spawned, by Nolte's count, twenty-six book-length treatments and more than a thousand articles. Furthermore, Nolte had not been "a" principal of the event. He was the instigator and *the* principal. I also knew that his apologia for Auschwitz was only one of many original interpretations he had created for Nazi deeds.

The man behind this turmoil appears, at first approach, to be all understatement. The egg-shaped, nearly bald head, the wisps of white hair, the rimless spectacles, all seem meek, almost apologetic. The stoop is almost unnoticeable. Mrs. Nolte called for coffee and the obligatory cake in the formal dining room. Nolte's small talk was fluid, worldly, almost painfully polite.

The mention of a cousin of mine, a historian, brought on the first hint of a ghastly orientation that I had thought long passé in civilized company. Smiling amiably, Nolte said he had known my cousin while he was teaching briefly in the United States in the 1970s. The smile persisted.

"Wasn't he of Polish origin?" he asked, placing a slightly undue emphasis on "origin." My ears caught fire. This was long familiar ground.

From my Berlin childhood in the thirties, I instantly recognized Nolte's probing for what it had once represented to an entire society and obviously still meant to him. "Origin" could be tantamount to a death sentence. It was the old synonym for "race," a buzzword once applied to Jews, potential deportees to Auschwitz, Nolte's successor to the gulag.

Throughout our talk, I found Nolte's mastery of words intimidating and symptomatic of his wish to hide his real message. So did others who had dealings with him. He was a virtuoso of camouflage, a wolf in professor's clothing, whose disguise invariably came undone.

An accident had long ago resulted in his losing several joints of two fingers. This minor disfigurement of the left hand obviously never ceased to cause Nolte serious psychic pain. He is forever fidgeting to hide it. Hide what, really? Weakness? Shame? A deviance from an eluded norm? It is said that Kaiser Wilhelm started wars because of a withered arm.

As Nolte talks, the imperfect hand keeps wandering furtively under his coat, under the other arm, darting, trying to hide, always to hide, to escape from being trapped in open view. He seems oblivious to the absurdity that the mannerism is so very visible, actually a distraction to the onlooker. Fairly or not, the hiding hand is reminiscent of the sinister Dr. Strangelove of movie fame. Was Nolte another Kaiser?

Occasionally, Nolte is hypersensitive to being watched. One of his colleagues told me that he once stopped himself in a lecture to demand why one of his listeners was staring at him so hard. "I see hate in your eyes," he reportedly said.

Watching Nolte is, in fact, a pastime. No contemporary historian's course has been more intently tracked within his profession or more incredulously quoted. He titillates. Except to his followers, he stands out like a feisty vessel steaming ever more aggressively into turbulent waters, oblivious to shoals and storms, seemingly blind to the risk of shipwreck by reason of, well, unreason. This was strange because the Nolte of the 1960s had been mild and courtly, even a trifle apologetic at having been trained as a mere philosopher, an adherent of Nietzsche and Heidegger.

He was an outsider, not in the ranks of the exclusive guild of historians. But he had been well liked at conferences all over Europe and the United States. Now he had become a puzzlement and would remain one.

The cascade of his books began with a stimulating splash in 1963, *Fascism in Its Epoch,* which experts judged an original and important analysis. Having previously taught below the college level, Nolte was thereupon extended his first appointment as a professor of history at the University of Marburg in 1965. The elevation was a watershed. Catholic and indeed conservative, Nolte suddenly came up against a loudly leftist — even Marxist — student body. The outsider became something of an outcast. Friends said the experience embittered him.

In 1974, a year after his transfer to the Free University of Berlin, Nolte struck back with *Germany and the Cold War* and clouds gathered.

The squeeze play to which the American and Soviet superpowers subjected the Germans was brilliantly presented. Nolte's treatment of the context, however, the conflict's Nazi roots, caused astonishment. Declarative sentences are not his tools, yet under the layers of the multilevel sentence structure, the diminutives, derisions, accusations, exhortations, pullbacks, appositions, and denials, certain centralities could be coaxed to the fore. More or less plainly the de-demonization of the Führer was under way. Nolte was scrutinizing him through a new, broad philosopher's lens that made everything appear relative.

"In point of fact," he declared, "every significant contemporary nation with extraordinary goals had its Hitler period with its monstrous side and its victims."

Further: "Viewed from the correct perspective, the destruction of the European Jews was nothing more than . . . the second . . . attempt to solve the problems of industrialization by the removal of a large group of people." Hitler, then, was a reflex, a reaction to Stalin's genocidal impulses, a measure against technological unemployment. Which made the Holocaust justifiable, a mere repeat performance legitimized by the Führer's "extraordinary goals."

Further: "Despite all differences in origins and goals, Zionism and National Socialism were closely related."

And moving into a later era: "In Vietnam, the United States put in place nothing less than an even more gruesome version of Auschwitz."

Protests from some insiders were emphatic. Peter Gay, the Berlin-born historian at Yale University, called Nolte's notions "trivialization through comparison" and argued that the "historical function" of the professor's thesis was to diminish the absolute singularity of Hitler's drive to wipe out a people as a matter of policy.

As yet, Nolte's audience was small, his access to the popular media limited. In 1985, he was still shadow-boxing in the hinterlands, but his energy found outlets. For a marathon treatise that appeared in the provincial *Stuttgarter Zeitung,* he bristled that "Hitler, like every other historical figure, has a right to be viewed in the context of the times . . . and should not be turned into an incomprehensible devil."

To Nolte, everything concerning the Führer remained in contemporary controversy. "Did Hitler definitively die in 1945?" he demanded. The professor had evidently taken the measure of the "Hitler wave" and noticed that Hitler lived.

Finally, in 1986, the year of Nolte came to pass. For June, a prestigious showcase, the Römerberg symposium of Frankfurt, was planning an all-out airing of the issue that they called "The Past That Will Not Pass." In most countries, such retrospection would get small notice. Not for the ruminative Germans. For them, the topic was about as dull as the sex habits of movie stars.

Nolte was invited. He accepted and reported that he was preparing an address. Details of what happened next were never fully clarified. A staff member of the symposium telephoned the professor, apparently about final arrangements, whereupon Nolte sulked that he had been made to feel persona non grata.

Avenging the perceived slight, he published a rump contribution in the *Frankfurter Allgemeine Zeitung,* casting himself as a victim of discrimination. He titled his entry "The Past That Will Not Pass: An Address That Could Be Written but Not Delivered," thereby hinting at censorship and assuring maximum public curiosity.

It was the opening salvo of the famous Historians' Dispute, which lasted eleven months. The original texts of the polemics themselves comprised 267 pages by twenty-nine authors — almost everyone who was anyone in the academia of history.

Nolte and his fellow conservatives declared that the time had come to place the Third Reich in its proper historical context — meaning a separation, in the historical analysis of those times, between Nazi Germany and the horrors traditionally associated with it. Nolte maintained that the vision of the Third Reich as an embodiment of absolute evil has made all attempts at comparison between Nazism and other forms of totalitarianism impossible. This was in support of Nolte's basic theory that genocide is a collateral effect of any political religion such as Bolshevism. The Nazis wanted to exterminate the Jews and the Bolsheviks wanted to eliminate the bourgeois. The debate, however, mainly regarded Nolte's notorious claim that the Nazi Holocaust was a consequence of Bolshevik genocide. Liberal left-wing historians argued (and heatedly so) that though Hitler linked Communism with the Jews, this was not his justification for ordering the systematic extermination of the entire race. As the debate grew, it went beyond Germany's boundaries to involve the most eminent historians around the world.

With his place in the long-envied historians' sun now assured, Nolte in 1987 launched his next broadside, *The European Civil War, 1917–1945*. Here the exoneration of Hitler was rendered as an unmistakable, systematized scenario, an echo of Bolshevism, which ignored the fact that Hitler had never shown much interest in the Communist revolution. In Nolte's construct of the Holocaust, as Hermann Graml, one of the leading Hitler scholars, pointed out, the Nazi crimes no longer even needed to be trivialized.

"Instead, they were withdrawn from discussion . . . clothed with the coat of historical necessity . . . and moved to a level where moral judgments like 'good' and 'evil,' even political values like 'right' and 'wrong,' appear inappropriate, indeed pointless."

Hitler's excesses had simply been colored inevitable.

Nolte did recognize that to institutionalize "the final solution of the Jewish problem" required a special gesture. Said Graml, "Even in this regard, Nolte did not shy away from tricks of advocacy in his attempts to correct historical reality and cancel the laws of logic."

To legitimize Hitler's war against the Jews, Nolte argued that "international Jewry" had already declared war on the Führer in September 1939 with a letter to the British prime minister, Neville Chamberlain, in which the Zionist leader Chaim Weizmann pledged Jewish support for the Allied war effort.

Graml pointed out that Nolte failed to note the six previous years of persecution in Germany, surely adequate justification for Jewish antagonism; that no conspiratorial coalition as "world Jewry" existed; and that Weizmann represented, if anyone, only a minority of his co-religionists.

More disgracefully, Nolte postulated that the mass deportations of Jews were "unavoidable" after the American government interned citizens of Japanese descent — a hardly comparable outrage that was in fact not launched until after Hitler's death trains were already rolling eastward to camps where people were not confined but slaughtered.

In 1993, the assembly line of the untiring Nolte's word factory produced his most explicit apologia for Hitler yet: *Points of Contention,* 493 pages of monstrous falsehoods, still embedded in word-rich casuistry, the booby traps only scantily covered up, if at all, but the overall effect still not shocking. The tone, doleful rather than angry, gave it the air of a well-intentioned manifesto by an earnest record keeper seeking to set history straight.

Here are some assertions I dug out during a night's search for Nolte's malodorous truffles:

• The Nuremberg Laws for racial discrimination were an attempt by the Hitler government to "rein in violent outbreaks of anti-Semitism."

• The gassing of Jews showed that "painless death was intended."

• Elie Wiesel's eyewitness reports of his concentration camp experiences are "hardly credible."

• In the denials of the Holocaust, "the last word to interpret findings of the technical experts is far from having been spoken."

• The figures cited for the mass murders are "excessive."

• "Jewry" maintains an "inner affinity" for "bolshevist ideas."

Nolte also was outraged by the postwar treatment given to some of the worst SS killer generals. Thus, *Brigadeführer* Otto Ohlendorf, who confessed to killing 90,000 Jews, was really an upright economics expert who was paid "much respect by prosecutors and judge" when he was sentenced to death.


When I had my talk with Nolte, he took me by surprise right off by quietly denying that he was a historian. I had not indicated that I had been tipped about the limits of his credentials. Did he already feel attacked? More likely, he sensed that I had been briefed by one of his rank-conscious peers and wanted to claim superiority.

"I never belonged to the union," he said. "I'm a philosopher, a humanist. We are more conscious of background and content (*hintergründiger und inhaltsvoller*). One should maintain one's distance toward many things that must be examined further."

I didn't jump the gun either. I had mentioned that I was a former Berliner (which was also discernible from my accent in German) and that I had left town in 1937. This made clear that I am Jewish, which — red blanket waving under the bull's nose — moved Nolte to charge, without having been pointed in any direction, into doubting whether all the agonies of the Holocaust had taken place as reported by the victims.

"It's a justifiable question," he allowed, amicably. "It can't be wiped away."

At a complete loss for words, I smiled amicably. Encouraged, Nolte proceeded, in tones of regret, to recount a meeting some years ago with Professor Saul Friedländer, the Holocaust scholar at the University of Tel Aviv and the University of California at Los Angeles, author of many respected books. Introducing the 1939 Chaim Weizmann letter as evidence that the world's Jews had unilaterally declared war upon Hitler, he said he had asked Friedländer whether any evidence existed that the German Jews had offered resistance to the Third Reich before 1939, as if only open rebellion could have immunized them against atrocities.

Friedländer had risen and stormed out, said Nolte, with the air of the aggrieved who cannot puzzle out what gets into some ornery people.

I changed the subject to the Historians' Dispute. After all, Nolte had been the star, so the topic should cheer him.

He beamed modestly.

"You loved the fencing, didn't you?" I asked, grinning.

"Well, I had the feeling that the weight of the argument was on my side."

"Didn't you think you really won?"

"People cannot claim I'm wrong," Nolte said archly. "There is silence in the forest now among my former opponents."

Why former? I didn't know whether these vanquished enemies had been slain or had only slinked away wounded.

So what about Hitler's standing today?

"I don't believe he was the embodiment of evil," said Nolte, whereupon he sounded his old war cry, by now compressed into a sound bite for TV audiences. The professor raised his voice and sang out triumphantly, "No Auschwitz without the gulag!" He was patently pleased to score the point yet again.

And what motivates the neo-Nazis?

"The skinheads are not children of Hitler," said Nolte firmly. "They are the children of a permissive society."

The professor had emerged from hiding.


Later, in Hamburg, I called on Dr. Monika Richarz, the director of the Institute for the History of German Jews, and asked about her view of Nolte.

"He is extremely dangerous," she said, "because he feels he is supported by public opinion."


Nolte's confidence in his public support was further buttressed in June 2000, when Nolte was awarded one of Germany's most prestigious literary prizes, the Konrad Adenauer Prize, which is given to works that "contribute to a better future." This prize is awarded by the pro-CDU Deutschland-Stiftung (Germany Foundation), which, though known to be conservative, had never shown its sympathies for revisionism so blatantly. The foundation justified its choice by saying it was a recognition of freedom in science. In his honoring speech, Horst Möller, director of the Institut für Zeitgeschichte

(Institute for History), ironically chose to use Rosa Luxemburg's words "Freiheit des Andersdenkenden" — freedom of those who think differently — in describing the Nazi apologist. Möller further praised Nolte for his "life's work of high rank," admitting that he agreed with the theory that National Socialism can be explained as a reaction to other great ideologies (i.e. Communism). Nolte's critics are, according to Möller, only attempting to censor open debate on the Holocaust in Germany.

Möller's honoring speech caused an overwhelming storm involving the Institute for History and the press. The institute had already lived through a major crisis when Helmut Kohl sponsored Möller's appointment as president in 1989. Up to that year, it had primarily busied itself with NS crimes, while under Möller the focus shifted radically to issues such as the "Red Holocaust." Many historians have been leaving it in disgust over the past ten years, and with this last scandal several of those who remained publicly called for Möller's resignation. In an open letter to Die Zeit, Heinrich August Winkler, a professor of history at the renowned Humboldt University in Berlin, wrote that "Herr Möller allowed himself to become party to an intellectual political offensive aimed at integrating rightist and revisionist positions in the conservative mainstream," and that his decision to make the speech had been a "big mistake."

Could it be that Herr Möller, under the guise of "free speech," was simply a victim of a latter-day strain of the Hitler virus?

# 21

## DIAGNOSIS

Have the Germans changed?"

This loaded inquiry, clearly meant to be rhetorical, was the opening shot of an extraordinarily forceful *j'accuse* in the August 1993 issue of *Psyche,* the leading German journal for psychoanalysts and psychologists.

"The longing for a repetition of Nazi barbarism, with its racism and contempt for humanity, is being openly expressed on the streets, among cronies in pubs, on the radio and television," the article observed. Skinhead youths would not be rampaging, it pointed out, "if they did not feel backed by the prejudices and resentments of the silent majority."

The author was Dr. Margarete Mitscherlich, Germany's most prestigious psychoanalyst and something of a guardian for the national conscience since 1967. That year, with her husband, the psychiatry professor Dr. Alexander Mitscherlich, she had produced a book whose title became a landmark: *The Inability to Mourn.* It deplored the incapacity of postwar Germans to feel pity for victims of the Nazi madness. Hitler, so the Mitscherlichs tried to instruct their fellow citizens, had taken over such inner functions.

Alexander Mitscherlich knew the record all too well and wasn't shy about holding up a mirror in front of his contemporaries. Professorial in manner, with an enormous bald forehead, he had dodged the Gestapo as an anti-Nazi resister, risking his life to arrange a hiding place for the Jewish wife of the philosopher Karl Jaspers, another prominent Hitler opponent.

"All levels of society, and especially those in positions of leadership — that is, industrialists, judges, university professors — had given the regime their decisive and enthusiastic support," the doctor charged in *The Inability to Mourn*.

And he explained why, after the nominal defeat of the Nazis, society made it easy for its guilty to whitewash themselves: "Defense against a collectively incurred guilt is easy when it, too, is carried out collectively, since the degree of guilt is then determined by universal consensus. Normally, a guilt-laden individual is isolated from society, but in a group he does not have to endure this fate, being merely a *sinner among sinners*" (emphasis added).

Mitscherlich's own colleagues, the German doctors, had for some time been subjected to his particular scorn. When they were called upon after the war to assess physical and mental damages sustained by Nazi victims, they "betrayed in many cases a terrifying lack of empathy," Mitscherlich wrote. "The evaluator is still thoroughly biased and unconsciously identified with the persecutors."

Mitscherlich knew his colleagues intimately. *The Inability to Mourn* was, in fact, an extension of his earlier groundbreaking book, *Doctors of Infamy: The Story of the Nazi Medical Crimes,* published in 1947. Along with revelations of murderous "experiments," that work described a psychological phenomenon so stark that it required a new vocabulary — "derealization," a stronger version of disassociation, for example, or what his American colleague, the psychiatrist Dr. Robert Jay Lifton, came to describe as "psychic numbing" and "doubling," reinforced by "selective inattention."

Accordingly, the Nazi medical killers in the concentration camps, like Hitler's other practitioners of genocide, felt empowered to commit unspeakable acts because these could be separated from any human feelings. The "work" of human extermination was not experienced as real. The emotions of the perpetrators were deadened or applied elsewhere.

The entire first printing of Mitscherlich's 1947 book quickly vanished from stores. Doctors bought them up to silence the disclosures. And while *The Inability to Mourn* was praised in the late 1960s by reviewers for its insights, it too gained little influence. The durability of the Nazi virus had seen to that.

To this day, many Germans counterattack by flinging an especially vibrant hate label at their accusers. The dirty word is *Selbstbeschmutzer*, a German ugliness for which no apt translation exists. It describes someone disgusting who soils his own nest.

Alexander Mitscherlich diagnosed that the seeds of the Nazi virus were planted in the Kaiser's time before World War I, if not earlier. He liked to cite a nineteenth-century sage who used to mourn, "It's the national misfortune of the Germans that nobody ever beheaded a ruler of the Hohenzollern family."

Dr. Lifton traced the onset of the disease to "historical dislocation and breakdown of symbols and meanings around which life had been organized" before the First World War. The German defeat of 1918, with its disastrously vengeful peace treaty and subsequent economic collapse, intensified the illness. Revitalization of German prosperity and pride made Hitler respectable and legitimized excuses for his barbarities.

Lifton appraised the Führer's rise shrewdly: "Like some of their Jewish compatriots, some ordinary Germans viewed Hitlerism as a temporary phenomenon that would pass. Many more Germans, attracted to Hitler, attributed cruel behavior to local excesses; the higher-ups would get these matters under control. Almost certainly the Führer knew nothing about them, and, once, informed, would surely stop them. The latter attitude enabled Germans to maintain their deification of Hitler, their obedience to authority and their sense of righteousness."

When Margarete Mitscherlich came to write her 1993 article in *Psyche,* the perniciousness of the virus had not cooled. "Nazi ideology had trained the Germans not to mourn," she recalled. "They were sworn to uphold a mentality of hero worship, of sweet death for fatherland and Führer. The annihilation of unvalued enemies was the highest law. Nor were they to forget the perversion of *Heldenmütter* [hero mothers] and women whose death notices publicly extolled their pride in the heroic deaths of their sons and husbands."

In psychiatric terms, it wasn't difficult to interpret the mentality that his people had inherited from Hitler's times. "The Germans were taught to practice a paranoid-schizoid orientation," Dr. Mitscherlich analyzed. "They needed enemies and scapegoats to idealize themselves, undisturbed, as a master people. Empathy, mourning and pity, especially with those who did not belong to the 'master race,' and who were to be regarded as despicable, were prohibited under penalty of death."

The doctor was not surprised that the memory of Hitler himself had gone underground beneath the mountains of rubble left behind by years of Allied bombings. It had been a vanishing act worthy of Houdini. One day he was strutting across the world stage, master of his universe, and the next day he was gone. Suddenly his name was taboo. He had turned into a land mine silently awaiting future reactivation. His time would come again, but not for now. Now was hunger and no firewood. For as Bertolt Brecht had Mack the Knife sing in the *Threepenny Opera,* "Food comes first, then comes morality."

The Germans followed Brecht's dictum in their typical way: vigorously and literally. Beginning in the late 1940s, well before the onset of the *Hitlerwelle* (Hitler wave), they plunged themselves into a *Fresswelle* (food-gorging wave), all but drowning in long-missed delicacies. And as Dr. Mitscherlich noted, all the while the deceased Führer lurked like an apparition, a ghost like Shakespeare's Banquo, a nonperson.

"They followed him into total war with such enthusiasm, but they could not mourn their idol Hitler," she wrote. "As if he and their love for him had never existed, the Germans identified with the victorious western powers without so much as a transition."

The switch was no switch at all. It was a symptom of "the German way of loving."

Dr. Mitscherlich explained: "One did not love Hitler as a person, not for himself, but because he was *part of one's own person,* the collective world of one's wishes" (emphasis added).

I put the article down in some excitement. Here was one of the wellsprings of Hitler's durability, perhaps the deepest of them all. To a German, Hitler was actually one's very self, part of one's heart and face and skin, of one's dreams, not of what is, but of fulfillment to come in the future.

It made sense. Over the decades I had been shaking my head at films of the immense, heiling throngs, not individuals but congealed masses, swaying in ecstasy, ocean waves of humanity pouring out at unison marching pace, unstoppable, the saluting arms snapping up and down like limbs of dolls, all accompanied by the swelling of the Hitler sounds, the orgiastic animal screaming, thunderclaps of joy and abandon, sometimes simply bellowing — emissions from cogs, not individual humans.

I had to refocus my contemporary lenses and bring back the Germans I knew in the 1930s and 1940s when I was a teenager in Berlin, and later while fighting the Nazis with the United States Army. Most of them were not really people at all. Hitler had pounded them into an amalgam. "Ein Reich, ein Volk, ein Führer," they shouted throughout my childhood, "one nation, one people, one leader." They kept roaring this battle cry as one — and with eerie consequences.

"I am only a little man," I remember the prisoners of war chorusing at us GI sergeants in our interrogation tents in Normandy during our 1944 invasion. Taken aback, my colleague and friend Stefan Heym had written for the *New York Times Magazine* as far back as in 1945 about these strangely shrunken members of the master race. They were all, remarkably, little men, dwarfs too insignificant to assume responsibility for their actions. And these "little men" were not mere foot soldiers: many were officers, and they included colonels.

And of course there was hardly a Nazi among them. "I was never a Nazi" became a comic cliché. All those heiling faces in all those limitless mobs of all those rallies in all those films had managed to turn themselves into phantoms, just about every one.

"The Germans love to put themselves down," the remarkably hale Dr. Mitscherlich diagnosed when I looked her up in 1994 at her homelike little office/apartment in a well-to-do Frankfurt residential district. "We're children who have been burned, and when the Cold War stopped, so did our intensive identification with the Americans. We no longer found ourselves on the side of victors. And so our old self-hate became virulent again."

In her *Psyche* article, the doctor had already pinpointed the one guiding light on which the Germans, and especially the disenchanted young people, could rely to steady themselves in their new vacuum.

That beacon was their Führer. "When we repress our history and thereby our self-hate," she wrote, "the result is what we experience today: youths in both parts of Germany attempt to awaken 'Hitler,' and everything he stands for, in order to achieve new life, to transform self-hate into a hate of foreigners. Silently, a large number of Germans support them."

And if the survival-in-death of the Führer was peculiar to Germans — who still can't mourn or empathize — so was the style of the hate with which the asylum seekers from poor nations were treated. Rightist extremists exist all over; German right-wingers were different. "Attacks of such primitive brutality happen only in Germany," said Dr. Mitscherlich as she rose with a therapist's promptness to end my hour of consultation. I had witnessed the diagnosis of a nation's loyalty to its godfather, cause and effect, in full continuity from its creation to the fallout on today's families, the widows and children and grandchildren of those involved in genocide.

# 22

## TAKING HITLER'S MEASURE:

## THE BIOGRAPHERS SPEAK

Remember "The Schmeed Memoirs"?

Friedrich Schmeed, whose pseudomemoirs were a creation of satirist Woody Allen, was Germany's highest-ranking barber. After his client Adolf Hitler — the fellow who gave such stern instructions ("Don't take too much off the top!") — no longer needed haircuts, Schmeed became a treasured historical resource, and he measured up to his postwar responsibilities.

"I have been asked if I was aware of the moral implications of what I was doing," he wrote in his best-selling record, an "incisive guide to innermost Nazi Germany."

"As I told the tribunal at Nürnberg, I did not know that Hitler was a Nazi. The truth was that for years I thought he worked for the phone company. When I finally did find out what a monster he was, it was too late to do anything, as I had made a down payment on some furniture. Once, toward the end of the war, I did contemplate loosening the Führer's neck napkin and allowing some tiny hairs to get down his back, but at the last minute my nerve failed me."

The Hitler legend survived many attacks and appraisals, none more enthusiastic than from the humorists. In *The Great Dictator*, Charlie Chaplin endowed his lookalike, the Führer named Hynkel, with the most guttural of Teutonic accents, and in his worst rages Hynkel actually chewed on carpets. In *The Producers*, Mel Brooks had his Führer's chorus girls kick up their heels to the tune of "Springtime for Hitler."

The 1991 German film comedy *Shtonk* even poked fun at his suicide by reenacting it in slapstick style and depicting the transfer of his last remains, a spoonful of ashes, from one con man to another in a public toilet. Indeed, the sport of mocking Hitler's postsuicide notoriety harks back to the postwar 1940s when a colleague of mine, Egon Jameson, published an essay lampooning the outpouring of memoirs from Hitler's retainers. He called it "I was Hitler's Toothbrush."

All such attempts at deflating Hitler failed among his disciples. Ridicule, perhaps the most merciless assassin, did not touch him. He was above it.

Until World War II unveiled him as master of the *Blitzkrieg*, it was his fate to be underestimated, and analysts who were ahead of their time and took his ravings seriously found themselves ignored. This was the initial fate of his very first major biographer, the little-remembered Konrad Heiden, who also turned out to be one of the most insightful.

A small, narrow-faced, mild-mannered journalist, luck placed him at the scene of Hitler's political birth in Munich. In that year of chaotic headlines, 1923, the most influential of the German newspapers, the liberal *Frankfurter Allgemeine,* assigned Heiden, at the age of twenty-two, to cover the floundering Nazis, then still known as Nasos.

Heiden witnessed the Beer Hall Putsch, Hitler's subsequent trial and entry into prison, and became known as "the man who kept Hitler waiting." Repeatedly, the Führer would not start a press conference until the correspondent from the great *Frankfurter* had made his appearance. Loyally, Heiden also trudged from one Hitler oration to another.

"It was only gradually that the effects of these speeches made me realize that behind all the nonsense there was unrivaled political cunning," he recalled many years later. Out of this prescience Heiden wrote his first book, *Hitler: A Biography,* published in Germany in 1935. It was widely ignored but sold for translation in England.

When the author visited London a year later, the translation was not yet under way. "The publishers were reluctant to issue a book about a dictator who tomorrow might be overthrown," Heiden remembered.

By 1944, when Heiden published his huge opus *Der Führer: Hitler's Rise to Power,* he was greeted by a large and respectful audience. The war was still on, however, and little attention was paid to the book's last lines about the long-term danger of the dictator's ascendancy.

"He could give them something that even the traditional religions could no longer provide," Heiden wrote, "the belief in a meaning to existence beyond the narrowest self-interest. The real degradation began when people realized that they were in league with the devil, but felt that even the devil was preferable to the emptiness of an existence which lacked a large significance. The problem today is to give that larger significance and dignity to a life that has been dwarfed by the world of material things. Until that problem is solved, the annihilation of Nazism will be no more than the removal of one symptom of the world's unrest."

Thus unmasked as a portentous societal symptom, Hitler nevertheless continued to be grossly underestimated by his later biographers. They killed him off, but he fooled them.

In his long-secret and prescient 1943 study for the OSS, *The Mind of Adolf Hitler,* the psychoanalyst Dr. Walter C. Langer became the first to detect and document Hitler's overwhelming yearning for immortality. Langer's most plausible prognosis was suicide, but immortality? The doctor did not predict — or even hint — that Hitler might actually realize this wildest of his visions.

Sebastian Haffner was still insisting just before the onset of the Hitler wave in the 1970s that the Führer was a forgotten cause. "Hitler is no longer a topic of conversation today," he wrote. He likened the dictator to an illness that had been successfully withstood and had, in that process, bestowed immunity. It was wishful thinking.

In his monumental 1977 work *The Psychopathic God,* Professor Robert G. L. Waite conceded that Hitler would survive, but only as a distant, mythical fantasy, "a darkly brooding Teutonic god enthroned in Valhalla, the shadowed hall of the dead." Suicide would enable the Führer to "rise far above time and space and the travail of mortal life." He would brood, but not stir up more trouble.

In 1982, Professor Gordon A. Craig, the grand old American master of German studies, also acknowledged that word of Hitler's death had been considerably exaggerated, yet he trivialized him as an apparition.

The Hitler wave, the professor asserted in his work *The Germans,* had run its course about as quickly as it started, and he reduced the dictator to a shadow, the annoying little man who wasn't there.[1] One would have dearly liked to see this pesky phantom vanish. More wishful thinking.

By the 1990s, the Hitler investigators had resorted to seeking perspective from historical personages with boots as big as the Führer's. It was the season for measuring Hitler by heroic comparisons, a theory of historical relativity.

In *The Duel,* John Lukacs matched Hitler against Winston Churchill as they stood poised, nose to nose, during eighty crucial days in the Battle of Britain in 1940. Under this looking glass, the outcome at first glance seemed vastly to favor the giant beloved as "good old Winnie."

"There are still admirers of Hitler," Lukacs observed, though "their number does not compare with those who admire Churchill. Even among Hitler's admirers there are few who are inclined to give the Nazi salute, the outstretched arm, or cry '*sieg Heil!*'; Churchill's wartime gesture of the V-sign, his two outstretched fingers, have become a nearly universal gesture of freedom."

In the end, however, cheery public relations didn't count. As Lukacs regretfully concluded, the British good failed to triumph over Nazi evil. Churchill's "grand vision" for the empire fell apart. Hitler's demagoguery lived. "The idea that Hitler incarnated and represented was a very powerful one," so Lukacs summed up. "This is why it is not only historically wrong but dangerous to see Hitler and Hitlerism as no more than a strange parenthesis in the history of the 20th century, the transitory rise and fall of a madman."

*Hitler and Stalin,* Lord Bullock's 1,081-page opus, applied another yardstick and found the Soviet dictator's crimes to have been no match for Hitler's evil. "The Stalinist system used terror, including mass murder, as an instrument to secure political and social, not biological objectives," Bullock wrote. "Nowhere was there a counterpart to the Holocaust, the planned extermination of all European

---

[1]In his book, Craig cited the entire ditty: "Last night I saw upon the stair / A little man who wasn't there./ He wasn't there again today / Oh, how I wish he'd go away."

Jews, the centerpiece of Nazi repression . . . in which mass murder became not an instrument but an end in itself."

Still further comparative discussions tried to shed light.

When I called on Professor Waite in the summer of 1994, he was preparing the publication of a new 1,000-page manuscript, *Hitler and the Kaiser,* on which he had been laboring since 1978. The parallel he drew was personal.

"Both men took their nation to war with catastrophic conse-quences," he pointed out to me, "and both were psychologically deeply impaired." Both were battered children. Hitler was savagely beaten by his father and was terrified of him. The Kaiser suffered through shock treatments and horrific indignities that were applied methodically to wipe away the consequences, mostly emotional, of an arm withered at birth.

"A bad childhood increased their yearning for power," said Waite. Any more detailed interpretation of Hitler's durability awaits a full reading of the professor's study. The matching of one important per-sonality's miserable early years against those of another may, however, not prove too educational, and in Hitler's case the parallel was drawn at least once before.

This daring operation was performed by Thomas Mann shortly before World War II. He entitled it *Brother Hitler (Bruder Hitler),* and its sibling relationship referred to Hitler and, of all people, the great Mann himself.

"He is a disagreeable and humiliating brother," wrote the author of *The Magic Mountain, Buddenbrooks,* and other memorable works, who won the Nobel Prize in 1929. "He gets on one's nerves, an embar-rassing relative . . . a catastrophe."

The style of the book is somewhat obfuscating to the contempo-rary reader, but by a stroke of luck I had been good friends for fifty years with Konrad Kellen, who was Mann's secretary in Santa Mon-ica, California, when his boss composed this surprising bit of nonfic-tion, and Mann had talked to him about it.

The two notable protagonists of the essay, the novelist and the dic-tator, had both suffered as depressed lost souls in their youth, or so Mann explained their "brotherhood" to Kellen. Neither could initially make his way in conventional life. Hitler was worthless as an artist; Mann saw himself permanently relegated to his early employment as a desperately bored bank clerk. Both ultimately achieved fame spectacularly, if outside of bourgeois society, one as a master artist, the other as a master politician. But I could find no explanation for the "catastrophe" called Hitler.

Churchill, Stalin, Kaiser Wilhelm, Thomas Mann. And still there was no definitive clarification for the phenomenon of Hitler's survival. It was like searching Madame Tussaud's wax museum. Perhaps the man was so singular as to remain, in the end, unknowable.

His close associates thought so. His foreign minister, Joachim von Ribbentrop, before he was hanged at Nuremberg, confessed, "I know very little about him; in fact nothing at all." And before the same end befell Field Marshal Alfred Jodl, who had known Hitler since 1923 and was his closest military adviser for six years of war, he wrote, "To this very day, I do not know what he thought or knew."

And so, for more than half a century, the unknown Führer was pursued even further, into the literally unknown, the hereafter. Public curiosity demanding an authoritative answer to the mystery of his remains was intense. Still, as of today, investigators have come no closer to the truth than the authors of *Shtonk* in the scene in which the specimen of the ashes changed hands in the toilet.

Two principal facts kept the hunt alive. First, Berlin had no functioning crematorium when Hitler killed himself, and human bodies do not completely turn to ashes in an open fire. Second, the remains were discovered by Russian troops and the secretive Soviets found it useful to manipulate the saga of Hitler's final whereabouts on and on until the mind boggled.

Bureaucratic fumbling and caprice motivated some of the Soviet behavior. Stalin's intense personal hatred of Hitler played a more significant role. So did fear that the Führer might become a hero figure in death if his remains were located. For a generation, the Soviets would not concede the dual mode of Hitler's death, long known to Western investigators from eyewitness accounts. To satisfy Moscow, he must not have shot himself. That suggested an honorable soldier's death. He had to have died of poison, "like a dog," as the best-informed Soviet investigator phrased it.

In 1992, *Der Spiegel* magazine attempted to add up the results of all this skeleton hunting. Its seven-page article, "Hitler's Last Trip," tracked nine possible burials, disinterments, and reburials. Some of the misadventures might have come from the screenplay for *Shtonk*.

Thus, in the spring of 1945, when Stalin was still telling the Americans at the Potsdam conference that Hitler was alive and in hiding (a lie that General Eisenhower accepted as truth as late as October), a Soviet military film crew was supposedly filming the remains in a Berlin bomb crater. At the same time, another Soviet military crew was burying another Hitler corpse nearby. That body was thought to be the true Hitler because the Hitler who was being filmed was reportedly wearing darned socks, which even the untidy Russians refused to accept.

The map of burial places that accompanied the *Der Spiegel* article led from the death site near Hitler's bunker, over the years, to a succession of small towns in Brandenburg province: Buch, Finow, Rathenow, Stendal, and then, for more than twenty years, to Magdeburg, where the counterintelligence service SMERSH maintained headquarters in a closed-off area around Westendstrasse.

There, in March 1994, the bulldozer of a construction crew happened to excavate a mass grave of twenty-one skeletons. *Bild,* a national newspaper that loves large, red headlines, bannered on the front page, "Are These skulls from Hitler's Bunker?" But no, by then the rumor mills of the veterans from Stalin's intelligence services were leaking word that the most famous corpse in history had long ago been spirited from Magdeburg to a secret site below a Moscow prison. Stay tuned.

A wider range of Hitler's universe in the hereafter remained to be explored, and at an unmarked grave site in the Central Cemetery of Vienna, a slightly built amateur historian, Hans O. A. Horvath, forty-four, believed he had located a productive target. A furniture restorer by trade, Horvath had resourcefully mobilized medical jurists on behalf of restoring bigger game. Its name was Adolf Hitler.

Horvath, whose desk at home was surrounded by life-size replicas of figures from the Nazi era, decided in the late 1980s that Hitler's reputation deserved humanizing and that the Führer's niece and greatest love, Angela (Geli) Raubal, was the likeliest witness. Although Geli had killed herself by a pistol shot in 1931 while alone in the Munich apartment she shared with Hitler, experts had assured Horvath that an exhumation of her remains might well reveal something about her still unknown motives, possibly even a pregnancy.

It became a moot question, because Vienna city authorities, enjoying their tranquillity, saw no reason to give permission to someone from outside the family of the deceased to, so to speak, dig up trouble.


I had become so conditioned by my reading about the incessant snooping through old graves that my mind did not respond when I opened the newspaper of April 20, 1994, and saw the headline "Adolf Hitler's Last Love." In the course of construction work at Potsdamer Platz in Berlin, the article said, the mortal remains of Hitler's German shepherd, Blondi, were discovered and secretly turned over to the German Historical Museum.

I should have smelled the proverbial rat instantly. April 20 was Hitler's ever-celebrated birthday. The newspaper was the *Taz,* the left-wing alternative sheet most likely to spoof Hitler's ghost. But the joke was encased in so much detailed, authentic history that I was fooled until I came to Hitler's darned socks.

Ha! These were obviously the same bogus darned socks that had fooled Soviet diggers half a century ago. I wondered how many readers had swallowed the story whole. The ending was especially persuasive. Chancellor Kohl had opened a file on the case, it is said, giving it the highest security classification. And rumor had already reached the film colony. A movie was being discussed.

Art was imitating life, and even the best-qualified minds were still divided on the question of questions: Why?

# 23

## WHY THE LEGEND LIVES:

## CONTEMPORARY AUTHORITIES TESTIFY

A *Blitzkrieg* required a *Blitz* life, and so Hitler could spare only three hours for Paris, from 6 to 9 A.M. Strutting, as the city's conqueror, for photographers in front of the Eiffel Tower on that crispest of summer mornings, June 28, 1940, he shared his transcendent joy with his fellow-traveler, friend, and architect, Albert Speer.

"It was the dream of my life to be allowed to see Paris," he confessed effusively. "I cannot tell you how happy I am that the dream came true today."[1]

They were sightseeing like any tourists: the Champs Elysées, the Trocadero, the Arc de Triomphe, and the Opera. Before Napoleon's tomb in the Dome des Invalides, the Führer's triumphant mood changed abruptly. Instead of being able to look up to the sarcophagus of the immortal warrior, he had to look down into a pit, and this agitated him.

"I shall never make such a mistake," he said suddenly. "I know how to keep my hold on people after I have passed on. I shall be the Führer they look up at and go home to talk of and remember. My life shall not end in the mere form of death. It will, on the contrary, begin then."

\*     \*     \*

---

[1]When the dream had faded in August 1944, he turned vengeful like a lover spurned. "Jodl!" he demanded of his chief of staff, "Is Paris burning?"

No strain was required for the Führer to measure himself against Napoleon, for already he considered himself immortal. "Hitler believes he is really the 'Chosen One,' and in his thinking he conceives of himself as a Second Christ." So wrote the psychiatrist Dr. Walter C. Langer in *The Mind of Adolf Hitler*, arguably still the shrewdest of many assessments.

Precedents exist. Napoleon surely is one. The Romans come to mind. Indeed, Shakespeare asked the question that keeps nagging: "Upon what meat does this our Caesar feed?"

It applies to Hitler as well.

Self-confidence and sense of mission to a psychopathic degree. Mesmerizing personality. Decisiveness. Lack of ethics and inhibitions. Cunning smell for the weaknesses of opponents . . . It took, after all, the combined might of nearly all the world, and 40 million casualties, to create but a pause in the continuum that "shall not end in the mere form of death." Even his suicide was interpreted by psychiatrists as an act of omnipotence, proof that he was master over life and death.

Such a personality is manifestly unique among power players, dictators, even criminals afflicted with megalomania. So it should come as small surprise that the waves Hitler made in life cannot subside in "mere" death.

But what keeps the vibrations so strong, so vivid, so constantly renewable?

I put the question to the most versatile cast of Hitler cognoscenti I could assemble on my tour of sources in Germany and the United States. The barrage of responses sent me reeling. They were penetrating, persuasive, imaginative — and almost all quite different. Everybody had answers, nobody had *the* answer. In the end, the question remained very much open. I found myself full of new sympathy for Diogenes.

The testimony of my expert witnesses follows, arranged according to their manifold themes.

*The Hitler Hangover*

The sheer pandemonium of the Hitler era left a twisted trail so littered with multigenerational questioning, pain, and nostalgia that the
ruins — and the appeal — simply never cooled.

"He's such a trauma that there never was a goodbye," said Dr. Margarete Mitscherlich.

"It's the persistent shadow of the Holocaust," said the historian
Christopher Simpson, "and the appeal of fascism can still be exploited
by demagogues."

"We are the sons of the perpetrator generation," said the historian
Jörg Friedrich. "We need perpetrators to explain the crimes. . . .
Hitler had power, he fascinated. He was a mass murderer but he was
also a sexy character." As for the films and books of the Hitler revival:
"They made him respectable and realistic and people got drunk on
that. He was no longer an idiot who ate carpets."

"From World War I on, German historical forces have been very
manifest in peoples' individual psychology," said Dr. Robert Jay
Lifton, the psychiatrist. "There was a tremendous dislocation from
which they never recovered. Hitler's total impact is perceived as
greatness, so today there is a romantic longing for Hitler. He did help
with regeneration and revitalization."

"I don't consider Hitler's [continuing popularity] surprising," said
Professor Norman Birnbaum. "His social policies were good, a
highly modernized form of socialism, even though it didn't work."


*Why the Extraordinary Intensity of the Hitler Memory?*

"Without him, everything would have turned out differently," said
the German TV impresario Guido Knopp. "He's our big bogeyman."

"The preoccupation with the Nazis is spooky," said Professor Eberhard Jäckel, "and I don't believe the attention will decrease [by the year
2000]. The interest of students at my university is unbelievable, greater
than in any other subject. I'm proud I'm working in this area. If we
didn't talk about Hitler, it would be said we want to avoid the subject."

"He's an icon," said Professor Wolfgang Wippermann. "The man never got out of the headlines! It's a morbid fascination. *Mein Kampf* is one of the most expensive books in the secondhand book shops, nearly 1,000 marks!"

"William Shirer's *Rise and Fall of the Third Reich* was one of the first books I ever bought," said the author Robert Harris. "I was fourteen and I read it like soap opera. Hitler had the most stupendous impact. There has never been such a case of evil dressed up as ideology. He encompassed a side of human nature that will never go away."

"It's the fascination of abomination," said Professor Robert Waite. "My grandson asked me to lecture on Hitler at his school. The questions were amazing: 'Was he all bad?' 'Why did people follow him?' And then a little girl got up and I explained Hitler's terrible childhood because she wanted to know, 'Did he come from a dysfunctional family?' "

## The Peculiar Germans

"It's the Hitler within us that's our problem," said the media expert Peter Boenisch. "Germans are pigheaded. The fascination of Hitler is a reaction to the complexity of the world, so complicated and so insoluble for the lower strata. There is no outlet for frustration."

"Hitler holds a romantic, perverse fascination of the total authoritarian power that appeals to German nationalism and is very deep-seated," said Professor Gerald Fleming.

"It's nostalgia and laziness," said the writer Rafael Seligmann. "Someone tells them the direction of the road. It's simple and you don't have to think. It's like the old slogan, 'Führer, give us your commands; we'll follow you!' "

"The loss of perspective is crazy," said Professor Wippermann. "In 1985 we started talking of 'liberation' instead of 'defeat.' Since the reunification in 1989 we're researching resistance against Honecker [in the old East Germany] and [the GDR prison] at Bautzen gets equated with Auschwitz. I tell my American audiences, 'Don't trust the Germans!' "

"Germans are in love with force," said the analyst Konrad Kellen. "They love to tremble before the master. We saw it during the war: why do they love to salute and kiss the ass of a general?"

"The Germans are susceptible to a perpetuation of the Hitler influence," said Professor Gordon A. Craig. "The memory of the Hitler figure will become more and more a myth, but it won't vanish. It'll continue to spook around and the memory will be used by whoever needs an excuse."

"There is a special German makeup," said Robert Harris, "that life is to suffer. This is an authentic German lunacy. They're all on edge."

"We're a potentially unstable country, a field for rat catchers," said Egon Bahr, Willy Brandt's man. But the danger is domestic and economic because vital differences distinguish the expansionist Hitler time from the present: (1) the German establishment no longer opposes democracy; (2) the military is not pro-war; (3) industry favors an integrated European economy; (4) the constitution and the government are essentially pacifist — there is no national command structure; even the military hospitals have been disbanded.

## Missing: A Democratic Tradition

"There's no experience of being in a multinational society," said Dr. Lifton. "The younger generation can have nostalgia for a simplicity of life as monolithic Germans without all those Turks and Jews."

"The key used to be held by the Russians and the Amis [Americans]," said Rolf Rietzler, the editor of Der Spiegel. "Now they're expected to have their own positions."

"We lack a democratic tradition," said the German filmmaker Edgar Reitz. "I've been traveling a lot and see how easy it is to get along if you're not German."

## The Media: Agitators or Messengers?

"The repetitions about Hitler have a magnifying effect," said Professor Wolfgang Benz, "and with Hitler you can sell everything."

"The media couldn't push the subject if the interest didn't exist," said Professor Jäckel.

Communications technology was seen as powerful in two opposing ways. After World War II (but before the flowering of television) Hitler's close friend, Albert Speer, believed that modern communications gave Hitler total control over his people and made his dictatorship possible.[2] But television might have had an unraveling effect. "Hitler on TV would have been Chaplinesque," said Peter Boenisch.

### The Neo-Nazi Message

"It started in the 1970s," said Jörg Friedrich, "when the neo-Nazis insisted, 'we're not some underage nation!'"

"Every form of Nazism appeals to the need for order and unity," said Dr. Lifton.

"This is how we escaped from the Allies," said Guido Knopp.

### The Jews: Scapegoats Forever

"The Jews are the seismograph," said Rafael Seligmann.

"They're sitting on packed suitcases," said Monika Richarz, "feeling unsafe, looking around again and asking, 'Where to?'"

### Enigma without End

"Here was a strange little man, a dropout, a psychopath," said Professor

---

[2] In an exculpatory but shrewd assessment before his judges at his Nuremberg war crimes trial, Speer said, "Hitler's dictatorship was the first of an industrial state in this age of modern technology, a dictatorship which employed to perfection the instruments of technology to dominate its own people. . . . By means of the radio and public address systems, eighty million persons could be made subject to the will of one individual. Telephone, teletype, and radio made it possible to transmit the commands of the highest levels directly to the lowest organs where, because of their high authority, they were executed uncritically."

Waite. "Questions about him seem absurd, but the intellectual problem is still open."

"I can't understand it," said Peter Boenisch. "Maybe we're victims of masochism, like the Japanese."

"Even today, we still have the problem of understanding ourselves," said Edgar Reitz. "We don't have the answer."

"Hitler never ceases to surprise you," said Klaus Lankheit, author and head of the archive at the Institut für Zeitgeschichte. "The research must stay with it even if we can't solve [the mystery]."

### Hitler in the Year 2000

"Historical memory is a very complicated, uneven process," said Dr. Lifton. "Each generation creates and recreates its own."

"More people than just the radicals hope that Germans will have a chance to become a real country," said Guido Knopp.

"How can Germans return to normality so Hitler will stop being the censor of our lives?" asked Edgar Reitz.

"It's back to the nineteenth-century empire, without the need for two hundred divisions," said Professor Wippermann. "It's not to the Memel [as the German national anthem phrases German expansion ambitions], it's on to the Dnieper!"

David Ceserani, the research director, sees hope in the young new German scholars: "They're allowing Germans to get back to their history in more honest fashion. They can look back without nostalgia and have a much bolder engagement with the past."

The potency of this mix suggests that the afterlife of the Führer will be of indefinite duration, and that the most dangerous and enduring force marshaled by him was mob control. The media master Peter Boenisch warned against a fairly new revulsion: the popular "reaction to the complexity of the world, so complicated and so insoluble for the lower strata." Hitler's intimate, Albert Speer, shuddered at the technical arsenal that made it possible for his beloved Führer as long as fifty years ago "to transmit the commands of the highest levels directly to the lowest organs."

It is no longer polite to speak of "lower strata," much less "the lowest organs." The word is, "power to the people." The open question is, "power to what end?"

# 24

## THE NAZI PROPAGANDA FACTORY

## IN NEBRASKA

I don't know what kind of suits he wears, but here we find his materials everywhere." That was the response from Dr. Hans-Gert Lange, spokesman in Cologne for the Verfassungsschutz, the German equivalent of the FBI.

I had mentioned that Gary Rex Lauck, the manufacturer and the world's largest supplier of Nazi propaganda materials from, of all places, Lincoln, Nebraska, was oddly seedy-looking for an operator little known in the United States but an ever-present figure of format throughout Germany. He lurks wherever one turns, a spooklike Kilroy, the character of the World War II graffiti.

I had run into Lauck's tracks at the Hitler birthday festivities of Curt and Ursula Müller in Mainz-Gonsenheim; in reports of closed conspiratorial meetings of extremist right-wing groups in Berlin and elsewhere; at Holocaust-denying lectures by David Irving; and throughout interviews and literature by and about neo-Nazis.

In his cheap, ill-fitting suit, with the little rectangular mustache and the Hitler forelock as his unmistakable trademarks, Lauck spouts racist slogans in an affected German accent that he sometimes explains as a "speech defect." The performance invites dismissal as a joke in poor taste, but it's no put-on. Lauck is so single-minded that he doesn't object to being disbelieved, and he can even turn flip about it. "I'm a politician," he told a writer from the *World Herald* of neighboring Omaha. "I lie."

As a political ideologue, however, Lauck is anything but a charlatan. Since the distribution of Nazi materials is illegal in Germany, Lauck's wholesale production of Hitler paraphernalia has been giving expression to the message of the neo-Nazi movement since 1973. Since 1990, his operations have been growing so fast that Lauck has been profitably devoting full time to them.

"The situation is getting worse the last three years, there is no doubt," said Dr. Lange. While he conceded that the police were able to seize only occasionally and incidentally, the number of such incidents have been multiplying. In 1991, Lauck's handiwork was captured in seventy-two raids. In 1992, there were over two hundred.

"His organizational skills are legendary in Europe," I was advised by Robert Wolfson, director of the Anti-Defamation League for the plains region. "He is sophisticated, computer literate, works with phony telephone numbers and mail drops, with cadres committed to violence, and he's the one central address."

World headquarters is a post office box, No. 6414, in Lincoln 68506, seat of the grandiose-sounding organization headed by Lauck, the NSDAP-AO. The letters purport to represent the foreign organization for the nomenclature of old, Hitler's National Socialist German Workers' Party (NSDAP). To penetrate beyond his post office facade is next to impossible for researchers. Lauck keeps office and home addresses strictly secret. The enterprising Mary de Zutter of the *Omaha World Herald* was able to find only county records indicating that Lauck and his wife, Janina, own a house in Syracuse, Nebraska, a village of 1,600 between Lincoln and Nebraska City.

Whether Lauck's secretiveness is dictated by genuine fears of violence or a promotional appetite for the conspiratorial, his precautions are elaborate. His monthly tabloid bugle, *Kampfruf,* or *Battle Cry,* expanded in recent years to appear in ten languages, including Russian, and distributed in thirty countries, always carries an eight-point program of "security instructions."

"Never write your real name on an envelope," it says, "use a false sender or none." And: "Do not register your letters." And: "Do not store national socialist propaganda material in your residence." Included is a call to help propagate the faith: "If you can receive national socialist propaganda material by the carton through friends in a neutral foreign country, for shipment into the Reich, please report this to us."

The German police believe that the bulk of Lauck's products are smuggled into the forbidden zone by mail and in the trunks of cars. Initially, Lauck often delivered the stuff in person, but he has been officially banned from travel into his favorite country since his arrest there (and a four-month prison sentence) in 1976 with 20,000 swastika stickers in his suitcase.

He hints that he still makes occasional secret trips to meet his friends in Germany, but only anonymously. Since most border controls have become loose or nonexistent in Europe with the advent of the European Community, he does get around. In the November 1993 issue of *The New Order*, the American version of *Battle Cry*, which principally promotes "white power," he reported ("Lauck in Europe") on a mission to Denmark, Croatia, and possibly elsewhere.

"Security considerations prevent me from revealing much," he wrote. "I met with comrades from several countries to discuss future operations. Even if I cannot reveal details, I can say one thing: the effects will be felt by the Bonn Treason Regime!"

What in fact frustrates the Bonn authorities the most is their inability to curb the flow of printed poison from Lauck's propaganda mill. The scope of his output cannot be determined. Lauck says it's "tons" and that his annual production budget is "in the six figures." The point is that large quantities of the materials do reach hands that eagerly pass Lauck's commercials along to impressionable minds.

His biggest hits are his bright red swastika stickers, neatly printed, two by four inches, efficiently gummed, each bearing a slogan in German, English, or several other languages, plus the box number of the source for resupplies in Lincoln, Nebraska. The stickers cost $3 per 100, $15 per 1,000, and their messages, in stark black-on-white lettering like the swastika prominent in the center, are incendiary.

Some of the English-language texts are: "Fight Crime — Deport Niggers"; "White Power!"; "Want Oil? Nuke Israel." For the German market, Lauck targets messages (given here in translation) that reflect his most urgent tactical aims: "Foreigners Out!" and "Lift the Prohibition on the Party!" For neo-Nazi morale-building, he offers:

"Reds, Die!" and "The Jews Are Our Misfortune"; both of the latter slogans are lifted verbatim from the repertoire of the Third Reich.

For shock effect, Lauck sells a sticker message designed as a wake-up call. It says simply: "We're back again!" Kilroy lives.

Lauck's determination to flood Germany with the forbidden swastika symbol bespeaks his first-rate talent for propaganda. A section in one of his German-language pamphlets is called "The Swastika As Wonder Weapon" and spells out his insight into the banned symbol's potential for mischief.

"Thanks to the swastika prohibition," he writes, "the massive distribution and pasting-up of propaganda material bearing the swastika suffice to put things on their head. The democrats get scared, the Communists scream, the entire press warns of the latest 'Nazi outrages' and the *Volk* can see that something serious is afoot. . . . The democrats in Bonn are more scared of the swastika than of red terrorist bombs. . . . We must exploit this exaggerated fear. We have to convert all Germany into a beautiful 'swastika!' "

To back up his stickers, Lauck also sells swastika stick pins ($4), swastika neck chains ($6), swastika key holders ($6), swastika flags (two by three feet) at $25, and swastika armbands for $5.

The price list in his *Battle Cry* features the neo-Nazi usual diet of books on "Jewish ritual murder," the "martyrdom" of Rudolf Hess, and "Hitler — The Unknown Artist." A good selection of Nazi marches is available on disks, and $10 buys a set of three 8½-by-10 posters of Hitler as a knight, as "Rider of Valsgaard," and as a Viking warrior. The spring issue of *Battle Cry*, doubtless to help celebrate the Führer's birthday, features a full-page reproduction of one such poster. It shows Hitler's profile floating above wisps of clouds, a god on duty.


Lauck was born in a German section of Milwaukee (he calls it "the little Germany") and remembers drawing swastikas at the age of four. "I was born a Nazi," he has said. His parents and grandparents were of German extraction, and Gary soon began calling himself Gerhard. He read *Mein Kampf* at the age of thirteen, was soon fluent in German, and recalls "identifying" with Hitler and standing apart, an outsider, at high school in Lincoln, where his father, who taught engineering at the University of Nebraska, had moved the family.

Gary attended the university for two years and became chief propagandist for a while for the National Socialist Party of America in Chicago. In the early 1970s he thought of relocating to Germany but then determined that he could be more helpful by operating from Nebraska.

"I realized that I could do more for the movement from abroad," he has written. "The legality in the USA offered the opportunity for supplying the cells in Germany with propaganda on a large, long-term scale." It was not the first time that an enemy of democracy owed his success to the benevolence of the First Amendment to the Constitution.

Lauck's importunings are one-dimensional. "I think Adolf Hitler was the greatest man who ever lived," he says, except that he was "too humane. . . . We National Socialists declare total war on World Jewry. We shall not rest until you have disappeared from the face of this earth."

Lauck markets videos such as *The Eternal Jew,* made more than half a century ago by Joseph Goebbels's film chief, Fritz Hippler. This is the production that likens Jews to rats, and on one of his American radio programs Lauck apologized to rats for making the comparison. He has remarkably little difficulty getting on the air. His regular TV shows appear on public access channels in Chicago, Milwaukee, Memphis, Seattle, Tampa, and eight smaller markets.

Whether Lauck merely theorizes or is instrumental in terrorist action is in dispute and under investigation. He heatedly denies advocating violence. German and American authorities have been consulting over his role for years. The Germans had vainly tried to persuade the Americans to interfere with Lauck's traffic by way of the postal laws. Lately, FBI director Louis Freeh had conferred about Lauck with the authorities in Bonn.

"There is a fairly fine line where an individual may go beyond mere free speech or expressions and begin to aid or abet [a crime in Germany]," Freeh pointed out.

Was Lauck aiding or abetting? According to a defected neo-Nazi leader, Ingo Hasselbach, who had to take to life in hiding, Lauck has begun not only to call secretly for terrorism but to supply technical how-to. Hasselbach told the *Dallas Morning News* that Lauck had sent him a computer disk containing a document entitled "An Armed Movement."

Hasselbach also said that Lauck had supplied his Berlin skinhead group with detailed instructions on making bombs and placing them so as to cause maximum damage. "That material came from U.S. Army explosives manuals," Hasselbach said.

More immediately threatening are Lauck's moves to knit together the fragmented extremist groups; to facilitate their communications with each other; and to amplify the volume of their propaganda by making it accessible to mass audiences through the most modern techniques. He talks to his German friends almost daily by phone; routinely supplies them with computers and fax machines; and, beginning in 1949, spreads the word about the extremists' latest weapon — sophisticated and omniscient, yet simple and cheap — the Info-Phone.

In 1995, however, Lauck's luck ran out. In March of that year, on one of his clandestine trips to Europe, while visiting a radical right group in Denmark he was arrested in Copenhagen. From there he was extradited to Germany, where he was charged with no fewer than thirty-eight counts of violating German law, including instances of disseminating forbidden material, from copies of *Mein Kampf* to swastikas in dozens of forms, from full-size three-by-five swastika flags to stick pins, key holders, and medallions; from copies of his *Battle Cry* to SS marches and battle songs on cassettes and CDs.

Lauck's subsequent trial points out some of the salient differences between laws regarding freedom of speech in the United States and several Western democracies, and those of postwar Germany. In America the dissemination of any material, even the worst hate literature, is protected under the Constitution. Wisely, the founding fathers understood that there can be no relativity when it comes to freedom of speech. In Germany, however, with its heavy recent history, restricting any possible resurgence of National Socialism or its offshoots is felt to be a necessity. Hartmat Wulf, the chief prosecutor in Lauck's Hamburg trial, who had been monitoring Lauck's activities for the past fourteen years, said in a pretrial interview, "In Germany there's an absolute consensus that these restrictions of freedom should exist. When you examine the history of the Third Reich, you have to recognize that we have a history different from that of any other country."

Much of Wulf's evidence against Lauck had been obtained through German court-authorized wiretaps to several of his Nebraska numbers. For years Wulf had tried to enlist the cooperation of the U.S. authorities, without success, simply because of Lauck's First Amendment rights. Lauck's defense lawyer, Hans-Otto Sieg, fully aware of the legal difference between Lauck's basic American rights and those of Germany, noted that "everything he's accused of is not punishable by law in the U.S.," adding half-jokingly but also in obvious frustration, "Maybe I'll bring a copy of the U.S. Constitution into the courtroom."

Wulf had lined up more than a hundred witnesses against Lauck, and despite the Americans' lack of aid and cooperation, which, noted the prosecutor, "would have helped us a lot," Lauck was convicted and spent four and a half years in a German prison.

Upon his return to the States in 1999, Lauck not only took up where he left off but increased his activities severalfold, thanks to a phenomenon virtually unknown, or unexploited, when he was imprisoned — the Internet. His Web site, which knows no boundaries, announces itself thus:

NSDAP/AO of Gerhard Lauck aka Gary Lauck publishes Nazi newspaper in twelve languages. Offers books on National Socialism or Nazism, NSDAP and Third Reich like Mein Kampf by Adolf Hitler, swastika flags/regalia and more. Order your *FREE SAMPLE COPY* and extensive *price list!*

There follows more than a dozen pages of literature, music, and assorted paraphernalia touting, to the four corners of the world, the virtues of National Socialism and an incredible array of hate material. For Gary Lauck, apparently, prison — as it did for his beloved Führer — served not as a deterrent but as a springboard to greater ambitions and further success.

A curious and ironic footnote to the Gary Lauck saga occurred after his return from Germany in the summer of 1999, when he applied for a handgun permit in his native Nebraska. His application — which was doubtless made with malice aforethought — was denied. The turndown was based on a federal law that states that anyone who has been convicted of felony in any court, domestic or foreign, and sentenced to more than one year in prison, is prohibited from obtaining a gun permit. Ironically, it was the ACLU arguing on Lauck's behalf. Why? Because Lauck contended, and the ACLU concurred, that the fundamental right of Lauck's free speech was being trampled on because he had been convicted and imprisoned for violating a foreign law — the distribution of material prohibited in Germany but totally protected under the U.S. Constitution.

Matt Lemieux, executive director of the Nebraska ACLU, explained why his organization went to bat for the so-called Farmbelt Führer. "This case raises a fascinating constitutional question," he said. "The question here is whether our government can treat someone as a felon for violating a foreign law which contradicts a fundamental American right. . . . Clearly, a foreign conviction based solely upon one's speech is contrary to our cherished right to freedom of speech."

The Lancaster County judge who had denied the Lauck application in essence punted, saying that Lauck should have appealed his permit denial not to a higher court, but to the Bureau of Alcohol, Tobacco and Firearms. Nevertheless, the Nebraska ACLU has announced that it will appeal the judge's decision to district court.

Whether Gary Lauck has any sense of the irony of his present judicial situation, he cannot help but be pleased at the added attention and notoriety that he — and his Web site — are receiving.

# 25

## THE HITLER SOUVENIR HUNTERS

Outrageous as it was, *Newsweek*'s belief that it almost didn't matter whether the Hitler diaries were forged turned out to be accurate in one respect: the scandal failed to deflate Hitler's popularity. It did nothing, for example, to dampen the eagerness of many affluent collectors — the estimates ran that there were 50,000, the majority of them Americans — to lose themselves in the perceived glamour of the Führer's glory days and all but spirit themselves into his exciting presence by gobbling up pieces of him and his world at astronomical (and constantly rising) prices.

In October 1984, only a little over a month after the two con men who had pulled off their hoax on *Stern* went on trial, the magazine published a four-page spread about Hitleriana collectors, entitled "Boom for Swastikas." The craze was (and is) international. Thus, the *Stern* reporters called upon the city manager of Independence, Missouri, Keith Wilson, a wealthy attorney in his mid-fifties and heir to a lumber fortune, who offered dinner with a heavy silver service used by Hitler on the Obersalzberg. The "R.K." on the silver platter for the roast stands for *Reichskanzlei,* Hitler's official residence and office in Berlin.

Wilson owned some 70,000 pieces of Nazi memorabilia worth untold hundreds of thousands of dollars: uniforms, busts, military decorations, swords, daggers, pistols, Hitler's personal poker chips, and his punch bowl, from which the Missouri fan often served drinks. Wilson volunteered that he was neither a Nazi nor crazy. Hitler simply fascinated him, so he insisted, because he changed the world "like Caesar, Martin Luther or Napoleon."

Back on their home ground, on Munich's most prestigious thoroughfare, the Maximilianstrasse, the *Stern* writers participated in one of the many auctions of "militaria" that have kept galleries flush with a business said to be grossing $40 million a year. Under the heading "The Third Reich," 360 lots came under hectic bidding by sixty heavily smoking, mostly elderly men. At times, they pushed up base prices by double and more.

A deed awarding the Oak Leaves for the Knight's Cross to an obscure general went for $12,000 because of the inked signature that read "A. Hitler." A few sheets of Hitler's bed linen from his Eagle's Nest, featuring stitched monograms and eagle insignia, fetched $1,500. A tiny ink sketch of a fireplace by the youthful artist A. Hitler went for $3,000 because it was accompanied by a sworn certificate of authenticity from Armaments Minister Albert Speer.

Fear of fakes had increased somewhat since the recent "affair" of the infamous diaries, according to the only mention of this disaster in the *Stern* article. Hong Kong, Austria, and the United States were named as principal sources of illegitimate resupplies. At least five pistols had been acquired by enthusiasts in their belief that they were capturing the weapon used by the Führer to ostensibly end his existence.

Fans lacking adequate funds for heirlooms touched by Hitler in person had to make do with the satisfaction derived from greatness by association. That is, Hitler's associations. While the con man Gerd Heidemann hosted drunken revels aboard Göring's yacht, other collectors took delight in the *Reichsmarschall*'s hand-painted dinner plates; his toiletry set ($2,200); and even one of his lowly shoe trees.

The hoarding of Hitler memorabilia kept on flourishing even though in Germany such paraphernalia were subject to life in legal twilight. According to paragraphs 86 and 86a of the German penal code, the "distribution," "storing," and "importing" of such meaningful souvenirs was *verboten* — strictly forbidden. Furthermore, "Decorations and honors from the time prior to 1945 also fall within this regulation if they show the swastika." But loopholes had been added so as to exempt such traffic when it served "citizen enlightenment" or "scholarly pursuits." In practice, this language translated into only occasional small fines for some of the biggest dealers. The "boom in swastikas" continued unimpeded.

*   *   *

On their inspection tour of American collectors, the *Stern* reporters were particularly enchanted by their visit to the comfortable home of Dr. Ronald Diestelhorst, an outgoing, well-spoken general practitioner in his early forties, who lived in the Chicago suburb of Inverness. Dr. Diestelhorst, who was born in Iowa, is the grandson of immigrants from Bavaria. Under dramatic track lighting in his subterranean fireproof vault of reinforced concrete, known to his friends as "The Bunker," the doctor had amassed some 10,000 Hitler treasures worth well into the six figures.

His trove included a storm trooper doll that could raise an arm in the Hitler salute at the push of a lever, and other prizes acquired at staggering cost. The doctor would not disclose what he paid for his greatest joy, Hitler's authenticated visor cap; experts estimated that he had to part with $40,000 for it. A dress uniform of Foreign Minister Joachim von Ribbentrop set Diestelhorst back $18,000. The document certifying the award of the Knight's Cross to the record-holding fighter ace Hans Ulrich Rudel cost him an astonishing $28,000.

Prices for Hitler memorabilia kept rising at rates varying between 10 and 20 percent per year, so Dr. Diestelhorst planned eventually to sell a few pieces to pay for his son's college education. Himself too young to have experienced the time of the Nazis, the doctor demonstrated celebratory feeling for the era. He had invested time and trouble to absorb the atmosphere according to his lights.

"Germany was the most exciting place in the world at that time," he bubbled to the writers from *Stern*. "The parades and formations exceeded everything known . . . there was employment for all . . . no disorder . . . no blacks, no sub-humans."

Was he a Nazi? No, no, of course not, just a collector with affinity for an avocation in which he had become steeped because of sentiment.

Not long before the visit from the German magazine, the congenial doctor had received a team from *Life* and had confessed to them that he had been acquiring beer steins, steel helmets, and other German souvenirs since the age of eight. Currently he was recognized among fellow collectors at their conclaves as a specialist in ceremonial daggers. He owned dozens, including Göring's hunt dagger, inlaid with rubies and diamonds, encased in a gold sheath with carved representations of every animal on the marshal's park-sized estate.

Along with some of the doctor's friends, the *Life* people were entertained in The Bunker, where talk was of new acquisitions. Then came respectful silence as the music box tootled the Nazi anthem "Die Fahne Hoch," or "Raise of the Flag."

*Life* made heady discoveries that had eluded the *Stern* researchers. In Los Angeles they located a retired museum employee who owned Ribbentrop's long SS greatcoat; the collector posed for the photographers in the uniform of a Wehrmacht colonel, flashing an Iron Cross. In Scottsdale, Arizona, Tom Barrett, a dealer in vintage cars, posed with his attractive daughter in an armor-plated convertible (weight: almost four tons), a 1938 Mercedes 540K roadster that had allegedly been a gift by Hitler to Eva Braun. The top was down, a swastika standard fluttered from the hood. Barrett estimated this seven-miles-a-gallon bargain to be worth $350,000.

*Life* was also initiated into the sizable market for Hitler's works of art by dropping in on Billy Price, an engineer in Houston, Texas, and viewing his private collection: thirty-three of the Führer's watercolors and oils. The quality of the work had not improved since the Vienna Academy of Art refused Hitler admission as a student in 1907, judging his samples "insufficient." Billy Price, however, the multimillionaire owner of the Price Compressor Company, manufacturers of almost all compressors used in underwater oil exploration, had spent $4 million on his holdings[1] and another $100,000 to assemble an illustrated history of Hitler as an artist that was eventually banned in Germany but published in America.

Price told a British visitor, the writer Robert Harris, that he had become fascinated by Hitler while serving in Germany with the U.S. Army in the 1950s and had sought out former Nazis and their families. Harris found a portrait of Hitler in the bathroom of Price's Texas

---

[1]This was not the largest collection of Hitler art. The Marquess of Bath owned sixty such paintings and kept them in his "Hitler Room" at Longleath, one of Britain's most stately homes. "Hitler did a hell of a lot for his country," said the Marquess. When Price was given a showing by the owner in 1982, he was much impressed, estimating the value of the collection at $10 million.

headquarters, and many more souvenirs were scattered about: a laundry list in Hitler's handwriting, two of Hitler's wartime photo albums, and a thick, obscene birthday card that the Führer had sent to his old pal, SS general Sepp Dietrich.

Price's paintings, taking up an entire wall of his conference room, were kept illuminated behind armor-plated glass, guarded by special alarm systems. Harris found them "lifeless and uninspired": an assortment of Viennese buildings, some flowers, a watercolor of Vienna's city hall, and a few architectural sketches.

No fool, Billy Price realized that he was indulging in an unusual pastime. "Most knowledgeable people say he was not the best artist in the world," he told Harris, "but I certainly think he was a good artist considering the amount of training he had." Price had assembled the paintings "in the interest of history," he said, and his admiration of the Führer transcended his defeat in war and even his posthumous victimization by con men.

"People say Hitler couldn't have kept diaries," he said *after* the forgeries had been unmasked. "They say he couldn't have done this, he couldn't have done that — shit, Hitler could paint paintings, he could write operas. Hell, he controlled more real estate than the Roman Empire, within three years. There's nothing Hitler couldn't have done if he set his mind to it."

At the time, Price had not yet learned that at least 170 of the paintings illustrated in his book — and probably a number in his collection — were the talented creations of Konrad Kujau, the hardworking forger of the putative Hitler diaries.

As the available remnants of Hitler's personal effects stretched ever thinner in recent years, more and more offerings were connected to lesser attractions. In the fall 1993 issue of the quarterly *Military Advisor*, Manion's International Auction House, Inc., of Kansas City ("Own a piece of history") offered an opportunity to bid on a "priceless" 1934 command flag once flown by SS chief Heinrich Himmler. From Long Beach, California, it was possible to order "Gau Berlin stickpins in silver." Jacksonville, Florida, was listed as the source of such books as *Headgear of Hitler Germany*.

Among the magazine's editorial fare was a profile of Leo Schlageter, "the first National Socialist martyr," a gunslinger so vicious that he came to regard Hitler as something of a sissy.

One of the best-known militaria auctioneers, Mohawk Arms, Inc., of Utica, New York, was offering a Waffen SS officer's "crusher-style visored cap" with "silver bullion cap cords" at a starting bid of $1,450. A court order for the wartime execution of a citizen, who had been heard to utter that the Führer had done nothing but commit murder and start the war, was listed at $300.

In a Mohawk catalogue for April 16, 1988, lot No. C19 was the pedigree for an Alsatian known as "Jupp of the Swastika," who once did security duty at the Hamburg-Altona railroad station. The document was considered special by reason of genes not totally unrelated to Hitler. Jupp had supposedly been the grandfather of Blondi, Hitler's favorite pooch.

Collectors cared for their Hitleriana tenderly. Marlin (Bud) Hasher's forty-five mannequins in Nazi uniforms, displayed in a special room of his New Jersey home, sparkled like gowns waiting for a fancy dress ball. His children were attached to the one dressed as Hitler, but Bud, who was Jewish, like many of the American fans, also possessed a model of a Dachau inmate in stained prison uniform. It all added up to a fortune; his ersatz Luftwaffe general alone was worth $4,000.

One wall was covered with swastika-bearing caps and helmets, another with swords, and a third with daggers. "I've always considered this better than the stock market," said Hasher. He planned to sell some of his holdings to pay for his travel in retirement.

Among the most revolting of all known keepsakes anywhere was a photo album said to be bound in human skin, with "SS" affixed on the cover. The Maryland dealer who owned it told the *New York Times* that he considered it no more chilling than his selection of scalps, originally collected by Indian warriors. The merchant had paid $5,000 for the album and hoped to get $75,000 for it.

Since hastily retreating Germans were surprisingly reluctant to destroy even the most secret documents, vast quantities of collectibles poured into the U.S. with the demobilized soldiers after the war and turned up in souvenir shops and flea markets. In recent years, desirable items tended to find their way into militaria magazines, catalogues of auction houses, and on display at the huge annual Militaria Antiques Xtravaganza in Baltimore.

As demand grew and supply dwindled, one taproot proved more fruitful than any other: the Berlin Document Center, operated since 1946 by the United States government. Lined up along an eight-mile maze of underground bombproof shelters, once the home of the Gestapo's wiretapping headquarters in suburban Zehlendorf, the center housed 30 million Nazi files, some 150 million pieces of paper, including seven million individual personnel records of party members.

While no uniforms or weapons were available in this repository, signatures and seals of Hitler, Himmler, and Eichmann, along with other precious paper items, were staples waiting to be filched. Locked gates, barbed wire, hidden surveillance cameras, military police, mirrors, and infrared lights supposedly held this arsenal sealed. In actuality, as one observer concluded, until the late 1980s the place was run like "Aunt Emma's grocery." No source of Hitler merchandise more wide open than this existed anywhere, and so thieves were drawn to these vaults much as the bank robber Willie Sutton used to like banks "because that's where the money is."

Matching its bizarre career, the Document Center was born under comic opera conditions. The first act opened at about 9 A.M. on April 15, 1945, two weeks before the end of World War II, when a car with an SS officer and a civilian pulled up in the courtyard of Hans Huber's paper mill some fifteen miles outside of Munich. A truck convoy would shortly arrive, so the perplexed Herr Huber was advised; he was to destroy the contents at once. The trucks came, as promised, a crew of SS men erected innumerable neat piles of boxes and crates from floor to ceiling of his storage rooms, and departed. Huber peeked inside several of the containers and ascertained that they were stuffed with official-looking papers. He had glimpsed the first sixty-five tons of the eventual Berlin Document Center.

While the SS man had warned Huber that he would be guilty of treason if he didn't follow orders, his radio told him that the Americans were already in the vicinity. By way of confirmation, fleeing German *Landser* (ground troops) were rushing past his mill. The SS was most unlikely to return and check up on him. The victorious Americans would hardly appreciate the last-moment destruction of enemy secrets. Besides, Huber was there alone; there was no way for him to process such an ocean of paper all by himself.

So he proceeded to do what most humans do best when torn by murky circumstances: nothing.

Act two commenced on the morning of May 1. An American jeep pulled up at Huber's mill on routine patrol and a friendly lieutenant greeted the miller in accent-free German. Delighted, Huber relieved himself of his secret. The lieutenant looked inside some of the boxes, speechless. It was my old friend and fellow warrior, Ernie Langendorf of the army's Psychological Warfare Division, who knew about secret German documents and what to do with them.

The exclusive status of the Berlin Document Center (BDC) as a utopia for Hitleriana collectors did not become public until the *Berliner Morgenpost* came out with a series of sensational investigative articles in February 1988. Even then, it could not be determined how many documents had been stolen. Nobody would ever know. Ultimately, prosecutors agreed that at least 10,000 were missing. But it could have been 20,000 or more; the trusting ways of the center's personnel made it easy for any visitor to walk off with anything. The reading facilities were loosely guarded, the files were unbound and unpaginated, body searches were unknown. Besides, many of the thefts — probably most — turned out to have been inside jobs.

The pilfering had been under way since the 1950s, so *Morgenpost* reporters were informed by the ubiquitous British historian and scout of Nazi documents, David Irving, ever eager for any publicity. "I knew an American officer and collector who was stationed in Germany at that time," Irving related. "He had a whole safe full of these things. He opened it for me once very proudly. He took all these papers back to the U.S. with him."

An early tip of mischief reached the West German Federal Archives at Koblenz on April 19, 1982, from a longtime collector, Jost W. Schneider. He enclosed copies of sixteen documents stolen from the

BDC and reported that trade in such contraband was brisk in West Berlin. A Nazi Party membership book was being offered to him for $2,500.

Ensuing investigations led nowhere. Finally, in the fall of 1987, the Berlin prosecutors came into possession of a suspicious catalogue from a Hamburg auction house offering "articles from the time between 1933 and 1945," and on December 11 they appeared on the premises with a search warrant. About a thousand documents with a street value of $175,000 or more were confiscated, and these could only have come out of the BDC; included were correspondence of SS chiefs and the espionage boss Wilhelm Canaris.

Interrogations led the authorities to a junk dealer, who told a strange tale. Some years before, the junkman said, he had met Alfred Darko, born on West Africa's Ivory Coast, a veteran staff member of the center and head of its photo and reproductions department. Darko was changing homes and wanted to rid himself of old furniture and oddments. Could the junkman find takers for "old Nazi papers that are going to be destroyed"?

The dealer soon located an enthusiastic fence who furnished him regularly with order lists. "He always wanted very particular papers," the junkman remembered. "He gave me slips of paper that set out precisely what he needed." Especially desirable were party membership books from 1924 to 1927, because the Führer personally signed them in those years, as well as Hitler letters.

Papers signed by lesser lights were not in clamorous demand. Indeed, Darko was eventually instructed to stop delivering "Himmlers" and "Heydrichs" and "Hesses" because the market was satiated and additional supplies would depress prices unduly.

Over the decades, the BDC also rendered legitimate services on a grand scale. Every year, tens of thousands of requests were filled from authorities checking for war criminals; agencies investigating applicants for pensions and jobs; courageous and curious relatives wanting certainty about the Nazi past of family members; and legitimate researchers reconstructing the historical past. In 1985 it supplied medical records that confirmed the identification of the late Dr. Josef Mengele, the Auschwitz "angel of death."

Not all research requests were prompted by impeccable motives. For some time, the extremist right-wing publisher Dr. Gerhard Frey paid David Irving and other middlemen fat fees for access to BDC documents that Frey used in publishing a popular reference work called *Prominent People without Mask*. Its biographical sketches were described by reviewers as "denunciatory." And Konrad Kujau managed to get access to at least ninety-six BDC documents that presumably helped him when he created Hitler's forged diaries.

Whether documents were also used as instruments for blackmail was never confirmed, although some of the files could have served as open invitations, especially the one million applications for party membership that were rejected on "racial" or other grounds; these could have been used by the applicants to claim that they had never been Nazis — falsehoods that blackmailers could have threatened to reveal.

The trial of Alfred Darko, the Hamburg auctioneer, and some lesser middlemen in December 1988 and January 1989 yielded other evidence that commerce in memorabilia of the Hitler era was prospering. The SS personnel file of Klaus Barbie, "the butcher of Lyon," so it was testified, had just been traced by the FBI to an attorney in Columbus, Ohio, who had bought it at an auction in St. Louis for $3,000.

And the American director of the BDC, Daniel Simon, who was accused of no wrongdoing, told the court that 158 papers relating to twenty-five SS officers had, believe it or not, been stolen twice. The bootlegged papers had been confiscated from a dealer in the Frankfurt area, returned to the BDC, and still had not been refiled four years later. Simon spotted them, but shortly afterward they had vanished once more.

Darko was sentenced to prison for two years and four months; the auctioneer and other defendants were fined and placed on probation. The judge in courtroom B-129 of the old palace of justice in the Moabit district was not pleased, however. Darko's story about the fencing of the stolen collectibles sounded thin to him. There had to have been higher-placed accomplices whom Darko refused to name. How come? "Fear," said the judge.

Shortly before the trial commenced, the U.S. government brought in another good friend of mine to shut down the BDC as a source for hobbyists: David Marwell of Washington, D.C., a professional historian of meticulous habits who formerly tracked major war criminals for the Department of Justice. His was the final act. By the summer of 1994, the center's riches had been turned over to the official German archives in a deal negotiated years before, with microfilmed copies deposited with the National Archives in Washington.

Although, of course, not all the papers that were once captured by the intrepid Ernie Langendorf were available.

Why would copies of Hitler stock photos fetch $700 because they were signed? Why could a Maryland dealer, Charles Snyder, charge $3,500 for a lock of Eva Braun's hair?

The collectors' motives range across an astonishingly diverse spectrum.

Some of the Nazi aficionados are plainly loonies; they collect Hitler in lieu of imagining themselves to be addressing party rallies in Nuremberg. "Quite a few have a crack in their bowl," observed a German collector of World War I spiked helmets. "They often have something hectic about them, as if they're being chased."

This loyalist was seeking the ancient comforts of the Kaiser's fatherland: the Nazi bug was not his department. Among the sane fans of Hitleriana, too, were some who used their souvenirs to cope with their own past. It is a German preoccupation of long standing and carries a formidable name, *Vergangenheitsbewältigung* (literally, "coverage of the past"), a word that denotes dealing with the bygone and suggests hard work to be done in the face of mighty obstacles. This is especially true for SS-men-manqué who belonged to the Hitler Youth but were not old enough for the real ranks.

"They couldn't become heroes because the war ended," said a dealer, "so they look for ersatz satisfaction by collecting Iron Crosses and close-combat medals."

Dr. Leon Rappoport, a professor at Kansas State College, studied the personality of American collectors and concluded, "Collecting Nazi regalia is a form of identification with the bizarre power of the

Nazis." For the many Jewish collectors, such identification may seem strange, but to at least one of them, Alec Tulkoff, it was not bizarre. "It's a matter of feeling victorious," he said. "You may have killed my relatives, but I own you now."

Overall, history exerted the strongest pull, or so the collector/ apologists insisted. Many cited its attraction routinely to legitimize their taste. Dr. Diestelhorst, the Chicago physician with the Horst Wessel music box, called himself a follower of "history you can touch," an apt phrase that skirted the distinction between history and genocide.

Robert Harris, the British writer, shrewdly detected one quality in Hitler that seemed to account for his appeal to self-made business successes like Billy Price, the art collector who believed Hitler could teach himself anything at all. "With his studied mannerisms, the cultivated habit of staring into people's eyes, his hunger to read manuals and absorb technical data, Hitler was self-help run riot," Harris wrote after visiting Price.

Susan Sontag, the author/philosopher, saw deeper meaning in the craze for Nazi regalia, especially the enthusiasm for the mysticism and symbols of the SS. "The SS has become a reference of sexual adventurism," she wrote. "Today it may be the Nazi past that people invoke . . . because it is that past . . . from which they hope a reserve of sexual energy can be tapped. . . . There is a master scenario available to everyone. The color is black, the material leather, the seduction is beauty, the aim is ecstasy, the fantasy is death."

Yes, death. Death is alive and well and a hot-button issue.

# 26

## THE FÜHRER STILL LIVES EVEN

## WHERE HE ALMOST DIED

The Führer Adolf Hitler is dead!"

So began the telex from Field Marshal Erwin von Witzleben to principal German command headquarters, moments after he had proclaimed himself commander-in-chief on July 20, 1944.

The sensational bulletin was almost true.

At 12:50 P.M., a bomb detonated by a Junker war hero and count, Colonel Claus von Stauffenberg, had blown up a top-level briefing in the "Situation Barracks" of Hitler's headquarters. Of the twenty-four men in the room, three were killed, eight were seriously wounded, almost all suffered ruptured eardrums, and many picked themselves off the floor with their hair in flames. At once, someone shouted into the thick smoke, "Where's the Führer?"

Hitler, miraculously, suffered only temporary hearing loss, the indignity of his uniform trousers hanging in shreds, and severe burns. The resistance organization behind Stauffenberg's attempted putsch proved surprisingly extensive, however, and came within a hair of succeeding.[1] Only a lone major loyal to Hitler saved the day, as detailed in chapter twelve.

---

[1]The organization behind Stauffenberg was extensive, but the putsch never really got started because right after the explosion at Wolf's lair, the news spread that Hitler might still be alive. Thus the orders to disarm the SS and attack several strategic sites were withheld until the count returned to headquarters, and then it was too late to act. The putsch proceeded only in Paris and Vienna (where news of Hitler's

Today this scene thrives as a tourist attraction operated largely (80 percent) for the profit of a chocolate manufacturer. Some 250,000 thrill seekers amble along on the hour-and-a-half tour of its ruins, although the location, because of Hitler's original planning, is hardly convenient. As noted, he called it his *Wolfsschanze* (Wolf's Lair), and work on it began in utmost secrecy during November 1940. Workers were told they were building a chemical factory.

The Führer officiated and lived there for almost a thousand days. It was the nerve center of the Reich, but the purpose of its location was military and specific. Hitler wanted a readily defended lair from which to run his planned invasion of the Soviet Union, still his partner in a celebrated nonaggression pact at the time. So he chose the deserted rural swamps and huge lakes — one of them is ten miles long — in the Masuria region of East Prussia, some six railroad hours northeast of Berlin. Thick woods provided cover and also made paratrooper assaults unlikely.

Eventually, this private universe would become known by the name of the nearby village, Rastenburg, now Ketrzyn, Poland. Some eighty buildings were put up, a rail station, two airports; the web of restrictions to protect the Führer's isolation was obsessive, ordered in detail by him personally, and the concrete walls of his personal bunker measured sixteen feet thick.

The reactions of sightseers these days, mostly Poles and Germans, reflect their divergent memories of the unforgettable master who hatched this once-forbidden labyrinth.

---

survival arrived much later), where the SS were disarmed, but by midnight "order" had been restored. One can say that Stauffenberg almost succeeded in killing Hitler; he had placed the bomb in a briefcase right beside the Führer, and it was only because one of the officers had moved the briefcase out of the way just before the bomb exploded that the dictator survived. That same night, Stauffenberg and fellow-conspirators Olbricht, von Häften, Ritter Merz von Quirnheim and Beck (who unsuccessfully attempted to commit suicide as soon as he was captured) were caught by the Nazis and shot. At first the conspirators were buried with their uniforms and decorations, then Himmler ordered the bodies to be dug out and burned. Later, Hitler had 7,000 suspects arrested, 200 of whom were killed as participants in the attempted putsch.

"The Poles, but also the British, the French, the Dutch, and the Russians that come here are predominantly interested in Hitler," reports Kasimierz Kolakowski, tour guide for nearly twenty years. "The Germans want above all to hear about Stauffenberg."

The symbolism of Rastenburg is all but palpable. Stauffenberg fascinates because he signifies pride that stouthearted Germans existed after all, who resisted Hitler and put up their lives to act on their hatred of him, even though the orientation of the putschists still remains controversial. Stauffenberg certainly was no democrat, but no matter; the interest displayed in him by the visitors to Rastenburg is but a fig leaf covering their preoccupation with Hitler, which drew them to this remote memorial in the first place.[2]

"The Germans behave in very different ways," says their shrewd shepherd, Kolakowski. "Some stay in the bus, refuse to participate in the inspection, thereby showing their contempt for Hitler or shunning a disagreeable confrontation with the past. Some follow me silently, visibly moved by the atmosphere. Most behave like normal tourists inspecting a sight. One or the other shows himself impressed by the construction achievement of the Führer."

---

[2]Even more controversial than Rastenburg is the proposed Holocaust museum in Berlin. The debate over the memorial began over a decade ago, when TV journalist Lea Rosh founded a private organization, to lobby for the museum. With the cooperation of the Federal government and the Berlin Senate, a 20,000 square meter lot, in the shadow of the Brandenburg Gate, was chosen. The initial design by Christine Jakob Marck, which depicted a massive gravestone on which the names of the murdered Jews were to be engraved, provoked such an outcry that then-Chancellor Helmut Kohl annulled the choice and called for a new competition. Ultimately, in June 1999, the German parliament approved a design by American architect Peter Eisenman, which consisted of 2,700 closely set pillars with, underground on the same site, an exhibition and multimedia center. Groundbreaking was set for "sometime in the year 2000." However, some critics complained that it was unfair to those, other than Jews, who had suffered at the hands of the Nazis, while Berlin Mayor Eberhard Diepgen argued that the Eisenman design was too overwhelming. Even Germany's Jews were divided: Michel Friedman, a member of the Central Council of Jews in Germany, argued that the museum should be dedicated solely to Jewish victims, while fellow council member Salomon Korn opposed him, saying that such a monument would give the impression that some Nazi victims were more important than others. As this book goes to press, groundbreaking has yet to begin.

The power of the past is at work once again, and the past of the *Wolfsschanze* itself — its vicissitudes even as a relic — echoes the half-century-plus of Hitler's afterexistence in the twilight.

*November 20, 1944.* Exactly four months after the Stauffenberg bombing, and with the Soviets pouring across the border of the Reich, Hitler leaves his command post for the last time.

*January 23 and 24, 1945.* Hurriedly, the *Wolfsschanze* is blown up by Wehrmacht troops. The explosion is so fierce that ice four and a half feet thick bursts into fragments across two nearby lakes.

*1955.* It has taken this long to remove 55,000 mines left hidden by the Germans.

*1959.* The *Wolfsschanze* is opened to the public under the orientation of the Communist Polish government, intent on discrediting the Stauffenberg resisters. "The conspirators actually were no opposition group," said the tourist guide; "they wanted only the best outcome of the war." The war crimes and defeat of the Germans, on the other hand, were dramatized in horror photos blown up to poster size and lining the walk to the remains of Hitler's Situation Barracks: bombed-out Coventry and starved concentration camp prisoners followed by the victory parade on Moscow's Red Square.

*1989.* With the Polish Communists out of power, the new premier agrees with Chancellor Kohl to erect a mutually satisfactory tablet at the Situation Barracks.

*1990.* The longtime administrator of the *Wolfsschanze,* the Polish state tourist office, goes bankrupt. The chocolate capitalists and their market economy take over — and their corporation, the Wolfsnest GMBH, becomes the area's biggest taxpayer.

*1991.* With the new German nationalism in full force, the photo reminders of Hitler's violent past are removed.

*July 20, 1992.* After two and a half years of negotiations between the German and the Polish heads of state, a bilingual tablet appears at the Situation Barracks to honor Count Stauffenberg and his associates in the agreed-upon words, unadorned, noncontroversial: "He and many others that rose up against the national socialist dictatorship paid with their lives."

*      *      *

The political underbrush of recent decades having been cleared away, visitors were given access to the details of why Count Stauffenberg managed to pierce Hitler's security measures and how he made his escape after planting his explosive.

Access to Hitler was possible only by passing through a sequence of forbidden zones surrounding several defense rings ordained by the Führer personally. With each circle that closed in on his presence, the cast of admissible staff personnel tightened to become more personalized and select. On September 20, 1943, Hitler had redesigned the precautions, creating a new Forbidden Zone A within Security Circle 1. It contained the Situation Barracks and the "guest bunker" where Hitler lived.

Stauffenberg owed his access to sheer brilliance. About to be appointed chief of staff to the general who commanded the Wehrmacht reserve armies, he had worked up a new plan of disposition for fresh troops assigned to block the advancing Russians. On June 7, he was asked to brief Hitler on the scheme at the Berghof on Obersalzberg in Berchtesgaden, which enabled him to make a crucial observation: "In the immediate environment of the Führer, it was possible to move about rather freely."

This was indispensable. The explosive, small enough to fit into a briefcase, would have to be positioned very close to Hitler's body to achieve a deadly effect. And Stauffenberg had to contend with physical restrictions. The war in Africa had left him blind in his left eye, and he had lost his right hand (and part of his arm) and the ring and little finger of his left hand.

On July 6, 7, and 11 he met again with Hitler at his Berchtesgaden home. Each time, the colonel carried his explosive, and each time he decided not to act because Himmler was not present. It was the same on July 14, when he briefed Hitler in Rastenburg for the first time. On the twentieth, with his by now extremely jittery fellow conspirators standing by in Berlin and around the country ready to take over, a now-or-never tension hung in the air.

Stauffenberg climbed into the Junkers Ju-52 courier plane at Berlin's Rangsdorf airport around 7 A.M. Shortly before 11 A.M. he was breakfasting at Rastenburg's Kasino II, the officer's mess of Forbidden Zone A. A little over an hour later, after politely turning down two offers for help with his briefcase, he entered the Situation Barracks and placed the case under the large table where maps were spread to be consulted by Hitler. The Führer entered promptly at 12:30.

Calling attention to his hearing loss, another aftereffect of the African campaign, Stauffenberg had asked to be placed near the table — and Hitler. As soon as he had completed his brief presentation, the colonel whispered a few words to someone, left the room, and got into his eight-cylinder Horch convertible. His departure caused no comment in the briefing room; officers routinely came and went, usually to use the phone.

Stauffenberg was approaching Guard House I of Forbidden Zone 1 on Rastenburg's outer periphery, urging his driver to hurry, when he saw a large smoke cloud over the Situation Barracks. Blackened scraps of paper whirled through the air, officers were running back and forth, soldiers were carrying the injured on stretchers. He was entitled to think that he had fulfilled his mission.

When he arrived at Guard House I, so little time had elapsed since the bomb went off that no alarm had been given. However, the guard, having heard the explosion, ordered his gate closed on his own initiative. Stauffenberg, with his injuries, his decorations, and his aristocratic bearing, identified himself as an insider of the general staff, and the lieutenant of the guard let him through. At the next and final checkpoint, the top sergeant in charge was harder to push around. But when Stauffenberg pushed him to call his superior, that officer turned out to be a friend of Stauffenberg who had no concern about letting the colonel through to the airport. A fellow conspirator had stationed a Heinkel He-111 there for Stauffenberg to return to Berlin.

Stauffenberg was executed that same night.

When the Hitler tourists pass through Rastenburg now, cows are grazing on the onetime airport and little but the foundation can be seen of the Situation Barracks and its long-negotiated memorial plaque. It is shaped like an open book. No telling what might transpire on further pages in the future — if the rendering of the past is any guide.

# 27

## THE PROOF IS IN THE POLLS

Since introspection is a favorite indoor sport of theirs, the Germans may be the most resolutely polled people on earth. And given their nervousness, reticence, and guilt feelings about their past, they represent a formidable challenge to their pollsters. By and large, the questioners have coped resourcefully. While their statistics cannot compete with brain scans for precision, they do supply structure for the interpretations of the historians, sociologists, journalists, and authors, myself included.

When not lured into trying to predict future behavior, polls make reasonably accurate evidence, mirrors of attitudes past and present. A truism holds that the phrasing of an inquiry in an opinion survey can grossly distort a poll result. So it comes as no surprise that the dynamite question, "Would you vote again today for a man like Hitler?" posed in 1993, brought a "yes" response from only 7 percent of the population — a figure that had not changed in a quarter century.

A seemingly trifling percentage, yes, but not to be ignored. It represents a sturdy core of incorrigibles, several million voters, presumably sane, who do not merely hanker nostalgically after a distant, idealized mystique of a long lost leader, but for whom Hitler remains a vibrant, contemporary model whose governance is considered desirable these days. They want their past to be prologue.

When the same issue was framed in a less blatant, slightly more impersonal (and therefore more socially acceptable) wording, the quota of open and unyielding Nazis climbed somewhat. An earlier (1982) survey by an impressive team of academics proposed this statement: "We should have a Führer again to govern Germany with a strong hand for the benefit of all." While only 4 percent of the 9,000 respondents called this martial assertion "completely correct," another 10 percent considered it "partly correct," and a further 7 percent claimed to have no opinion. So the total came to 21 percent who felt positively or were fence-sitters.

Such results hardly reflect reality, however, because the questions are invitations to lie. It was like asking a burglar about property rights. Every child is taught the right and wrong of mine and thine; Hitler was a criminal. Moreover, German pollsters are mistrusted by their audience. In a poll about their own credibility, only 55 percent of respondents considered their questioners "reliable and credible." In this cynical climate, unusual vigilance must guard against fibbing.

Rather than pushing the Hitler button, a more neutral question, posed in 1989, flushed out more reliable truth about models of leadership. Citizens were invited to name the Germans they most admired. The runaway winner was the foxy Chancellor Konrad Adenauer, a generation out of office, nearly a generation dead, ultranationalist, enemy of denazification, Cold Warrior supreme, strong-willed protector of high-ranking Nazis. He stood firm as the model German, applauded by 61 percent. The gap in standing between him and two Nobel Prize winners was remarkable. Willy Brandt, then still alive, was an also-ran at 28 percent; Thomas Mann scored 21.

For the typical voter, Adenauer, Hitler's successor, was the displaced ideal, the leader who laundered some of the Third Reich values, but discarded few. The Old Fox hung on for fourteen years because he listened to his electorate with the ear of a Toscanini taking the measure of his orchestra. And listening also to what the master pollster, Elisabeth Noelle Neumann, told him about the minds of his countrymen.

By 1988, the durable Noelle Neumann could show the next conservative chancellor, Helmut Kohl, who likewise employed her as chief pollster and valued confidante, how closely in harmony Adenauer had been with the voters when he reemployed Nazis for high posts.

Here is how Neumann phrased this delicate subject: "In the postwar period, many persons who held high office in the Third Reich again were given important positions. Two people are taking opposite positions about this. With whom are you inclined to agree?"

The view attributed to Citizen No. 1 was "I think it's a scandal that such people got big jobs after 1945. Their past incriminated these people so severely that they should not have been allowed to rise again." This proposal was approved by 37 percent.

Citizen No. 2 was said to hold: "One can't say this in a general way. It all depends on what an individual did during the Third Reich. Many of these people helped during our reconstruction period and turned out to be good democrats." This point of view was adopted by 42 percent, somewhat more voters than considered big-time Nazis to be unemployable in high places. An additional significant 21 percent voted "undecided," some of whom undoubtedly being among the Nazi-tolerating plurality.

In 1992, with Chancellor Kohl by then ten years in office, Noelle Neumann was still traveling to Bonn once a month to counsel the chancellor on his political standing, and in that year her pollsters asked the electorate, "Would you say that without the war and the persecution of the Jews Hitler would have been one of Germany's greatest statesmen?"

There were 27 percent "yes" votes. That same year, 42 percent also held that National Socialism had offered "good as well as bad qualities."

To be sure, defenders of the Third Reich became fewer as mortality reduced the ranks of eyewitnesses. In 1964, 28 percent denied that Hitler had run a "regime of criminals." In 1979, 21 percent felt that this demonstrable truth was really untrue; in 1990, the contingent of deniers was at only 11 percent.

When the pollsters cleverly depersonalized past history so that interviewees could finger-point at peers without disclosing their own views, more Nazi loyalists emerged. Thus, the Noelle Neumann interviewers read this statement to their population sample: "During the Third Reich, a lot of Germans were National Socialists. How do you suppose matters stand today? Are there still a lot of National Socialists among us, or only a few?"

Suddenly, when voters no longer felt they had to claim, "I was never a Nazi!" Nazis did show up; 26 percent said there were "quite a few," another 19 percent begged off by shrugging, "impossible to say."

Kohl, an old-line conservative as wily as Adenauer, albeit more folksy in manner and utterance, has always reminded me of the old Kansas senator of whom it was said that he sat on the fence with both ears on the ground. Having listened to the sounds from the grass roots with his left ear, Kohl — it was during a trip to Israel — invoked the "blessing of late birth"; that is, his own. He was a teenager in the early 1940s and cannot therefore be taxed with guilt like his elders.

When pollsters asked whether it was OK for a politician to hide behind his late birth, ambivalence reigned. The defense of "I wasn't there" was endorsed by 25 percent; labeled improper by 48; and was voted "impossible to say" by another 27 percent, presumably fence-sitters, liars, or dim in the head.

Then again, listening with his right ear, Kohl stoked the embers of Hitler's soul many times, not only with his homage at the SS cemetery in Bitburg. "Herr Kohl can go where he will and talk whereof he will," observed the German critic and poet Hans Magnus Enzes-berger, "everything reminds him of Goebbels or Hitler or the Hitler Youth. Fascism is his obsession."

Deploying, I suppose, his third ear, Kohl has not renounced one popular see-no-evil, hear-no-evil way out. It calls for drawing a *Schlusstrich* under the past in its entirety — literally, a bottom line, but not as in the balancing of books. It really means, "that's all," no further data is desired. In various polls, this ostrich device has been endorsed over the years by 62 to 66 percent of Germans.

Anti-Semitism, while publicly practiced by few adults other than hooligans, has never relaxed its grip on the postwar Germans. In 1947, with the photos of concentration camp liberations still in fresh memory, three-quarters of the population turned its collective back dismissively toward the crimes and asserted that Jews "belong to a different race [*sic!*] than ourselves." Nearly as many stated they would never marry a Jew.

In 1952, one-third said that "Jewish characteristics" were the primary cause of anti-Semitism. Only one-fifth had ever discussed the persecution of the Jews with their children, and 37 percent said it was better for Germany to have no Jews at all in its midst.

By 1965, that last figure had declined to 19 percent, but then, in the 1980s, along with full prosperity and reviving nationalism, anti-Jewish sentiments began to rise again. Research classified at least six million Germans as anti-Semitic, about two million of that number constituting a hard core of diehards. Jews were popularly characterized as "shrewd and money-grubbing," and too eager to exploit the Nazis' past for compensation and other financial advantage.

In 1982, the statement "The influence of Jews and freemasons in our country is still too great today" was called either "completely correct" or "partially correct" by 25 percent of voters.

By 1986, fewer than half of all interviewees troubled to take a defensive view toward their anti-Semitic past; 46 percent said that "only a minority" had been against the Jews during the Hitler period. And in the 1990s, with the reunification giving a further boost to nationalism, anti-Semitism was openly recognized (accepted?) by the Germans as a permanent feature of their culture.

While only 26 percent still clung to the lie that accounts of the Holocaust were "exaggerated," or that they couldn't make up their minds about what happened in the concentration camps, 43 percent conceded that half a century later "many" of their countrymen were still "against the Jews."

And the following question elicited an unequivocal verdict: "Will anti-Semitism slowly die out in Germany, will it always exist to a certain degree, or will it increase?" Almost one-fifth (18 percent) said that anti-Jewish prejudice would rise further; 60 percent felt it would continue "to a certain degree."

Most revelatory of all has been the popular response to a particularly sickening brand of anti-Semitic humor: not standard jokes about supposed Jewish characteristics or behavior, but banter that the pollsters described as distinctly "pogromistic"; that is, laughter about mass murder. The EMNID polling organization, showing enviable fortitude, first probed attitudes toward such atrocious witticisms in 1981. When the question was next repeated in the summer of 1993, the results were released under the heading "Jokes about the annihilation of Jews are still far from taboo."

While the questioners did not consider it their business to address the ethics and taste of such so-called humor existing at all, they did comment astutely on the usefulness of jokes as mirrors of attitudes: "Jokes can be valves for the release of pent-up aggression, they can establish connections between the likeminded, and they bring out attitudes that otherwise surface rarely."

It was found that attitudes toward black humor about the annihilation of Jews have abated somewhat, but not by much. In 1981, 48 percent labeled such humor "very bad"; in 1993, 63 percent did so. In 1981, 21 percent considered the jokes "not worth talking about"; in 1993, only 11 percent still wanted to dismiss them from discussion.

Investigators in a particularly large-scale survey concluded as long ago as 1982 that the attitudes among 13 percent of the electorate were governed by an "extreme rightist world picture." Beginning in the summer of 1991, the EMNID pollsters fine-tuned the issue further. They wanted to identify a larger and more significant but mostly silent, similarly oriented segment among the electorate.

This was how they posed the question: "The problem of the foreigners has brought on right-radical tendencies. Do you have understanding of these tendencies or no understanding?" In September 1991, 38 percent of West Germans and 21 percent of East Germans said they felt right-wing sympathies. In January 1992, the corresponding figures were 28 percent and 14 percent respectively. The views of a powerful minority had thus been tapped.

The rise of the new nationalism, tracked in general terms by all observers, has been pinpointed by the pollsters through a variety of revealing sample taking. Even before reunification, in January 1989, Frau Noelle Neumann's questioners had asked, "Can a German today feel as proud of his country as an American, a Frenchman, or a Britisher?" A thunderous 84 percent voted themselves "equally proud."

By 1992, the interviewees from EMNID had detected not-so-latent stirrings of old master race ("*Herrenvolk*") ambitions. Their question came in the form of a trump-card statement, the flat assertion "We

Germans are superior to other nations." This reactivated jingoism was rejected by only a slim majority; 27 agreed with it, 17 percent were undecided. So the jingoists plus the undecideds almost matched the moderates.

Whenever the issue is raised in a neutral style, feelings of pride in being German have not wavered over the decades: in 1975, 76 percent voted themselves as "unconditionally" or "predominantly" proud; it was 76 percent again in 1985, 66 percent in 1990.

In 1989, when reunification infused tough new muscle into patriotic pride, the question was "Should one have national pride today or do you consider that unimportant?" The "should" vote ran 57 percent.

By 1992, even a more aggressively worded test elicited a strong response. Now the question was phrased this way: "The word 'Fatherland' — does it have a good sound to you or does the word no longer fit today's times?" Fifty percent admitted that they liked the sound.

Patriotic music was also gaining favor. Beginning in 1990, the two principal television networks, ARD and ZDF, which are publicly financed and tend to rate as reliable weather vanes of general opinion, played the national anthem ("Deutschlandlied") nightly before going off the air. The hymn had once been highly controversial. The fire had gone out of the debate. One-third of the interviewees claimed to have no opinion; half said that ending the day with martial evidence of one's patriotism was "a good idea."

"Patriotism" has always been the equivalent of chauvinism among Germans, and although Joseph Goebbels was no longer present in the flesh, his style of propaganda was still feeding hate, and it was flowing most conspicuously from a very odd source.

# 28

## A VERY OPINIONATED POLLSTER:

## THE TWO FACES OF ELISABETH

## NOELLE NEUMANN

The attainments of Elisabeth Noelle Neumann would be notable anywhere; in the anti-feminist German business world, her ratings are not measurable by any chart.

As the dean of the public opinion research industry, she has counseled the conservative chancellors of her country privately for more than forty years. She still issues regular public reports on political trends; predicts elections of her clients and other politicians; wins international research awards; co-publishes the *International Journal of Public Opinion Research;* and, until 1991, lectured regularly at the University of Chicago, which published many of her books.

The news magazine *Der Spiegel* coined the word *Päbstin* to describe her. It means "female pope," and it is an apt summation of her singular status and her Teflon skin. It took nearly half a century for her Nazi past to catch up with her, and even when the dirt hit, it left her stature untarnished.

The rules governing practitioners of Neumann's profession seem not to apply to this wizard. Pollsters usually make a point of staying reasonably neutral, above partisan battles. Noelle Neumann — brainy, feisty, and exuding charm — relishes life in the eye of the storm.

A careerist and partisan from the start, she was a "cell director" and held posts in four Nazi student organizations as a teenager in Berlin and Munich. On the strength of these credentials, party authorities selected her in 1937, at the age of twenty-one, for a prized exchange student fellowship at the University of Missouri.

Feeling qualified as an authority on National Socialism, she gave Americans advice. In an article for the campus newspaper, *The Missourian,* she urged the United States to guard its racial purity in order to avoid the nation's "downfall." Germany was immune to such a fate: "National Socialism is opposed to a mixing of the races because it sees herein a danger of the maintenance of national character."

She learned polling in America; the techniques were just being systematized by another young journalist, Dr. George Gallup, at his newly established American Institute of Public Opinion. Fortunately, Gallup was not Jewish, for when Noelle returned home and published her government-financed Ph.D. dissertation as a 166-page book, *American Mass Surveys for Politics and Press,* Jewish colleagues did not fare favorably.

Walter Lippmann, then the most influential of the columnists, became "the Jew Lippmann," and his coreligionists were hateful: "They monopolize much of American intellectual life and concentrate their demagogish talents to agitate against Germany."

Finding employment at *Das Reich,* a slick-paper weekly published by Propaganda Minister Joseph Goebbels and directed at intellectuals, she continued — with assistance from officials of the Goebbels office — to disseminate her version of who shaped American public opinion. Her prize exhibit was "Who Informs America?" a two-page spread on June 8, 1941.

Her answer: Jews. "Jews write in the newspapers, own them, have virtually monopolized the advertising agencies and can therefore open or shut the gates of advertising income as they wish. They control the film industry, own the biggest radio stations, and all the theaters."

In 1944, when her husband was propaganda aide to the *Gauleiter* of Dresden, she was still crusading against the United States, calling it a "pseudo-democracy" controlled "by the money power."

Her postwar conversion to democratic ways began by the grace of the French military authorities. They paid her 4,000 marks a month for secret opinion surveys in their occupation zone, thereby becoming, in 1947, the godfathers of the polling organization that she still directs: the Allensbach Institut für Demoskopie at Allensbach on Lake Constance.

Not until July 1950, when evidence of old Nazi careers was entombed by wholesale forgiveness, did she wrangle her *Persilschein* from a German denazification tribunal. Persil is a detergent; to hold a *Persilschein* was to have laundered one's political past. Noelle Neumann's slip certified her as "unincriminated" — meaning that she never shot at Jews with more than words.

In the 1980s, Noelle Neumann published a book that sparked a stir among political scientists. It argued that polls are prejudiced by a "bandwagon effect," because a lot of people blur issues by shyly conforming to what they suppose is the majority view. She called her work *Spiral of Silence,* and soon, paradoxically, the long-hidden story of her own silence came into print, first in Germany and then in the United States, where she still taught polling briefly every year as a visiting professor. Not until Leo Bogart, a New York sociologist, published a critical article in the August 1991 issue of *Commentary* magazine did the University of Chicago campus wake up to the presence of the old Nazi.

The resonance was mild. Even Professor John J. Mearsheimer, who spearheaded a campaign for an apology, told me that he did not consider Noelle Neumann a "Nazi" but only "an anti-Semite." The pollster wrote to *Commentary,* "I am terribly sorry if any hurt was caused by what I wrote 50 years ago. I certainly can say that when I wrote that passage [*sic*] at that time, I had no intention of doing any harm to the Jews." In a letter to the *New York Times,* she insisted, "I was not a Nazi and I am anguished by the suffering of the Jews in Nazi Germany."

Some faculty members and students considered her reaction adequate. Others, including Professor Mearsheimer, did not. In any event, the incident died quickly. And while Noelle Neumann did not reappear to teach in Chicago, and in 1992 declined an invitation to speak at the university's National Opinion Research Center, the impact of the disclosures in Germany was nil.

# 29

## THE HAIDER PHENOMENON

In October 1999 a shudder went through Europe and the United States when the results of the national elections in Austria were announced. The ruling Social Democrats (SPÖ) had obtained 33.4 percent of the vote, the conservative People's Party (ÖVP) 26.9 percent, and the Liberal, or Freedom, Party (FPÖ) 27.2 percent. Suddenly the world realized that the FPÖ, which had always been disregarded as a minor extreme-right-wing movement, was now officially the second largest party in Austria. Suddenly Jörg Haider, head of the FPÖ, thanks to a coalition with the ÖVP, was destined to become vice chancellor of Austria.

In Austria, the system of proportional representation had allowed the *Große Koalition* (Big Coalition) between the SPÖ and the ÖVP to maintain a firm grip on power for thirteen years, guaranteeing, since 1987, stability and growth. As trade unions were absorbed into the state apparatus from the start, the government coalition had no true opposition. Until now.

In the 1950s, the right wing, misnamed the Liberal Party, which was then called Verband der Unabhängigen (VdU) — Association of Independents — had never attained more than 4 percent of the popular vote in the general elections. In 1956 the VdU was dissolved and replaced by the Freiheitliche Partei Österreich (FPÖ). In the early 1990s, the ruling *Große Koalition* began to reveal some fissures and flaws: corruption scandals (which had tainted many European governments over the previous decade) began to surface. Also, between 1981 and 1991, immigration into Austria had increased by 75 percent. The Austrian people no longer felt represented by the two governing coalition parties, and as trade unions were not considered an alternative, many turned to the FPÖ to voice their concern and disapproval.

The flow of immigrants into Austria had always been high. For one thing, Austria was a democratic, socialist state with excellent social services. For another, Vienna was the most important city close to the Iron Curtain, which meant that refugees and immigrants from Eastern Europe often headed here. That proximity to the Eastern Bloc also resulted in the presence of large international institutions such as the United Nations and OPEC and their international staffs. In the 1980s there was a sizable increase in immigration from Turkey and North Africa, mainly to Vienna but also to the rest of the country. After the fall of the Iron Curtain, in the early 1990s the Balkan War provoked a huge wave of immigration as Serbs, Croats, and Bosnians sought refuge in neighboring Austria. So it was not only the vulnerability of the ruling coalition but also the disquieting (to many Austrians) increase in immigration that led to the extraordinary, unanticipated election results in 1999. To those factors had to be added the personal success of one Jörg Haider, who had been chairman of the Freedom Party for more than a decade. During the thirteen-year rule of the *Große Koalition,* the FPÖ's popularity had grown under Haider's leadership, gradually increasing its meager 5 percent of the Austrian vote to an impressive 27 percent. Who was this man who, almost overnight, vaulted himself from virtual obscurity to one of Austria's most powerful — and potentially dangerous — political figures?

Haider was born in 1950, the son of two active members of the Nazi Party, who were, as such, severely penalized at the end of the war — his father was arrested and his mother lost her job as a teacher. Though he condemns the Nazi dictatorship, Haider has always defended the Austrian war generation by saying that they were "only doing their duty." Most notoriously, in 1995 he addressed a group of SS veterans in Krumpendorf, in the traditionally nationalistic southern province of Carinthia, in the following words: "In these turbulent times there are still decent people, people of character, who stick to their conviction even when they have to face resistance, and who have remained loyal to their conviction to the present day. And that's

the foundation, my dear friends, that's the foundation that you transmit to us, the young generation. A nation that doesn't honor its
ancestors will perish anyway." In other words, remembering — or
even honoring — the Nazi past was essential to a strong Austria.

In 1968, having completed high school, Haider went to Vienna to
study law, and there joined the nationalist movement Silvania. Later
he was elected leader of the young Freiheitlichen (the FPÖ youth)
and eventually joined the FPÖ itself. It was the 1970s, and in those
days the FPÖ was headed by Friedrich Peter, a former member of
the SS. In the early 1980s, Haider became the local leader of the FPÖ
in Carinthia.

In 1983, the SPÖ formed a coalition with the FPÖ, which was
then led by Norbert Steger, a less fervent nationalist than his prede-
cessors. This coalition lasted until the Social Democrats, under Franz
Vranitzky, unilaterally broke it off when Jörg Haider became leader
of the FPÖ in 1986, their slogan being "no coalition with Haider."
As a result of this rupture, in 1987 the *Große Koalition* between the
SPÖ and the ÖVP was formed, leaving the FPÖ as the only opposition party. That same year, former Nazi and convicted war criminal
Walter Reder was released from prison and returned to his native
Austria. The Austrian defense minister Friedhelm Frischenschlager
of the FPÖ greeted him with a warm handshake, a gesture that
caused outrage both in Austria and abroad, especially in Israel, where
the furor was such that the good minister made a public apology. But
it was Haider who stole the show in this affair by declaring publicly
that Reder was a man who had only "done his duty" and that the
defense minister's apology to Israel had been "superfluous."

In 1989, Haider was elected governor of Carinthia, a position he
lost in 1991 for having declared that he would decrease unemployment in the region by putting pressure on those people who simply
did not want to work. When a socialist deputy compared this policy
to that of the Nazis, Haider replied, "In the Third Reich they made a
proper policy of employment, something that your government in
Vienna never accomplished." When public opinion and the press expressed outrage at this statement, Haider attempted to clarify what he
had said: "All I said was based on fact: that the Third Reich created a

great number of jobs through an intensive policy of employment, and thus eliminated unemployment. And I said it in the context of a debate we were having, as more and more people in Austria are losing their jobs, and at the same time we are importing more and more foreigners who take our jobs." In any event, Haider was voted out of his job as governor of Carinthia.

In the early 1990s, the more moderate elements of the FPÖ slowly started to abandon the party. Most of them left in 1993 because they disagreed with the referendum against *Überfremdung* — foreign penetration — that Haider was ardently promoting. One of the issues in the referendum was the strict segregation of schools along ethnic lines. Haider lost the battle and the racist referendum did not take place. That same year, he faced another political defeat when the Austrians were called to vote on a referendum for membership in the European Union. Haider opposed the idea arguing that membership would lead to a loss of Austrian independence and launched a huge "no" campaign that did not succeed. Sixty percent of the Austrians voted yes, and Austria did become a member of the EU. Yet, thanks largely to Haider's campaign, 40 percent of Austrian voters had sided with him.

In spite of this political setback, in the 1994 elections in Carinthia Haider received the largest number of votes of any candidate. But in order to become governor he needed the support of either the SPÖ or the ÖVP. Both parties refused to back him, which first gave rise to Haider's claim that he was a "victim of political exclusion." With the FPÖ as the biggest party in the region, Haider finally regained his post as governor of Carinthia in 1998.

The uneasiness many Austrians felt as they saw increasing numbers of foreigners entering their country found voice in many of Haider's statements. In a television news program in May 1991, he explained that "those who haven't learned the trade of work and labor will never be able to build prosperity — and that must also be mentioned with respect to Eastern Europeans," thus implying that Eastern Europeans who emigrate to Austria do not know how to (or want to) work because under the Communist regimes they did not need to. It is only the competitiveness of the free market that teaches "the trade of work and labor" necessary to "build prosperity."

But Haider's racism is not directed only against Eastern Europeans and Turks. After a trip to Namibia in 1995, he made the following report on a morning news program: "I visited friends in Namibia, formerly German Southwest Africa, together with my family, because I wanted to probe how it is to live with black people when they have the [political] majority. There is definitely a problem with the blacks. Even where they are in majority, they fail to get their act together. It's simply a hopeless case." The press service of the FPÖ reported, in a simple equation, pointedly accessible to all, that "There are 300,000 unemployed people in Austria and 300,000 foreigners." In this context it is interesting to note that among those who voted for Haider in 1999, 45 percent are workers and 35 percent are people under thirty — those most likely to lose their jobs or to remain unemployed as immigration continues to rise.

The Freiheitliche ideology is based on a combination of Austrian nationalism, strict law and order, anti-immigration, and conservative social policies. The third chapter of the FPÖ program, entitled "Öster-reich zuerst" (Austria First), explains that the historic and cultural legacy of Austria justifies pride in the achievements and traditions of the country. The ensuing patriotism should lead to self-conscious Austrian politics and to a firm opposition to any denigration of that proud Austrian tradition. The fourth chapter, entitled "Recht auf Heimat" (Right to Home) refers to a specific selection of peoples who are traditionally part of the old Austrian Empire: German, Croatian, Roma, Slovak, Slovenian, Czech, and Hungarian. Only these peoples are considered Austrian and yet have the right to main-tain their cultural identities. A further article in this chapter declares that because of Austria's topography, demography, and scarcity of resources, it cannot be a land of immigration. Finally, multicultural "experiments" are refused because they create social conflicts.

The FPÖ based its 1999 election campaign on the issue of Über-fremdung. Vienna was covered in posters that cried out "Stop For-eignization!" and "Stop Asylum Abuse!" In an intensive countrywide mail campaign, letters were sent to Viennese households warning of the risks of foreign penetration. "Did you know that . . . our children are forced to read entire pages of Turkish and Serbo-Croatian in their German readers? . . . It is only possible in Vienna under the SPÖ that black African applicants for asylum in designer suits toting luxury cell phones can pursue their drug dealing unhindered. . . . The Vienna SPÖ confers Austrian citizenship on thousands of foreigners every year, which entitles them to vote and makes them eligible for public housing." But there's more: "Who cares for our young mothers? Not the SPÖ and ÖVP, because if they did they would not allow the Viennese community kindergartens to be overrun by foreign children." And in conclusion: "We must defend ourselves against an overly quick eastern expansion, since the potential emigration from the east would increase immediately and the consequence thereof would be further foreignization." In other words, now that Communism has fallen, look out for immigration dangers from that part of the world as well.

But let us take a closer look at the country where the "Haider phenomenon" is taking place. Since 1945 there have been 28,000 trials against former Nazis in Austria, and 13,600 of the accused were found guilty. In the process of *Entnazifizierung* (denazification) 70,000 Austrian civil servants lost their jobs, as did 60,000 people working in the private sector. Between 1955 and 1975, of forty-six people accused of Nazi-related crimes, only eighteen were found guilty. In the first half of the year 2000, the number of charges of extreme-right, foreigner-hostile, and anti-Semitic occurrences increased by 48 percent — from 157 charges in the period between January and June 1999 to 232 in the same period of the year 2000. Today, out of every thousand Austrians questioned, 70 percent believe that Austria was responsible for the mass murder of the Jews. Of those over sixty-five years of age, only 56 percent are of this opinion, while 84 percent of those nineteen or younger feel that Austria was responsible. In other words, those who were there are more disinclined to accept responsibility or guilt than those who were not. In the same poll, 83 percent of the Austrians asked confirmed that millions of Jews were killed during NS times, almost 8 percent claim that this fact has not yet been convincingly proven, and 10 percent had no opinion. Sixty percent of the Austrians believe that it is important to continue discussing Nazism so that such events do not happen again. In a press conference in Klagenfurt in 1985, Haider declared, "The FPÖ is not a successor of the NSDAP. Because if it were, then it would have the absolute majority [of votes]." What he was saying, or implying, was that if the FPÖ was more radically right, it would attract even more votes.

When in October 1999 the results of the elections became known, there were several strong reactions both in Austria and around the world. Shimon Peres, the Nobel Peace laureate and former prime minister of Israel, reminded the world that Hitler too had come to power through "democratic means." Nobel Prize winner and Holocaust survivor Elie Wiesel said he would never set foot in Austria again if the FPÖ ever became part of the government. The Israeli government recalled its ambassador, and the United States soon followed suit. For three weeks, thousands of Austrians (mainly students) took to the streets to protest the new coalition government. The Ministry of Social Affairs was occupied by demonstrators who hung a banner from the windows that read: "Wiederstand!" — Resistance.

In January 2000, the European Parliament in Strasbourg judged the FPÖ racist and hostile to foreigners. When the new conservative–right-wing coalition was formally sworn in, the European Union, for the first time in its history, imposed diplomatic sanctions on a member country. All bilateral diplomatic relations between the fourteen EU members and Austria were frozen. No more contacts or ambassadorial meetings were allowed at an intergovernmental level, and when EU international offices were assigned, Austrian candidates were not considered. Only relations of a technical nature were allowed. At the end of that month, Jörg Haider resigned as chairman of the FPÖ, claiming that he did not wish to be seen as the *Schattenkanzler* — shadow chancellor — of the governing coalition. Susanne Riess-Passer took Haider's place at the head of the party and in the government, which assigned five ministries to the FPÖ (Finance, Defense, Justice, Social Affairs, and Infrastructure) as well as the vice chancellorship.

Vice chancellor Susanne Riess-Passer, who is thirty-nine, has been active with the FPÖ for thirteen years and, unlike Haider, has never been known to make debatable statements about National Socialism. For the last three years she has been Haider's closest collaborator. A strong-willed, ambitious woman who never compromises, Susi (as Haider tenderly calls her) has been nicknamed *Königskobra* — King Cobra — by her FPÖ colleagues. This is a nickname she sees as "positive." Though her promotion to head of the FPÖ (making her Haider's superior) was clearly an attempt to distance the party from Haider's international bad-guy reputation, the *Königskobra* feels that "to be described as the female version of Haider is a compliment. For that is how I understand my political line." This young vice chancellor-snake does not seem willing to stray far from her nest.

The EU sanctions and Haider's retirement from the head of his party provoked a series of reactions. As for the sanctions, most Austrians were outraged, feeling this was direct interference on the part of the EU in their country's internal politics. Minority right-wing parties throughout Europe — including Belgium's Vlaams Block, Italy's Northern League, and Switzerland's SVP Party — gave Haider their full support. The Northern League stronghold of Jesolo in Italy gave Haider the honorary key to the city. Yet when Haider visited Venice to promote tourism in Carinthia, hundreds of people pelted him with coins and tomatoes, hung out a banner that read "Haider out," and Venice mayor Paolo Costa said that Mr. Haider was not welcome there.

According to Haider, the sanctions confirmed both his belief that EU membership was undesirable and his oft stated claim of "political exclusion." Haider gained the sympathy of many moderate Austrians who had not voted for him in October but found the EU sanctions unacceptable. With the melodramatic move of renouncing the post of FPÖ chairman (though he remains governor of Carinthia), Haider increased his chances of winning the elections for chancellor. As he himself claimed, "The EU is apparently preparing my political comeback. Because what they are doing brings about an astounding solidarity inside and beyond the Austrian borders."

By July 2000 the EU freeze began to thaw. After a close analysis, as there were as yet no racist laws in place in Austria and the FPÖ had not taken any action to that effect, it was decided sanctions were no longer required or useful. Similar movements, it was noted, had been gaining support throughout Europe over the years and the EU had never found it necessary to intervene.

An example of a similar phenomenon can be found in the recent political history of Italy. Alessandra Mussolini, granddaughter of the fascist dictator and a member of the right-wing party Alleanza Nazionale (AN) — National Alliance (formerly Movimento Sociale — Social Movement — Benito Mussolini's party) — sits, per her request, in her grandfather's seat in parliament. Gianfranco Fini, the chairman of AN, has participated in several governments as part of the coalition with media magnate Silvio Berlusconi. He is a cunning politician who has carefully refrained from making anti-Semitic remarks, but has nevertheless made all sorts of ominous, Haider-like statements, the most notorious being that homosexuals should not be allowed to teach. Umberto Bossi and his separatist Northern League, which has (on and off) been part of Berlusconi and Fini's coalition, is concerned with issues such as immigration, security, and unemployment, often proposing solutions similar to those of the FPÖ. These people have been actively participating in the Italian government for the past ten years without provoking any reaction whatsoever from the EU, or the world.


Many Austrians, and others around the world, tend to minimize the potential impact or danger of the Haider phenomenon. Despite his official resignation as party head, he remains the real power in the FPÖ (as his supporters emphasize). As such, Haider's mistakes affect the whole party, and he is known to often trip and blunder, then try to retract, only to make things worse. What is more, Haider is surrounded by men whose statements are often subject to widespread ridicule, giving the overall impression of a group of provincial lunatics rather than a political party. Most of the absurd statements uttered by the Freiheitlichen provoke incredulous smiles rather than awe. But wasn't that the case in Hitler's early years? "Don't worry," Germans reassured one another, "he's a crazy demagogue, a passing phenomenon. He'll be gone before you know it."

In any event, certain of Haider's statements — and those of his followers — cannot be taken lightly. In 1991, for example, Carinthian cultural adviser and ideologue Andreas Mölzer explained that persecuted peoples such as the Jews and the Armenians knew how to make their adversity a virtue: "Trade and the business of money changing even when currency was replaced by a bottle of vodka or salami, characterized these races so thoroughly that craftsmanship, agriculture or industrial work must seem utterly unnatural to them."

In October 1995, Haider told the *Salzburger Nachrichten* (Salzburg News) that "an Austrian's right to his homeland is stronger than the foreigner's right to live with his family. Therefore we should not follow the European Convention of Human Rights." More recently, on February 3, 2000, in *Die Zeit,* Haider was reported to have said, "All this fuss about being apologetic for the [Nazi] past in the end only stirs up people's emotions and makes them ask why is all this still necessary after so many decades. At some point we have to break free from our past." Reinhard Gaugg, chairman of the FPÖ in Carinthia and vice mayor of Klagenfurt, when asked what the word "Nazi" meant to him, replied, "Nazi? New, attractive, zealous, inventive. It has nothing to do with the past."

Today the FPÖ has only 40,000 members, not much more than it had in the 1980s. However, in a recent poll conducted in January 2000, 33 percent of the 850 people questioned said they would vote for the FPÖ if the national elections were to take place the following Sunday. The Freiheitliche policies as described in the FPÖ program are often simplistic and not likely to work in practice. As for the need to reduce the immigration quota, this is a policy many European parties — not just the FPÖ — have proposed in their platforms today. What is especially worrisome about Haider and the FPÖ is the way they have gained support, the type of feelings they arouse and play with. It is the new millennium and here is a political party, only two generations removed from the long shadow of Adolf Hitler, playing on the same twin fears and feelings that sixty-seven years ago propelled him to power — nationalism and xenophobia. Haider may be no Hitler, but then when Adolf became chancellor in 1933 — again one must recall, through the electoral process — most people had no inkling what he and his policies would ultimately become. Five and a half decades ago, when Hitler in his bunker declared that his death would not end his legacy, who ever would have predicted that the virus would resurface so quickly, and so effectively, in the country of his birth?

# BOOK 6

## PROGNOSIS POSITIVE: THE GENERATION FACTOR

# 30

## SINS OF THE FATHERS

The year is 1992 and Renate Röder, fifty-one, a petite Cologne schoolteacher, soft-spoken and gentle, is displaying her World War II family photos and letters for BBC television from London. A documentary film is in the making. It is called *A Child for Hitler,* and Renate is that child.

Now her mother, a *Hausfrau* over eighty, holds up pictures of Renate's father, the SS general, in uniform, stone-faced, medals and death head emblem blazing. With maternal pride, the mother tells how vividly Renate reminds her of him. The resemblance in appearance, manner, speech, and, above all, in determination — it is all quite uncanny, the mother reports, smiling warmly.

Renate is not smiling. Much of the time she is in tears, obviously feeling branded, greatly upset to be so graphically identified with SS general Friedrich Jeckeln. Because today's Germans generally veil such family skeletons with silence, she has known about her *Vati's* record for only a few years.

The newly gained knowledge took her into fruitless psychotherapy. It caused her to suffer ostracism at her job when she began to lecture her high school students about the Nazis. And it sent her on a tormenting pilgrimage to Jewish Holocaust survivors in Riga, Latvia, where her father, the SS general, was hanged by the Russians before a big crowd in the main square in 1946.

The BBC film researchers are known for their relentlessness, so the hanging scene is shown in the film where she is doing penance now. She is guilty of nothing but her resemblance to her father, yet she feels accused of awful deeds. Has he damned her soul forever? "There must be something evil in me," she said. So Renate went on TV to atone. This shy, fragile teacher is revealing herself to an international audience of millions[1] to ask forgiveness.

Now a book appears on the screen. Called the *Einsatzgruppen* by Helmut Krausnick, it is the history of "Hitler's ideological warriors," the SS mass murder squads. Jeckeln is not a household name — there were too many like him — but he appears in the book, his crimes briefly sketched. As one of SS chief Heinrich Himmler's intimates, he supervised the "liquidation" (that is the official word in the German records) of some 500,000 Jews over his two years of service in the East. The figure brings disbelief, but the details are on record and the numbers add up.

In the last days of September 1941, for example, Jeckeln organized the historic two-day shooting orgy where 33,371 fell into the ravine outside of Babi Yar, near Kiev, in Ukraine. On November 30, he led the murder of 27,000 "deportees" from Berlin and other cities in snowbound pits of the Rumbuli forest outside of Riga. And so on. Eager to prove himself as an up-front role model to his killers, he emptied his pistol into the shivering, naked bodies. At his three-day trial in Riga after the war, he testified, unmoved, unrepentant, "I, Jeckeln, took part in the shootings on three occasions."

Renate uncovered the truth about her father almost imperceptibly. As a little girl, her mother having lied that her adored *Vati* was missing in action, she fantasized that he would return late on any afternoon and stationed herself at the top of the stairs to spot him. When she was fifteen and her mother revealed, without details, that he had been tried and executed, she concluded that he had simply been guilty of holding a high position.

But the family streak of determination — that of Renate and General Jeckeln, too — would not allow her to desist. The search for the father's true self became something of an obsession, and she never

---

[1] The documentary was shown in the U.S. on the Arts and Entertainment Channel.

married. Voraciously, she dug through accounts of the killings in the East, and when she ultimately hit upon the Helmut Krausnick history of the murder squads, with its references to her father, she placed the book in front of her mother, who turned white and cried. Eventually the mother reported that she had read the book but she would say nothing about it.

Further questioning and reading pierced the family silence for Renate. Gradually, her investigations revealed that she had been one of eight children. She was the only one who was illegitimate, her mother having only been a mistress of this bedeviled patriarch, the general. His embrace of the Nazi cause in 1929 had been an escape from family chaos and hated dependency. His first father-in-law had been his employer, and when Jeckeln concluded from a book, *The Sin Against the Blood,* that this benefactor had to be Jewish, divorce brought him relief from "contamination." In his second marriage, he was supported by a wealthy wife.

Her woman therapist tried to tell Renate the obvious: she couldn't possibly be responsible for this dreadful man. It didn't help. The ghost of Adolf Hitler, having energized her father and made him a "success," could not be denied, not by shrugging off accountability.

At her job, Renate's campaign to enlighten her students came under fierce fire from protesting parents. "They said I bring up only the negative side," she reported. "They say there were also good things about Hitler." She was asked to "stop," but the old Jeckeln stubbornness prevailed. "As a teacher, I hope I can bring about a significant change in my students," she said. "This period of history hasn't been dealt with properly. It's still unfinished business."

Frau Röder offered these observations to a Jewish psychologist of her own age with whom she also had much else in common. He was another determined searcher for difficult truth: Dr. Dan Bar-On, professor at the Ben Gurion University of the Negev at Beersheba, Israel. I had first seen them together on the CBS television program *Sixty Minutes,* where Bar-On had brought together a mesmerizing assemblage of Holocaust survivors who did not fit the usual mold. These were gentiles who had not been harmed physically, people like Renate, Martin Bormann, Jr., and a hippie nephew of Reinhard Heydrich, the Gestapo hangman.

Softly, patiently, kindly, the Israeli researcher questioned these descendants from evil about the psychological scars left by their unspeakable fathers. Renate, fighting back tears, was the most thoughtful and appealing of these witnesses, and exceptional in the depth of her remorse.

Dr. Bar-On — reserved, thin as a nail, almost inaudibly soft-spoken — had by then succeeded in opening up fifty-one such sinned-against Nazi offspring. He had been born in Israel five years after his parents arrived as refugees from Hamburg, Germany, where his father had been a physician. Dan's German was fluent, if halting, and he had long been aware of what his German colleagues later came to call "the collective silence." It resembled the inability of many Jewish concentration camp survivors to tell their children how they survived. "It was like covering a volcano with cement," Dr. Bar-On wrote in his empathetic collection of fourteen long interviews with German sons and daughters of genocidals, *Legacy of Silence,* published in 1989.

In 1984, he had entered this minefield of then novel research after he received a nudge toward reconciliation from an Israeli friend, Naomi, a survivor of the Lodz ghetto. "I have no mercy for those who did it to us," she told him, "but I care about ourselves and I am afraid we might have come out of it lacking the human capacities we had before — to hope, to trust, to love."

Providentially, a German professor from the University of Wuppertal dropped in at Dr. Bar-On's university. "What do you think happened to the children of Holocaust perpetrators?" the Israeli asked.

The German professor's wife said, "Let me tell you from my own experience . . ."

Bar-On remembered, "We talked for two more hours. When I returned home, I was upset, yet also stimulated. I felt that I could do it. I could go to Germany."

With the help of his new colleagues at Wuppertal, he advertised for interviewees. Slowly, they came. So did more contacts suggested by twenty-five clergymen and twenty-nine doctors, nurses, and psychotherapists. Bar-On wrote how the conversations began. "I am very angry," he recalled. "I have not yet worked through my own need for revenge. But gradually my anger fades . . ."

The cover-ups in the family histories were pervasive. Two fathers actually bragged at home about what they "accomplished" during the war, including the killing of Jews and partisans and the torching of villages. Generally, however, reactions to the violent past were flat. "We had a perfectly normal family life," was the standard response from the children. "We found that the parents could not provide answers which could help their children develop a healthy moral self," concluded Bar-On's 1988 report. "We move into the future without a real desire to learn from the past."

Indeed, even the worst of the past is worshiped by its children. At least three names with a historic ring still help to keep the Nazi mold vibrant for these days. The daughters of Heinrich Himmler and Hermann Göring and the son of Rudolf Hess have made it clear that they remain proud of their fathers and the beliefs these leaders embraced. To their adoring children, the genocidal fathers did no wrong. They were heroes then and are heroes now.

The daughter of a Prussian Junker family, Dörte von Westernhagen was still striving to come to terms with her father at the age of fifty-one, exactly like Renate Röder. Dörte never knew her father. A colonel in the most elite of the SS units, the *Leibstandarte Adolf Hitler*, Heinz von Westernhagen had died in the final days of World War II.

When I met the daughter in Berlin in 1993, she lived in an almost vacant apartment, was divorced, unemployed, and despondent. Her sad state did not jibe with the elegance and intellectual sophistication of this aristocrat. In fact, von Westernhagen held a law degree and used to work as senior administrative officer in the court system. She surrendered her status in the 1970s to devote herself to a preoccupation that had taken more and more space in her mind: her father's past and her connection with it.

With the zeal of a prosecutor, she searched documents and buttonholed family members, her father's war comrades, and sons and daughters of other old Nazis. She found that Heinz was a very "old fighter," having joined the party in 1932, before Hitler assumed power. Prior to volunteering for combat he served in the national headquarters of the feared SD, the security service, and, at the very least, acquired extensive knowledge of Nazi crimes. His daughter discovered that his officer training took place at Dachau, across the fence from the concentration camp guards. In December 1944, during the Battle of the Bulge, he fought with the *Kampfgruppe Pfeiffer* that massacred seventy-two disarmed American prisoners of war and then moved on at leisurely pace, joking and laughing.

Digging with mounting passion, Dörte interviewed dozens of other descendants of genocidals and wrote one of the first research reports about her own kind. As if describing herself, she concluded, "The postwar generation came to put their parents on trial, pursuing them with rage and hatred, and in doing so became persecutors themselves."

Other children, she found, "learned to avoid touching exposed nerves" and watched helplessly as "the biographies of the parents appeared blurred and disfigured or fraught with lies. Mothers as well as implicated fathers contributed to the psychological deformation of their children."

Like Renate Röder, Dörte had placed herself in psychoanalysis. And like Renate, she gained little self-esteem. "My confrontation with my family's past and that of my country has changed me," she wrote, "but I do not believe that this has made me a better person."

Obviously, Hitler is keeping millions of his children and grandchildren embroiled in psychological chaos. Repression, guilt, accusations, and abuse proliferate and boomerang within these families, as if the guns of World War II went silent only yesterday. Beginning in the 1970s, a small but determined international effort has grown to lift the fog of noncomprehension and provide assistance to victims, by now mostly middle-aged or older, who seek relief.

Laboring at the center of the reformers is an extraordinary professor of psychiatry, a psychoanalyst, officially retired from New York University, Dr. Judith S. Kestenberg of Long Island, New York — eighty-eight years old but exuding the energy and organizing skills of someone decades younger. Child development is her specialty. As founder of the International Study of Organized Persecution of Children, she first established worldwide forums for Jewish child victims of the Holocaust. Then she addressed the emerging need to help the gentile victims, Hitler's children, too — and she quickly uncovered profound similarities and impossible dreams:

"Whereas Jewish children wanted to help their parents reconstitute the people they lost and change history in fantasy, the German younger generation wanted to help their parents repent, not to be Nazis anymore and make good. Neither succeeded in this transposition endeavor."

The quiet that envelops German parents struck her as poisonous. "Their silence is denial, a lie," she told the Children in War Congress at Hamburg in 1993.

She voiced support for the German psychoanalyst Dr. Erich Simenauer, who first spotted the same "persecutor mentality" of second-generation patients that was later displayed by Dörte von Westernhagen. Kestenberg also sided with another German colleague, Dr. George Hardtman, who found that, in turn, "many children felt they had been their parents' Jews" — maligned and persecuted.

The dubious prospects for the psychological liberation of the second post-Holocaust generation of Germans prompted Kestenberg to shift her attention to the third. She did so in 1993 with a unique children's book of drawings and large-lettered German text, *When Your Grandparents Were Young*. "The Germans were good people," it begins, "and were friendly with their neighbors — until the time, when your grandparents were still young, a small, bad man, whose name was Hitler, became their Führer. . . ."

When Kestenberg told an assembly of German psychiatrists that she wanted even small children to absorb the message of the book and her colleagues voiced skepticism, the tiny, white-haired doctor from Long Island instructed them firmly that they were wrong. "The best time to tell the story of one's country is when children begin to ask questions and already have enough words to explain what they are thinking," she said. "This capacity may exist at the age of two and a half. With three year olds it is mature, although often they only ask, 'Why?'"

Wise people like Dr. Kestenberg will not accept "no" for an answer.


Yes, sure, I hear some readers responding as they contemplate the unenviable situation of the trapped Second Generation, but aren't they leaving us, isn't death moving the end within sight? To these optimists I recommend *Murderous Science* (1982), a book by Professor Benno Müller-Hill, a geneticist at Cologne University, that looks not only at surviving criminal academics but their descendants who will be with us for decades to come.

In the course of his teaching, Müller-Hill had found himself handicapped by the postwar "collective silence." A black hole had swallowed the past. The quiet was particularly deafening among psychiatrists, anthropologists, and other scientists who had participated in unconventional experiments. Müller-Hill found that not one had written an autobiography. So he dug through old records and set out to interview survivors, their assistants, and next of kin.

To him, the perpetrators were absolutely "evil," yet, not wishing to add further inhumanity to brutality, he gave his interviewees the right to approve transcripts of their recollections. The results were revealing. All the academics who permitted publication of their approved words claimed they knew nothing about criminal experiments and were not anti-Semitic. But at least eight principals had a change of mind. They told the researcher, often through their lawyers, that they refused to review their notes and wished to hush them up.

One witness who didn't join the scientists' resistance was a lawyer, Helmut von Verschuer, son of Professor Otmar von Verschuer, director of the Kaiser Wilhelm Society for the Advancement of Sciences (he died in 1969). Dr. Joseph Mengele, the most notoriously aggressive of the concentration camp extermination doctors, had been an assistant to the elder von Verschuer and had sent him eyes of murdered Jewish twins from Auschwitz for "research."

The memories of the younger von Verschuer were benign. He told Professor Müller-Hill that he knew Mengele as "a friendly man" who was "called 'Papa Mengele' by the ladies on account of his kindliness." The son defended his father's discreet behavior after the war: "He maintained silence about everything he thought to be slander." People simply don't understand the realities, so the son argued: "Were people aware of the inevitable ambiguity of every action of persons in positions such as his? And are we any more aware of it today?"

"Inevitable ambiguity" and silence were what the son best remembered about his father's practices. Anti-Semitism? "We never spoke about Jews" or "about his party membership," the son said. How about his father's court report condemning a defendant of "racial dishonor"? The son's reply: "Perhaps a co-worker wrote it." What about the eyes of murdered concentration camp inmates? "I can't really form an opinion on this matter since the events weren't known to me at the time and weren't explained to me later by my father."

No word of embarrassment, no regret about Hitler or his works.

My wife, Elaine, and I have a deep emotional stake in rooting out the brotherhood of the genocidal mentality (happily, there are not many sisters). A personal detour is required here to explain how and why we were able to match faces — and at least one name — to the crime. It is a family affair.

In seven years of interviewing, we attempted to identify the genocidal murderers responsible for the deaths of much of Elaine's family, and in our search from Beverly Hills, California, to Montevideo, Uruguay, to Israel, and (twice) into the lonely hills of the most rural Ukraine, we were able to establish closer intimacy with the breed than we had thought possible.

Our core scene was Misocz, Ukraine,[2] some 250 miles southeast of Warsaw, a village still without running water or indoor toilets. Chickens are the principal pedestrians on the central square. My late

---

[2]The town of Misocz has had a checkered geographical past. Before World War I it was Russian; between World War I and World War II it was Polish; after World War II it became part of the Soviet Union. It became part of Ukraine only after the demise of the Soviet Union.

father-in-law, the fiercely proud and energetic Louis (originally Leib) Mazlish, ran away from there to New York as a teenager before World War I, the only member of a large family ever to leave home.

Others were shot by an assembly-line system in a deep ravine in the outskirts, together with all of the town's other 1,200 Jews. The procedure caused them to fall in neat labor-saving layers on top of one another. This was standard practice, we learned, repeated in hundreds of eastern communities. Our village was exceptional only in that we found, at the Yad Vashem archive in Jerusalem, a sequence of five photos documenting the mass murder step by step. In the final picture, Germans are shown wading through the corpses pumping bullets at anything still moving.[3]

The shooters were an SS squad of about fifteen full-time assassins who came in two personnel carriers from provincial headquarters at Rovno, forty-five minutes to the north. Since they were scheduled to massacre the Jews of neighboring Ostrog promptly the next day, they were too hurried to linger long. They did spend the night in the home of Volodymir Silidyev and his wife, with whom we talked.

The Silidyevs remembered watching the soldier-assassins, drunk, taking potshots at peeping children and bolting upright from sleep, evidently stung by nightmares. They particularly recalled one redhead who, with eyes wildly rolling, babbled about the people he had already shot in nearby Korets (home of the Leonard Bernstein family).

The shadowy memories of the Silidyevs were as close as anyone ever came to identifying the Misocz triggermen. They got away with all their crimes; not even one of their names became known to the authorities or to us. We did establish the identity of our killer *Kommando*'s chief: *Obersturmbannführer* Dr. Karl Pütz, thirty-four, a brilliant, good-looking lawyer and prosecutor from Aachen. He dispatched the triggermen to Misocz and neighboring ghettos.

Pütz was a fanatic, the very prototype of the genocidal mentality. Eyewitnesses in Rovno fingered him as no mere *Schreibtischtäter*. He also ordered the execution of a Jewish family whom his wife and daughter had adopted as friends. The wife protested tearfully. Pütz

---

[3]The German orderliness was not infallible. In Uruguay, we found Yankel Mendiuk, who had been covered by his mother's blood but not hit and ran away at nightfall.

could not be moved. Under the New Order, no exceptions could be permitted, he said.

Pütz killed himself with a shot through the temple — not because he was crushed by guilt but because he despaired over the death of his Führer a few days earlier and the failure of his genocidal ideology, the ideal of racial purity, and the rest. So we were told by his daughter, Dagmar, who spent five years, off and on, in mental hospitals trying to cope with the guilt triggered by the sins of her father, triggered in the days when the Führer was on his way to becoming the ruler of the universe.

# 31

## DEAR FATHER, DAMNED FATHER

Dagmar Pütz is a most unlikely Holocaust survivor. She denies the role, doesn't act it or look it, and she isn't Jewish. She has never been near a concentration camp nor been threatened by Nazis. She is an affluent, uncommonly pretty, petite blonde Parisian housewife, cheery and hyperbusy with her family.

And yet, although she speaks French without accent, Dagmar reminds me of a type I knew well, too well, when I grew up Jewish in Berlin. Her bright blue eyes and her demeanor — the abrupt briskness, the surges of energy bursts — suggest the fervor of a Hitler Youth. The impression, though not totally off the facts, is grossly unfair. So what is Dagmar's world, what *is* she truly?

In our first conversation, over the phone, she had told me about the youngest of her three children, Eliza, aged ten, and the little girl's life with Down's syndrome. Dagmar made clear that her entire family is focused, seven days a week and with remarkable success, on the mission of creating as normal and warm an environment as love and money can provide for the incurably handicapped child.

"In my father's time, she would have had to be killed," Dagmar calmly volunteered to me, a stranger, on the phone.

Many conversations and letters later, I detected another, unspoken horror in her assessment of her father, the war criminal. Quite probably, this Nazi fanatic, the sort that academics now call "genocidal personality," would personally have ordered the child killed. Possibly, he would have murdered Eliza himself.

This is no random speculation. Dagmar was four when her father,

SS *Obersturmbannführer* Dr. Karl Pütz, put his service revolver to his temple. Most of what she knew about him had to be elicited in interrogations lasting more than a decade. The clues to her identity were dropped in sparse fragments in the course of ruminations by her mother, Maria, known as Mia. One evening when Dagmar was in her teens, her persistent questioning yielded a particularly telling reminiscence.

It was during World War II in German-occupied Poland. As representatives of the Nazi rulers, the Pütz family of Aachen, in westernmost Germany, was settled in a comfortable requisitioned city house. Another local family lived close by, possibly in the same premises. When Dagmar first relayed the event to me, she called these neighbors "friends." Later, she speculated that they may have been brought around to help with the housekeeping. She was certain that they were Jews and that they had a child who indeed became her friend, a playmate.

One day her little pal was gone. Dagmar could not recall what questions she asked about the disappearance at the time, but, in the dialogue with her mother when she was growing up, Mia revealed that the Jewish family had been taken away to be killed. Mia had been horrified and had exploded at her husband, Karl, with unaccustomed vehemence.

"She pleaded for these people," Dagmar reported. "It was not right that they were taken."

Dr. Pütz would hear none of that. "My father said nobody could be spared," Dagmar told me. "It had to be for the good of humanity."

When Mia continued to protest, her husband responded with a long, impassioned prosecutor's writ arguing that the necessity was indisputable: all Jews had to be eliminated to ensure the purity of the German race. His eloquence, then and on other occasions, left the mother literally "speechless," too tongue-tied to press her own case for mercy.

"He could talk and talk and talk and make you see that black is white," Dagmar said, "and that no exceptions could be made."

She reported this to me in a tone of bemusement, conveying simultaneous admiration and strong disapproval, and her ambivalence did not seem unreasonable. There was something satisfying about being the daughter of a brilliant advocate, even if his brain worked for unspeakable ends.

I asked whether her mother had seemed troubled because she lost her argument on behalf of the Jewish friends. Dagmar didn't think so. Did it strain her parents' marriage that the father had friends slaughtered for impersonal ideological reasons? Dagmar could cite no evidence of such an aftermath. Long after the event, her mother still acted helpless at the husband's dazzling gifts.

The impression that the father left with both women was of a masterful barrister acting out immutable convictions on behalf of his life's idolized client and leader, the Führer. If Hitler had ruled that the earth was flat, Dr. Pütz could not have argued otherwise.

"Hitler was like a Messiah for him," said Dagmar.


This daughter is indeed a Holocaust survivor. And there are hundreds like her, German children, now middle-aged, whose fathers committed mass murders and other unspeakable crimes on behalf of Hitler. Millions more of these innocents were fathered by rank-and-file Nazi activists. Almost all these offspring are haunted to some degree by shame and dread of their heritage. *Born Guilty* was the apt title of a book suggesting the taint carried through life by these contemporary victims of the Führer, their suffering largely ignored for half a century.

The weight of this widespread psychological torment is still in the process of coming to light, and the reaction of the victims is enormously diverse. Some silence their memories by suppressing them. Some deny them angrily. Some seek absolution by invoking the distance of time and place. Some try to ignore the past, especially if the details of parental crimes were hushed up or kept murky.

For the more sensitive descendants, such ostrich defenses settle nothing. These survivors remain perpetual underachievers. They dodge marriage, cannot maintain loving relationships, much less bear the thought of giving birth to children. They seek help from psychiatrists or from sedatives, take flight in depression or suicide. Many carry on stoically, sleeplessly, sometimes on the brink of madness, especially if they are afflicted by a dreaded family name like Heydrich. Martin Bormann, Jr., insulated himself through religious conversion. Others, including those named Himmler, Göring, and Hess, hide behind walls of self-righteousness, the drawbridges closed shut.

Inner tumult remains endemic even among the anonymous. The self-questioning forms a litany. How could a father, any father, my father, ever, ever perpetrate such acts? Is his guilt so indelible that it has become mine as well? Is it perhaps rooted in the genes and trans-ferable? Must it be exorcised somehow? Was my father a monster? Must I hate him? Can he be somehow pardoned? Should he be excused? Forgiven? Accepted? Perhaps even loved?

Dagmar's emergence from this whirlpool of emotions is excep-tional. Now in her sixties, she is fully functional, happy in marriage and motherhood, her small, alert face almost as unlined as a teenager's. She alone has been responsible for her liberation and she does not con-sider herself a victim. Her outcome is the result of insight, courage, resilience, and an old-fashioned quality called goodness. It is some-thing of a wonder, a triumph of sanity over demons. I see Dagmar as a quadriplegic who willed herself to walk.

Her journey took nearly half a lifetime — an evolutionary self-rescue progressing in stages that unreeled in excruciating slow motion. It required, first of all, more than a decade before the full force of her father's sins merely became clear in her mind; then fol-lowed another twenty years of denial and descent into an abyss of breakdown, near-suicide, and extended mental illness; she needed additional years for painful recovery, and finally, for mature search into the meaning — and the cause — of her father's evil, for release that is almost, though not yet entirely, complete.

For about the first thirty-five years of her life, then, Dagmar was torn by a war within herself, a quest for her father's self, his divided identity. She articulated the paradox for me precisely: "On one side a wonder-ful, generous, brilliant young man and on the other side a criminal, a monster, an evil person. I had to find the key to this mystery."

How could Pütz be called *wonderful?*

"When I was a child, my father was everything," Dagmar recalled. The memories were few and dim but happy. There was her father on all fours, whooping as he played hide-and-seek with her on the floor. She could also hear him talking to subordinates in his office, Dagmar peeking from outside through a gap under the closed door.

She was spotted in her eavesdropping, whereupon her father and his colleagues took her into his private office and they all laughed because she was such a persistent little spy. They joshed playfully with her, making her feel pleased to have penetrated Daddy's domain, the heart of Gestapo headquarters when he was boss, dreaded by all but a few select insiders, of whom she had become one, on that occasion, childishly and fleetingly.

Dagmar believes deeply in life after death, so after she survived a total collapse in the 1970s she set herself a stark dual task for the second, adult phase of her discoveries about herself and her father. "I felt my duty was to liberate him," she told Elaine and me. "How could I help him to find peace?" Only if she succeeded would she be freed of him.

Though dead nearly half a century, the loved and accursed father is yet with her in something eerily close to physical state. Many years after the war, the Red Cross sent her mother his official death photograph. He is in SS uniform, his eyes open, his face perhaps at peace, perhaps searching — Dagmar could never decide. Blood dribbles from a small wound in his left temple.

Appalled, Dagmar burned the rolled-up picture after her mother passed away, relieved by the belief that she had finally wiped out this last palpable evidence of hate and violence incarnate. Then, shortly thereafter, another Nazi in the family, the authoritarian Aunt Else, died, she who had taken over much of Dagmar's upbringing when her mother, Mia, kept the clan going by working extra long hours. A cousin sorted through Aunt Else's belongings and handed Dagmar an envelope. Her heart stopped. Here it was again, another copy of the damned and shameful photo, the eerie reminder of the collision within herself.

When Elaine and I last left Dagmar several summers ago during her family vacation in the French Alps, she was making plans to destroy the ubiquitous heirloom once again, this time in a formal ceremony. By now, this event has doubtless taken place.

Elaine was participating in the encounters with Dagmar because she is, by happenstance, our living link to *Obersturmbannführer* Dr. Pütz. By phenomenal coincidence, he was responsible for the death of her grandmother and eight other close relatives in October 1942.

As commander in Rovno, Ukraine, of the SD, the elite *Sicherheitsdienst,* the intelligence arm of the SS, he was in charge of executing a secret and explicitly defined top-level assignment: the elimination of the region's remaining 70,000 Jews. We possess documentary evidence showing that the order was signed by Hitler personally.

We had also succeeded in reconstructing the wartime career of our family's killer in some detail. Surviving German colleagues had testified that he was an "unforgettable" personality, brilliant, obsessed with carrying out Hitler's Final Solution, often seen drunk, but long enough sober to push his mission with fanatical hands-on zeal.

Our family had been a speck in his day's work. Actually, they had been ciphers in a three-day sweep, October 12 to 14. We could never verify that he went along on this assignment — perhaps it was too trivial a sideshow — but within seventy-two hours three small villages, Misocz, Zdolbunov, and Ostrog, were efficiently "cleansed" of Jews. The killers ordered every Jewish man, woman, and child to disrobe and lie facedown in a ravine to be shot in the neck. The next victim was commanded to lie down on top of the corpses. The sequence in Misocz is documented in very clear photographs. The close-knot bloody stack of bodies from that village accounted for an estimated 1,500 targets, and Misocz was *our* town.

Elaine had not looked forward to meeting the killer's daughter. Understandably, she had wanted to keep her distance. While Dagmar was hardly to be treated as a guilty party, Elaine had illogically expected her to be somehow contaminated by her father's genes, his hatred. Instead, my wife's apprehensions melted almost on sight under Dagmar's smile and embrace. No trace of hate was detectable in this still girlish, lean witness to the Hitler legacy. The face was unclouded.

No trace of suffering was evident. Her movements were generally without restraint; she darted about birdlike, quick and free.

Her bubbly and exuberant speech conveyed tension, outright nervousness at times. We registered a sense of control, occasional hesitations that suggested she was choosing her words with utmost care, almost a self-censorship. Sometimes she stopped as if startled like a deer caught in a headlight, as if to ask, "Who, me?"

As our acquaintance deepened, her overall softness, openness, and astonishing lack of inhibitions would confirm: there was no hate here and nothing *to* hate. The word LOVE emblazoned in capital letters on her gold choker was no shibboleth. It was a statement, a considered reversal of her father's ruling four-letter passion, HATE. Dagmar uses "love" often in conversation and letters. Ingenuous or not, it is the commandment she lives by.

During our research in dust-poor Misocz and its forgotten hinterlands in 1989 and 1992, three weeks in all, I had come to identify Elaine's family more than ever as my own as well. I had known my late father-in-law as a somewhat formal, immaculately turned-out successful New York entrepreneur of dignified and conservative habits. The "ifs" implicit in his departure from Misocz all by himself, in 1914 at the age of sixteen, were awesome: if he hadn't run away from home . . . if he hadn't made it to New York . . . if he hadn't happened to meet my mother-in-law there...who knows whom I would have married? To think that his daughter might have ended stacked in those bodies at Misocz . . .

Some memories require no interpretation: the facts speak for themselves. Dagmar's mother was an unquestioning Hitler supporter, working for the Nazi civil service when she married Dr. Karl Pütz in 1939, the year World War II began. She was a secretary in the Cologne city hall. He was twenty-eight, a promising lawyer and head of the feared SD in nearby Düsseldorf.

The script is plain, but while Dagmar's recall about her personal life is stunning, the gaps in her historical inventory are extraordinary.

Some may be self-induced to reinforce remnants of her armor, her innocence when she was very young, self-protective techniques known to psychologists as avoidance behavior and coping mechanisms.

The earliest missing links reach back to her hometown and that of her father, Aachen, where she returns several times each year to visit family. What Dagmar, college-educated, doesn't know about her city is notable. Although less than twenty-five miles from the Belgian border and once known as Aix-la-Chapelle, this cosmopolitan center, while never a Nazi stronghold because its population is predominantly Roman Catholic, had fallen into the hands of a few fanatics. I was stationed near there during the war and remember the frustration and vain efforts by several of my colleagues to get the place to surrender before it was bombed to pieces. After the war, "werewolves" assassinated Aachen's American-appointed mayor, a unique event.

Dagmar knew none of this, and when I appointed myself to be her history coach and informed her of her background, she smiled in gentle astonishment, receiving the belated news with interest but considerable detachment. I was telling her about antecedents as remote as Charlemagne.

Her memory of her father's career is likewise limited. She has absorbed numerous books about Hitler and the Holocaust but tries to maintain a distance from what she considers excessive and needless detail. "I am not interested in finding more historical facts of the horrors of the Holocaust because digging in the horrors only feeds the flame of hate." So she had written me in one of her early letters. She does inform acquaintances of her father's guilt, but almost never more than the euphemism "He was involved in Nazi war crimes."

At one point she told me more: "I'm not interested whether he killed a hundred or thousands. I'm interested in *why*."

As further example of her selective sweep across the Nazi period, I discovered that she had simply never heard of the infamous Julius Streicher, hanged as a war criminal following his conviction at the Nuremberg trials, or of his pornographic Jew-baiting weekly, *Der Stürmer*.

Of course she knows that her father, Karl, was born in 1911, the son of Peter Pütz, a ranking civil servant, chief postal inspector, and that

Karl received his Ph.D. in jurisprudence from the nearby University of Cologne in 1934. She had, however, kept away from his readily available doctoral dissertation. I sent it to her and she was relieved that it was a skillful but dull technical treatise about real estate law.

Equally accessible — yet also unknown to her — was her father's Nazi personnel file. It told of her parents' marriage and Dagmar's birth in 1941. The father's party history was less conventional. He joined the Nazis very early — on May 1, 1933 to be precise — very shortly after Hitler assumed power, and went to work for the local SD as a full-time operative in the agency's infancy, during 1937.

"Despite much resistance, he built it up into a hard-hitting instrument," says the party record.

Dagmar had never heard of Rovno until I mentioned the city. She does recall summer heat so intense that her mother stuck her in the bathtub to cool off. As an adult, her research never led her as far as the open files of the Zentrale Stelle in Ludwigsburg, near Stuttgart, where I had found the graphic testimony of her father screaming with religious fervor as he led wholesale executions, sometimes stepping across bloody corpses littering the streets.

Dagmar had convinced herself that her father officiated as an ideologue and *Schreibtischtäter* ("desk perpetrator"), above the gore. "He knew all that was going on," she told me, but she believed that he dealt with death at second hand. "He was like a *Gauleiter,* she said, "directing, giving orders." I did not have the heart to inform her otherwise.

Of her father's final days Dagmar retains fragments, mostly of a fearful scene she draws partly from her own memory, partly from the received recollections of her mother. It was May 1945. The family was at an inn, passing hurriedly through the Black Forest, retreating from the father's last post in the undamaged luxury spa Baden-Baden.

Hitler had killed himself a few days earlier. The father announced he would do the same.

Dagmar heard him say this, but at that point she was discovered hiding behind a curtain and sent from the room. Her mother much later recalled having kept on pleading with her husband, by then thoroughly distraught. He should flee across the nearby border to Switzerland, she shouted at him, move on to South America, escape, save his hide as so many *Parteigenossen* were doing at that very moment!

The mother remembered that her husband was adamant about not wishing for escape, and she reported why he could no longer face living. Dagmar said, "She told me it was more than having lost [the war]. That was not the real reason. It was the enormity of the wrong that had been done. His whole belief [system] collapsed." He was overwhelmed by remorse — or so Dagmar had convinced herself.

Dagmar was told he was missing in action, a hero, and his death was kept mysterious until she was in her teens.

Her memories suddenly turned vivid with her account of herself as a victim of the war in its last days. She was perched atop a handcart pulled by her newly widowed mother and her aunt Else. They were without shoes, fleeing south, escaping toward the Swiss border from the attacking French troops. Straining to pull over the 5,000-foot Feldberg, her mother failed to feel that the strap of the money belt around her waist had broken; all the family's resources were lost. They piled onto a bus. A dive-bomber strafed it as it crossed a bridge, and it burst into flames.

"We got out of the bus with nothing," Dagmar said, "and my mother lay on top of me. I see the face of the pilot . . ."

The family settled in a suburb of Aachen and Dagmar became sickly. For months she was hospitalized with diphtheria, and its after-effects left her long unable to speak. In school she was bright but phobic and hyperactive: "I couldn't sit still."

At home she became a rebel. "I was wild, nobody could handle me," she said. "Aunt Else came after me with a broom." She was desperate for a dog, but Aunt Else, the family's other ardent Nazi, refused: "Too dirty." Dagmar ran away repeatedly, a day at a time. Locked in her room as punishment, she held lengthy conversations with the pets she hid in a kerchief. They were worms, destined to become bait. "They were my dolls," Dagmar said. It is graphic evidence of her sensitivity and inner resources.

Her repressive home failed to get her down. Rather, it made her an exuberant escape artist. "With my scarf blowing in the wind I thought, I'm an angel," she said. "I created my own world." It was an early success at what she does best: liberating herself from repression.

At seventeen she escaped to live with a relative in London and became a nurse assistant. Aunt Else disapproved. Nurses were not good enough. But Dagmar loved the dirty work: "I felt I was able to help, to respond to suffering." (This is another fascinating coping mechanism. It parallels the predominant life choice of the so-called Second Generation Holocaust survivors, the sons and daughters of concentration camp victims. They, too, tend to become attracted to social work, teaching, psychotherapy, and other "helping professions.")

At eighteen, Dagmar drifted to Paris for a year, despite the fact that Germans and their accents were often not welcome in formerly Nazi-occupied countries during the 1950s. What persuaded her to seek out "enemy" territory? Probably the same quality that ultimately made her whole again. She hoped to train as an airline stewardess, but was rejected as too young and became a waitress.

At nineteen, she went back to Aachen to finish school, returning at twenty-one to her present hometown, Paris. This time she made the scene as a fashion model and a chaotically addictive personality. The slowly assembled knowledge of her past was beginning to make an impact on her present.

Modeling was enjoyable, easy, and earned her so much that she could live for three weeks by working a single day. Freedom exacted its price, however. She smoked three to four packs of cigarettes a day until her lungs threatened to give up. She drank — any hard liquor would do — until the doctor warned that her liver was endangered. She went on pot, even tried LSD. "I was completely addicted," she recognizes now.

While looking for a new apartment, she was introduced to one of her neighbors in Montmartre, a rock singer I shall call "Robert" (since I promised the couple anonymity). They dated for three years — initially, Dagmar claims, because she had gone on the wagon and Robert was the lone person of her acquaintance who didn't drink. Dagmar and Robert ultimately married and had two sons, the elder of which is now a commercial airline pilot. Today Robert is a successful and highly regarded composer and musician.

\*　　　\*　　　\*

Dagmar kept pressing her cross-examinations about her father, off and on, until firsthand information was shut off by her mother's unexpected death at fifty-eight in 1974. For the daughter of Karl Pütz, the SS executioner, that was the year of the ultimate descent. Her old questions remained in ferment: Was her father adrift in the sea of the damned who could find no peace in the hereafter? And why, oh why, had he turned so possessed, so perverted, so crazily consumed with fulfilling the Final Solution?

Dagmar never articulated the extreme degree of the father's fervor, but our conversations made obvious that she realized perfectly well: he was no stereotypical Nazi. Some of the prime war criminals hanged at Nuremberg came to judgment with hands less bloody than his.

With Mia gone, Dagmar decided that she had only herself to talk to about her festering questions concerning her father, and these introspections plunged her, at unpredictable intervals, into four years of mental illness. At first she tried to treat herself, mostly by endlessly practicing yoga and transcendental meditation. The TM rules called for twenty-minute sessions. Compulsively she lost herself in self-induced catatonic spells for two hours at a stretch. "I wanted results," she says with some vehemence. "I suppose at some point perhaps I wouldn't have come back."

Robert was severely shaken. His pretty wife did nothing around the house. She neglected the children and sat withdrawn on the floor in a corner, meditating or crying.

That summer of 1974, while on vacation with Robert's family in Nice, his hometown on the Riviera, Dagmar became extremely agitated and had wild paranoid hallucinations. "I felt I couldn't breathe, I was in water; I thought I was drowning." But sleep deprivation was her worst symptom.

"I didn't sleep, I was like on speed," she says. Robert took her to a psychiatric hospital. "I was manic, I felt on top of the world," Dagmar says, "they just couldn't put me to sleep." Eventually, she did sleep for the better part of six weeks, thanks to extremely high dosages of sedatives. Discharged, she felt calm, empty, lost: "I looked like a hundred years old."

The doctors said she was manic-depressive and schizophrenic. The diagnosis was lost on her. She cannot recall talking to any doctors, cannot remember their names, faces, or anything else about anyone who treated her — and she is unaware of taking any medications except the sedatives.

The next time, her psyche snapped at home in Paris. By then, Robert could discern when confinement should become mandatory. Because of quirky French laws, he drove three hundred-plus miles with her by ambulance to Aachen for more weeks of hospitalization — a fascinating coincidence: returning to the source of illness for cure. Again she suffered horrifying visions, again she now claims to remember almost nothing of her treatment.

She recalls talking about her father to her — again faceless — doctors, though she cannot so far bring to mind what she may have disclosed about his heinous crimes or her continuing preoccupation with his fate.

Although Robert employed household and child care help, he became increasingly stressed at the necessity to be mother as well as father to his sons and the worry of whether Dagmar would ever be well again. "Friends said, 'Why don't you get rid of this burden,'" Dagmar recalled, "but Robert stuck with me." On the other hand, he could not be expected to withstand permanently the strains caused by an invalided spouse. I have not yet had the opportunity to talk to this very friendly and receptive husband about any of this.

Dagmar's final acute ordeal overcame her in 1977 while she was staying with an aunt in London. "It started the way it always started," she reports. "I couldn't sleep and I cried and cried. I could tell I was in trouble. I was shaking, I was suicidal."

This time she was determined to stay out of hospitals and pull herself out of her dysfunctional state on her own. "Psychiatry had not helped me," she insists, ignoring that her ego — her stubbornness? — had barred her from giving psychotherapy a chance. She stopped taking prescribed medication, and, unlike quite a few descendants of culpable Nazis, she never entered treatment while she was functional.

As Dagmar's breakdown in London progressed, she experienced what appeared to her as an actual conversation with her father. "He was with me," she reports. "I asked him about his guilt, and he said, 'I have regrets and I cannot find peace.' I told him I loved him and forgave him. This is when the burden came off my shoulders. When I finally could forgive him, I was cured."

Yet, as I will show below, some burden, in vastly reduced form, still clings. And the psychotic episode in London ended only after a near-disastrous turn.

Dagmar heard voices shout, "Get out! Get out! The house is on fire!" These voices were real, although the house fortunately was not burning, merely smoky and at risk. In her need to exculpate, to expunge the spirits besetting her father after so many years, to liberate him at last, she had dashed into the garden and set fire to whatever pictures she could quickly snatch up in the house. Pictures represented the intolerable past.

Her hostess remained supportive, her agitation passed, and help was on the way. At a London gathering she had met an unconventional therapist, Dr. Richard Alpert, author of *Be Here Now*. He had recommended that she seek out the spiritual counsel of a famous Indian guru, Meher Baba, who had died in 1969 after maintaining silence for forty-four years. His disciples were keeping his teachings alive in a pilgrimage center built around his tomb, where "Baba lovers" still flock by the thousands from all over the world.

Dagmar had been given a smiling photo of Meher Baba — the name, eloquently to her, means "benevolent father" — and she had tucked it into the frame of the mirror in her room. His artless gospel, the mantra-like slogan of the elementary sort so common for hundreds of Indian gurus, held immense appeal for her. It remains her "open-sesame" to inner peace, no less. "Don't worry, be happy!" was Meher Baba's overarching and magical directive for a liberated life. Simplistic? Certainly. For Dagmar it carried the power of Dr. Ehrlich's magic bullet.

Dagmar regards the late Meher Baba as her daily healer and savior. Since 1977 she has traveled to his tomb at Ahmadnagar, in the hills about 125 miles east of Bombay, at least once a year, and describes her encounters glowingly.

"When I went to the tomb," she says, "that was Home with a big 'H.'"

Robert is accepting. Initially, he had distrusted his wife's conversion to mysticism. On the basis of rationality, he brought the same skepticism to cult worship as I do. "He couldn't handle spirituality," Dagmar says. His attitude turned, however, when the effect on his wife became visible and evidently permanent. She is serene and has known no emotional crises since she burned the photos in 1977.

Finally at peace, the couple decided to have another child, and Eliza, the hoped-for daughter, was born in 1983. Her mongoloid features were emblematic, perhaps even more than heartache, of renewed punishment for the sins of Karl Pütz.

"The doctor said, 'Just forget about this child,'" Dagmar reports. This was standard medical advice given to parents of children with Down's syndrome.

Eliza was placed in the finest special Paris nursing home, and three months later came desperate news. "She refused to eat," says Dagmar, "she was dying." Dagmar and Robert rushed to the home and were devastated. "She was brown like a shrunken apple," Dagmar remembers, but Meher Baba had taught her the answer: "She needed love! We took her home and just cured her with love. She made me fall in love with her."

To love Eliza required, first, to reach her. Dagmar's doctors and nurses were appalled at the way this mother applied her mothering instincts. She spoke to her daughter in German, and she still does so, much of the time. "You can't do that!" she was told. "You'll confuse her terribly."

Dagmar refused to be dissuaded. She told me that after thirty years in France and notwithstanding her perfect command of French and English, she still felt she was German.

I found this somewhat odd, because Dagmar conducts herself as an international citizen, if there ever was one. So this self-label needs considerable probing. Is it a generalized loyalty to birth ("This above all, to thine own self be true . . .")? Is it a loving wish not to desert the father who has no other defenders left? Or what? Home is where the heart is, yes, and in German the word *Heimat,* which I have yet to discuss with Dagmar, has unusually evocative connotations.

I find it difficult to see her as a true citizen of Aachen, where some years ago I spent a week, but the issue of "belonging" requires airing. I face it whenever a stranger asks about my past and then says, "So you're a Berliner!" Well, yes and no . . .

At any rate, being Eliza's mother, why shouldn't Dagmar talk to her in her own *Muttersprache,* her mother tongue? There is no such word as *Vatersprache,* or father tongue, and I have not yet dared to ask Dagmar whether she would feel differently about speaking German if the term existed.

As a result of her mother's unconventional decision, Eliza manages nicely in German, French, and, to a lesser degree, in English.

She was three years old when a friend told Dagmar and Robert of a television film about a fascinating scientist, Dr. Glenn Doman, who might be able to help the retarded child. The Pütz family investigated, and, annually for four years until 1990, they took Eliza for a week's training with Doman at his institute in Chestnut Hill, outside Philadelphia.

Doman coaxes remarkable (if necessarily limited) advancement from children who were, for whatever reason, given up as more or less hopelessly retarded. He pioneered with persistently — even insistently — applied physical exercises, especially creeping and developing the muscles of the hands. Since he started out, the concept that exercise stimulates brain development, even in the very young, has been validated elsewhere.

My wife and I observed Eliza playing and reading with Dagmar in German, doing homework with Robert in French, joshing with us in English, and whooping off to activities with children who are well: to a trampoline contest, a picnic for painted-up "Indians," a sleep-out camping expedition. She truly is a love child, obviously secure, happy, eager to learn, and attends age-appropriate classes for children who have speech problems only.

"She is a gift," Dagmar says. "She has given us so much more than what is lacking. She understands through the heart."

While some parents of Down's syndrome children still tend to institutionalize them or to keep them hidden in shame, Eliza gets taken most anywhere, even India, and is clearly thriving on all the attention and warmth of so much human contact. From age three to seven, her training, programmed by Doman, was arduous. She would run for an hour a day and managed thirty trips along the horizontal ladders that dominate the child-friendly clutter of the living rooms in both of the family's penthouse homes: in Paris and in a resort, facing the 8,000-foot French and Italian Alps.

Ten years ago, the family's pilgrimages to Chestnut Hill ceased. Dagmar and Robert accepted that Eliza is susceptible to infections, her life span is uncertain. "That's why we stopped," Dagmar explains. "We want her to have a normal life, to enjoy, not to be pushed."


Dagmar's searches for answers about her father, for the why of his obsession, calmed but also intensified in recent years. A trip to his rural grave and interviews with the farmers who found his body yielded no clues. Neither did conferences with Frédéric Lionel, an aged and distinguished French investigator of Nazi "black magic." I have yet to question Dagmar about the circumstances that led her to this sociologist and about the give-and-take of her several conversations, the questions that he asked about her father and the data she gave him. I gathered that it was Lionel who directed her to the occult for explanations of the father's fury, much as she had turned to Meher Baba in search of inner peace. And her line of inquiry gained momentum when, during one of her trips to London, she met a British historian, Trevor Ravenscroft.

His book, *The Spear of Destiny,* published in 1972, proposed elaborate fresh theories about Hitler's manipulations of the occult. Given the serenity that Dagmar derived from her flight into the mysticism of Meher Baba, she seized gratefully upon Ravenscroft's intricate and fanciful notions and concluded, "Hitler practiced a form of black magic on my father."

All members of the SS, but especially insiders like Pütz and other bright young disciples of ambition who were promoted rapidly and entrusted with executive responsibilities requiring tunnel vision and merciless brutality, were driven by the Nazi hierarchy to become adherents of the occult. The Nazi movement was drenched in these macabre, otherworldly beliefs. They were integral to the environment. A four-volume series of documentary video tapes is devoted to *The Occult History of the Third Reich,* and a large literature on the subject exists.

For the purposes of this summary, the following should suffice. While Ravenscroft's speculations have been discredited, the influence of "Ariosophy" and its fanatically anti-Semitic pushers, especially Dietrich Eckart, Hitler's principal early intellectual mentor, has been reliably researched.

A solid work by another British historian, Nicholas Goodrick-Clarke, *The Occult Roots of Nazism* (1992), uncovered investigations of occult phenomena by the SS in the very area of the Black Forest where the SS fanatic Pütz killed himself.

The occult was a hobby also avidly pursued by Pütz's boss, SS chief Heinrich Himmler, who liked to interfere with the personal lives of his men in astonishing detail.

Himmler was a relentless letter writer. At the height of assisting in the administration of a losing total war, he was still dispatching long notes to his followers counseling them about the management of their girlfriends. Pütz's spiritual link to Himmler must be taken for granted; it was part of the SS covenant.

More light was shed on Pütz's enthrallment by an old secretary of his in Cologne, whom Dagmar visited for the first time. And I interviewed Father Paul Mackels, an eighty-two-year-old retired priest I discovered in Aachen, who had attended school with Pütz from 1920 to 1929 and remembered him as a happy, puckish kid. Mackels had recollections of visits to the Pütz home, and reported that Pütz's mother was ardently religious and hoped that her son would become a priest. Father Mackels pointed out that Pütz's formal break with the Catholic Church virtually coincided with his entry into the Gestapo. Sometimes such desertions triggered radical personality changes in Nazi disciples. Pütz also compelled his wife to leave the church.

In a fervently Catholic city like Aachen, the import of loyalty and disloyalty to the church can hardly be overestimated. I have a secret 1935 internal morale report by the head of the Aachen Gestapo to his chiefs in Berlin complaining in the strongest terms about the ideological foot-dragging of the locals, especially the clergy. There can be no doubt that Pütz's decision to turn away from his mother, and from the Mother Church, strengthened his Nazi zealotry to a powerful degree, probably crucially.

*    *    *

"His bible was Goethe's *Faust*," Dagmar told me, and so I introduced her to the ideas of my psychiatrist friend and occasional adviser, Dr. Robert Jay Lifton, especially on transcendence ("a psychic state so intense that time and death disappear") and on "doubling," the Faustian bargain that divides the self into two functioning wholes, good and evil. Dagmar has given me pages from her father's copy of *Faust* with his handwritten annotations. One such passage, which Lifton independently cites as meaningful, reads, "Two souls, alas, reside within my breast/and each withdraws from and repels its brother."

# 32

## NEW HOPE FOR DACHAU

I feared it would be rude of me to ask Sybille Steinbacher for her weight or her waist size. Such personal data would not have been uncalled for, however. Steinbacher, a woman in her early thirties, is a professional historian who grew up near Dachau in Bavaria. She is such a tiny wisp of a woman that she comes close to being unnoticeable.

Back in 1994, however, she had become very noticeable indeed. With one stroke of research as precise as brain surgery, her book *Dachau: The Town and the Concentration Camp* succeeded for the first time in stripping away half a century of historical cover-up. The cozy kinship linking the first Nazi murder camp with its civilian neighbors, professing ignorance three miles down the road, was finally laid out beyond denial.

"Fairytale Time Is over for Dachau," said a headline in the leading newspaper of nearby Munich.

Even as fairytales go, the cocoon of lies that the Dachauers had woven around themselves defied facts that were hard to wish away. Starting in 1933, considerably more than 32,000 innocent people died in the camp next door; a full count was never possible.[1] The smoke from the crematoria stank to the heavens. Here was the model for all of Hitler's murder factories, the training place for almost all the commandants of the other killing grounds.

---

[1]That number indicates those who "officially died" at Dachau; that is, the figures taken from the camp registers. That figure is clearly but a fraction of those who were killed there, including many thousands of Russian POWs summarily executed — or beaten to death — upon or shortly after their arrival.

And yet, three years after the camp was liberated, Franz Klug, the town's party chairman, still insisted before his denazification trial board, "Until this day I don't know what happened there." Indifference and fear made them withdraw from reality, so said the citizens, over and over, when questioned by the many interviewers who descended upon Dachau over the decades without ever learning much of the truth about the people who called it home.

"It's as in a family that has a mental case," explained a television commentator. "Everybody knows about it but it's not talked about."

When the prodding for truth would not subside, the Dachauers felt increasingly indignant, indeed libeled, by the deathly reputation that had made the name of their picturesque hometown synonymous with genocide. And over the years their defenses grew more and more elaborate.

Stories made the rounds that the citizenry had been against the establishment of a concentration camp on the edge of town in 1933; that the camp was not really part of Dachau but of Prittlbach and should have been named after that neighboring village to erase the stain on innocent Dachau; that the subsequent incorporation of the camp within the Dachau city limits had been opposed by the town authorities; that Dachau was saved from sacking by American troops because of a heroic appeal of the town priest on bended knee.

As Sybille Steinbacher long suspected — but couldn't prove while she was still studying history at her university in Munich, twelve miles away — these all were inventions. Indeed, the priest proved to have been about the most duplicitous of the collaborators.

The lies made her angry. "I disliked the hypocrisy," she told me in her Bavarian accent, less guttural than most. "It was intolerable." And so her book was born of a logical hypothesis: Unlike Auschwitz in rural Poland, the Dachau camp was so accessible, so closely adjacent to a sizable, educated metropolitan area, that citizens could not possibly have remained ignorant of its evil.

The Dachau officials were less than enthusiastic about Steinbacher's enterprise. The city archivist suggested that she investigate the Thirty Years War instead. Steinbacher was not surprised. As far back as 1985, Lord Mayor Lorenz Reitmeister, protesting Dachau's odious reputation, went beyond the usual claim that his townspeople had seen no evil and heard no evil. He lamented that they were victims, "a minority persecuted by defamation."

The mayor was by no means oblivious to the crimes committed at Dachau, and certainly he was no Holocaust denier. Having been elected in 1966 by a thin margin of 240 votes, he focused his efforts as townsfather on destigmatizing his constituents by struggling to replace their KZ image with the pastoral memory of the nineteenth-century Dachau artists' colony. That his platform paid off well is shown by the fact that he was reelected again and again for the next quarter century. In the 1990 elections, he won by an overwhelming margin of over three to one, garnering 10,841 votes against 3,337. Still, he never failed to remember the suffering of the Jews and he appeared reverently at all memorial occasions.

"Mayor Reitmeier sets an important example for the citizens of Dachau," said Nikolaus Lehner, a Jewish ex-inmate of the camp who stayed and runs a lumber and building supply business in the town. "He has always shown a great deal of sensitivity and consideration in these matters." Which did not, however, keep the mayor from also asserting the innocence of his voters and their forefathers.

In a rare editorial aside of her academically framed book, Steinbacher would refer to the establishment's defensive strategies as "irrational self-pity." By then she had dug out the real entanglements of Dachau's love/hate relationship with its infamous neighbor.

It started with a peace treaty that Hitler made his arch bugaboo. In just about every speech he railed against "the shame dictate of Versailles." Politics aside, the pact that ended World War I also triggered the closing of Dachau's principal industry, the big munitions factory just east of town. It was an economic catastrophe. During the 1920s Dachau reported the highest percentage of unemployment among all the unemployment-ridden cities in Germany. Men loitered around the streets in droves.

So the town authorities were elated when they heard that a concentration camp with an SS staff of 3,000 would come to Dachau's rescue. The Bavarian minister of the interior told the then mayor that he was "optimistic" about the impact of "the concentration camp's purchases on Dachau's businessmen." And on the day the place opened, the *Dachauer Zeitung* hailed it as a "great economic advantage."

Townspeople welcomed the camp as a "legitimate institution" where inmates "alienated from society" — mostly Communists, social-ists, union leaders, and later Jews — were being constructively "reed-ucated." Thus sold on the economic and social worthiness of the acquisition, by which Hitler and Himmler had decreed the revoca-tion of their misfortune, the citizenry joined joyfully in cultural hap-penings sponsored by their economic rescuers, the camp's SS leadership. On June 15, 1933, Steinbacher discovered, the *Dachauer Zeitung* published an account of one such occasion:

"At 11 A.M., a stand-up concert took place before the concentra-tion camp. . . . The prisoners, closely packed behind the gate, were engrossed in listening to music from a dashing stormtrooper band. . . . Around 3 P.M., a strong SS detachment trailed the ringing instruments of the stormtrooper band, in procession, from the con-centration camp through the city to the Ziegelkeller restaurant where a big concert took place. The camp commandant, Party Comrade Hilmar Wäckerle, was in the lead, high on horseback. . . . It was a heart-quickening picture."

On April 1, 1939, the ties between the town and the camp were formalized with the incorporation of the KZ site within the city lim-its. The town officials had competed for the privilege insistently, cit-ing their hope of collecting taxes from the SS staff on beer and other goods while also "solidifying" the mutually rewarding social relation-ships. Numerous meetings ensued. The villages of Prittlbach and Etzenhausen were likewise competing for administrative possession of the camp. The Dachau negotiators, more assiduous in their court-ship, wound up victorious, proud to be "awarded" the prize, accord-ing to contemporaneous documents.

Starting in 1942, the increasingly desperate Nazi war effort pres-sured the SS into lowering the physical barriers separating civilian from camp populations. Every day, more than a thousand prisoners were marched to twelve major factories and to smaller businesses to perform slave labor. As a special privilege of rank, the major was given a prisoner for use at his discretion.

Until then, citizens had been occasionally exposed to the cruelties of the SS, usually at a distance, when Russian and Polish prisoners of war were beaten as they were herded to the camp from the railroad station. Now, at close range in the workplaces, the civilians saw that the inmates were emaciated and starving. While many of the Dachauers registered shock, Sybille Steinbacher discovered only a single case of a citizen sufficiently repelled to blame the Nazi system and take political action.[2]

Individual co-workers were, however, capable of pity in some cases. After the war, documented reports told of bread, apples, and cigarettes being smuggled to prisoners while they were at work. A prisoner testified that his employer gave inmate workers beer, bread, potatoes and sometimes a hot lunch. A seamstress in an SS tailor shop watched prisoners search the garbage cans when they reported for the twelve-hour night shift, so she left her radish sandwich under her sewing machine.

Sometimes, too, individual SS men displayed signs of humanity. An elderly local housewife saw prisoners laboring in the old cemetery and innocently asked an SS guard if she could give them something to eat.

"Little mother, it's a good thing you're asking just me," the SS man said. "Don't ever ask another post or you'll be in the KZ yourself." Then he winked and said, "If you happen to lose something, nobody can do anything." Years later, the woman said, "So I often went to the cemetery and lost bread and apples."

Such examples of courage and compassion were crowded out by postwar recollections of a different sort: mobs, mostly women and youths, who vociferously demonstrated contempt for prisoners — by then mostly Polish civilians and Jews, as they were marched from the rail station to the camp.

---

[2]An employee of a gypsum plant, Sepp Mukof, arranged for inmate laborers to contact an anti-Nazi group in Munich. Although the Munich resisters were captured, Mukof was never identified.

A Polish ex-inmate, Branz Brückl, testified, "All the way down Friedensstrasse we were spat upon. Some threatened us with fists and had to be pulled back by the SS. . . . Umpteen times we were spat upon . . . by women and youth, especially young males. It was terrible."

The disdain of the Dachauers toward the prisoners, dead and alive, remained virulent right along, even *after* the liberation of the camp, when ignorance of its horrors could no longer be claimed. The locals behaved as if Hitler's preachment that Jews and other alien folk were no worthier than "rodents" had always been — and still was — a biological truth.


When American soldiers first entered the camp on Sunday, April 29, 1945, the sight beggared credence. Hugh Carlton Greene of the BBC (later its chairman) saw soldiers writhing on the ground, vomiting. More than 2,000 corpses littered the terrain in varying stages of decay. Another 2,300 bodies jammed thirty-nine cars of a freight train, forgotten on a railroad siding, presumably a transport from Buchenwald. Some 32,000 survivors lay or staggered about, many of them mortally weakened;[3] 2,000 died of typhus in peacetime, between May and July.

The death train, by remarkable coincidence, had been a jolting event in Mayor Reitmeister's life; it lent weight to his claim of having experienced the Holocaust at close range and as a thinking person, not a mindless child.

The mayor did not publicly disclose this confrontation until he had been in office for nearly twenty years. When he did so, however, he chose a sanctified occasion — the fortieth anniversary of the camp's liberation. He revealed that he had been taken by a Polish priest, when he was twelve years old, to view the corpses of the prisoners

---

[3]I have been unable to produce a solid explanation of a news photo, widely circulated in postwar German publications, including a book published by the West German government, showing fit-appearing Dachau survivors cheering their liberators lustily, even climbing on flagpoles and waving. Barbara Distel, director of the Dachau Memorial, speculates that these must have been among the most recent arrivals.

on the train. The victims had been given rations for a day to survive a trip lasting almost three weeks; virtually all had succumbed to starvation or exposure.

"At the sight of this gruesome scene," Mayor Reitmeister movingly declared in 1985, "I felt a sense of terror and anguish that I have never been able to forget, and that I am certain will be with me for the rest of my life."

Not all his contemporaries who saw the train horror reacted the same way.

A *New York Times* correspondent listened to the cheerful chattering of civilians looting an SS depot near the death train: "They avoided glancing in the direction of the boxcars full of corpses and acted as if they did not exist. . . . Not a single good German had the decency to stop and place a cloth over the corpses. . . . Evidently they believed it was none of their business."

In May 1945, when interrogators from my U.S. Army Psychological Warfare Division reminded townspeople of the truck convoys then driving through town daily, bearing corpses, the response was profession of ignorance. "We were lied to," was the standard phrase. Nobody seemed to know of crimes committed at the camp.

Furious, the Americans recruited Dachau women to clean up the boxcars of the death train. Leading party members were made to bury the dead. On May 9, a mere thirty town dignitaries were compelled to inspect the camp, still filled with piles of the dead. Films were made that later became part of the widely avoided "reeducation" film *Todesmühlen* (*Death Mills*). The mandatory tour of the camp was the only such punishment to be staged.

According to eyewitnesses, a few of the notables fainted, some cried, many shook their heads. Typically, they turned away, eager to leave the scene. Outside, they were heard to whisper, "Unglaublich!" — "Unbelievable!"

Actually, credibility was an issue only in fantasy, a question of citizen image. "The chimney of the crematorium stank and stank, day and night," said Mrs. H., a housewife, when she was questioned in the less defensive days of the 1980s. "Everybody in Dachau knew it," said a Mrs. P. "When Russians, bound in chains, were herded from the station to the camp, the SS beat them with carbine butts so that the heads were cracking!"

And still many fantasies continued to flourish in the heads of Dachauers who could not help feeling persecuted, as well as in the newspapers. One of these fairytales had the town priest, Father Friedrich Pfanzelt, save the city from being sacked by American troops in 1945. In a 1981 series of articles, the *Dachauer Nachrichten* still kept this drama alive: "On his knees, the prelate pleaded for mercy for Dachau."

Sybille Steinbacher unwrapped the kernel of relevance that spawned this legend. The occasion was the camp visit of the thirty town VIPs. Angrily, the American town commandant allowed himself to fulminate in front of them: "As punishment for the brutality that the town tolerated next door to it, it should be sacked and turned into ashes!"

Father Pfanzelt, who was among the visitors, remonstrated, which was a significant act of resistance since 90 percent of the 8,234 Dachauers were Catholic. Then, from the pulpit of his St. Jacob's Church three days later, the priest set in motion Dachau's great trauma, the protestation of innocence, the denial of guilt that would never leave the community.

"We Dachauers," he cried out, "let it be sworn to the skies and assured to all humanity on our honor and conscience for all eternity, are not guilty and had not the most minor part in this." He deplored what happened behind "locked walls," failing to mention that the camp's walls were not locked to him. For years the SS had extended him the privilege of conducting Sunday services in the KZ. And he had reciprocated with many ingratiating letters (which Steinbacher found) and had taken pride in his cordial relations with most of the camp commandants.

The claim of "salvation" for Dachau from American vengeance was never confirmed or denied by the priest. No reference to it appeared in his very detailed private diary, and his silence served him well. He continued to be held high in honor, not only as the town's chief man of God but as a local representative of the CDU, the ruling conservative party, until his death in 1958.

*       *       *

The postwar history of the Dachau camp was a case of radical reversal. Quickly, the fate of the former KZ turned as noisy and controversial as its earlier incarnation had been more or less hushed up and monolithic. The institution simply kept stirring too many emotions in too many directions to fade away as a quiet tomb for terrible memories, and the tumult is still far from over.

Once again, inventors of malignant fiction sowed seeds of trouble. And this time, not only the good name of the Dachauers was in contention, but that of all the Germans. The odor of the Dachau smokestacks.

With the war not long past, spokesmen for right-wing causes produced "witnesses" who asserted a bizarre claim. The story held that, in 1945, the American military had compelled SS prisoners to build gas ovens from the ground up. Over the years, this yarn gained believers, and eventually the extremist *National-Zeitung* of Dr. Gerhard Frey trumpeted the fantasy into a cause.

"Gas Chamber Swindle Revealed" said a headline in 1960. An article declared that everything still remaining of the concentration camp was "a dummy without documentary value."

The actuality was innocent, though strange. In addition to the old crematory, a windowless gas chamber and four big new brick crematory ovens had indeed been constructed at a cost of 350,000 marks and was ominously designated "Barrack X" when deaths multiplied in 1942. The sign on the heavy iron door of the separate gas chamber said, "Shower Bath." Prominent on the structure's western wall was a death head and the lettering "Caution! Gas! Danger to life! Do Not Open." Yet for reasons never revealed, this facility was never used. Nor did officials confirm any claim that it went into operation. Prisoners were hanged and shot in Dachau. They died of disease or starvation or torture or criminal medical experiments. Bodies were cremated by the tens of thousands. Yet nobody was gassed.

Nevertheless, the lie of dummy ovens was kept in circulation by numerous extremist outlets until, in 1978, with the "Hitler wave" still rising, it gained respectable sponsorship in the authoritatively titled *History of the Germans*. The publisher was the Prophyläen Verlag of Berlin, a long-honorable house owned by the Jewish Ullstein family but then "aryanized" and later very quietly converted into a sanitizing haven for ultra-conservative authors.[4] The author was Helmut Diewals, professor of history at Erlangen University, with no Nazi affiliations, past or present.

Diewals characterized the concentration camps as a necessity dictated by "reasons of state" and dismissed Hitler's destruction of the Jews as an act of "disrespect." In the case of Dachau, the professor accepted as gospel the old yarn that its death installations were "dummies which the American military forced SS prisoners to build after the capitulation."

The chain of lies continued unbroken. Thus, in 1983, the *Lechkurier* of Landsberg, the Bavarian city where Hitler had once served a brief prison sentence, carried a four-part exposé of "victor justice" in which it offered its version of the "Dachau trial" of November 1945. Forty of the most brutal Dachau SS personnel stood accused before a U.S. military court of mistreating and murdering prisoners, medical experiments upon prisoners, and killings of the sick. Of the defendants, twenty-eight were eventually executed.

The Landsberg newspaper expressed "doubt whether there was any search for justice." The accusers had been "professional witnesses" and, according to the weightiest claim of the paper's investigation, "there were no defense witnesses at the time because, as was stated, none could be found." In fact, ninety-four defense witnesses were heard. The prosecution called sixty-nine, including numerous former camp inmates.

---

[4]Ullstein today is owned by a man named Herbert Fleissner, who, starting in the 1950s, began buying up a number of German publishing houses (Bogen, Amalthea, Universitas, and Molden S. Seewald). In 1985 he succeeded in fusing Springer-Konzern (which includes the Ullstein and Prophyläen publishing houses) into the Langen Müller group. Fleissner published books by Nolte, Irving (who now calls Fleissner a cheat for unfair contract conditions), Fest, Christa Schröder, Haider, and Waldheim. He also published books by Elie Wiesel and Simon Wiesenthal, claiming that he is simply giving space to open debate and to "plurality of opinions," a claim buttressed by Ullstein's appointment in 1996 of Wolfram Göbel as its head. Göbel claims Ullstein has broken all ties with the neo-right. Nonetheless, Fleissner financially supports a series of right-wing papers and is a member of the neo-fascist Witiko association, which advocates the return to Germany of the Sudentenland (where Fleissner was born) and other territories annexed by the Nazis. Fleissner, who is currently head of the Langen Müller/Herbig publishing group, is the third-largest publisher in Germany.

Barbara Distel has a polite name for all this fakery. She calls it "defamation" and believes that its goal is to follow up the destruction of the Dachau victims with the eradication of their memory.

Frau Distel had come to Dachau as a twenty-one-year-old librarian in 1964, just before the opening of the appropriately bleak Dachau Memorial. It is an assault upon the heart, an exhibition of explicit historical photos and documents, remnants of the crematorium, and some reconstructed barracks. The enterprise, run by Distel at the site of the camp, is the outcome of a ten-year bureaucratic struggle by an international committee of former prisoners lobbying the reluctant Bavarian state government.

"The place was never accepted by German society," said Frau Distel, director since 1975. Her head was bowed, her face partly hidden by her hand, as if in some embarrassment. She was a professor's wife and the couple had lived in the United States for two years.

Overtly, nothing seemed amiss at the Memorial. Annual visitors number 600,000, about half of them Germans. This is down from 900,000 of some years ago but still respectable. The first road signs directing tourists to the site from the edge of town display good-sized lettering and are prominently placed. And while the Memorial has budget problems, so that only half of the roofing can be repaired, what institution doesn't have money worries?

Closer up, other evidence makes clear that the Memorial is in fact an unwanted orphan. Moving toward the intricate approaches to the site, the direction signs become fewer and their type is hard to read, as if the Memorial was best left unfound. This is not a problem of sign painting; the easy-to-read signs were put up by the state, the others by the town. But the real malaise is national, not local: the decline in visitors is heaviest among Germans; nearly all the people who do come are classes of schoolchildren, from all over the country, for to the Germans' credit, attendance at the Memorial is mandatory for students.

How effective is the Memorial as an instrument of education? Frau Distel reported that virtually no students with right-wing extremist views make the trip; they find ways to dodge this history lesson. Whatever happens in the heads of youngsters who do come is largely the function of individual teachers. Some turn the trip into a tour of the entertainments for which Munich is famous. Others make the Holocaust come alive as vital and hardly impersonal contemporary history.

Occasionally, appalling acts of tactlessness get converted into poignant reproof. Some years ago, a Munich high school class that included one Jewish girl was discussing an impending journey to Dachau. "When we go we can use you as a guinea pig," a fellow student sneered at the Jewish student. The ensuing discussion was intense and maintained a constructive note.

German sentiments, as recorded in the guestbooks, show a split between old and young. Most youths are indignant: "How could this have happened?" they write, or "I never thought it was this bad." Many make appeals: "We've got to be watchful" and "Something like this mustn't happen again." Only a small minority shrug off their Dachau experience: "Why should this concern me today?" or "I hate Jews and Turks."

Differing parental views get reported too: "My parents don't think it's a good idea for us to come here. Only hate against the Germans gets stirred up here. One shouldn't constantly dig up the past." And: "Everything gets exaggerated here."

Increasingly, the often hostile views of adult visitors include remarks such as, "Israel is doing exactly the same!" A letter writer from Munich suggested tearing down the Memorial and sending the pieces to Israel. And a writer from Wiesbaden proposed that Frau Distel's museum put up a memorial "for the victims of Israeli barbarism as a reminder that even victims don't learn from the past."

Frau Distel said she was appalled at Lord Mayor Reitmeister's consistent efforts to trivialize the Memorial by trying to shift attention to the local scenery and the old artists' colony, but she did concede receiving quiet assistance from some local officials. Whenever violence was threatened against the institution by right-wing extremists, the police chief called her with a warning and sent extra patrol cars.

The Memorial's long-range future looked bleak to her, however. Her principal supporters, the former camp inmates, were rapidly dying out. "What will happen when they are gone?" she asked. "I'm very pessimistic. Sometimes I ask myself, 'Why am I here?'"

It was Frau Distel who first told me of Sybille Steinbacher's book and of its closing note regretting that a "conscious confrontation of the town with the camp has never taken place" and is "badly needed today."

Half a century late, such a discussion had finally been sparked by the Steinbacher book with help from outside — but not too far outside. The leading Munich newspaper, *Süddeutsche Zeitung,* arguably Germany's best, published a long, favorable, and pointed review that also recognized the connection between Steinbacher's findings and the nationalist travail of contemporary Germans.

"After reading this work," the reviewer said, "the phrase that 'such a thing' could no longer happen today sounds somewhat more hollow to the ears."

Locals were snapping up the 289-page book at $50 per copy, but Lord Mayor Reitmeister remained unmoved by its many fresh revelations. "We lived through that time and see things more objectively," he told the Munich reporters. "The book was written subjectively from the viewpoint of a young woman in the 1990s. Only if you experienced that time can you write about it."

In response, Steinbacher attacked Reitmeister as a "cheery circulator of untenable little stories" about Dachau's Nazi past and dismissed as "absurd" the lord mayor's assertion that his personal experience made him "an expert in Nazi research." When the concentration camp was built, Steinbacher noted, Reitmeister was two and a half years old. At the time of its controversial incorporation into the city, he was eight and a half.

Reitmeister attempted one more return volley. He had been a "fairly conscious" eyewitness of the Nazi time, he argued, and was therefore "entitled to take a position out of my own experience, which younger people cannot do in the same way." For him, Hitler was still the great savior: "The privation prior to 1933 was enormous," he declared.

Steinbacher was unperturbed and no longer seemed so tiny. She viewed Reitmeister as an increasingly isolated lame-duck reactionary attempting to play "king of Dachau," and took delight that his temper was getting short. "Shut up and sit down," he reportedly told a woman who questioned him about a traffic problem at a community meeting. "No wonder you are so unpopular," countered the woman. "I am not unpopular," replied Reitmeister. It sounded much like President Nixon declaring, "I am not a crook."

The lord mayor was ineligible to run again in 1996. What might happen then to Dachau's leadership and the citizens' views of their Nazi past? The apologist old guard was fading, just like the KZ victims. In actuality, rays of self-recognition had been seeping into the public perception for years. While the fresh and incontrovertible details amassed by Steinbacher's research created a more fact-based level of debate, the essential truth had long made the rounds. Harsh charges and countercharges faded with the years, aided by insistent nudging from the media beyond Dachau. So, backed into the defensive, the town authorities embarked on a campaign of artful stalling.

The tortuous road toward accommodation between Holocaust survivors and the besieged Dachauers began with a conciliatory suggestion put forward in June 1980. Scrupulously, though without resolution, the ensuing twists were traced by a seventeen-page "Report from Dachau" in the August 13, 1992, issue of the *New Yorker*.

The five-page 1980 letter that instigated the extravaganza in bureaucracy was jointly written by Nikolaus Lehner, the lumber man, and a local high school principal. It was addressed to Mayor Reitmeister and proposed the creation of a "House of Encounter" in the town — "a framework of conscience, responsibility, tolerance, and dialogue."

After four months, Reitmeister replied with the town council's decision: No. The project wouldn't help with the town's concentration camp image. Also, Dachau shouldn't shoulder a responsibility that really belonged to all Germans.

*November 1984.* Supporters of the project, including former camp inmates, organized an "Advocacy Group for International Youth Encounter in Dachau."

*July 1985.* Members of the advocacy group met with local and national representatives of the dominant political party, the Christian Democrats. The politicians turned down the project summarily. The advocates countered by drumming up support from national and international leaders.

*March 1987.* During a vehement discussion by the town council, one member declared that the proposed center would "never" be allowed to put the "mark of Cain" on Dachau. Speaking in World War II Nazi imagery, the councilor cried, "We will defend ourselves with all our might to the very last drop of blood."

*October 1987.* The town council voted twenty-four to fifteen against the project. The decision prompted wide and unfavorable media comment.

*December 1989.* With criticism still mounting, the state of Bavaria agreed to finance construction of a meeting place, and the town donated a vacant lot. The "encounter" center proposal was watered down to become a "Youth Guest House" where no "political" issues were to be discussed.

*April 1992.* The town council voted to go ahead with the project, an architect was hired, public hearings were held. However, the project's board of directors included no one from the advocacy group, nor any former camp inmates. Construction was to start in 1995.

In the fall of 1994, a group of homeowners, potential neighbors of the center, hired a lawyer to stop the project because it would lead to too much noise. The Bavarian state authorities estimated that the center would still become a reality, probably by 1998. Its advocates wondered whether it would ever be built. It was, in fact, built May 1998 by the city of Dachau and the State of Bavaria.

Were the Dachauers merely offering grudging knee-jerk concessions, or were they really acknowledging complicity? The answer was still uncertain.

I told Steinbacher the old Washington story, probably apocryphal, about the senator who changed his vote after debating with himself for a long time. "I didn't see the light," he said, "but I felt the heat."

Steinbacher laughed and shrugged, encouraged but not entirely assured of where her neighbors stood. She had received a prestigious appointment to the staff of the Institute for Contemporary History in Munich and was preparing for her next self-assigned task: an examination of Auschwitz, the town and the camp, which was published in the early part of 2000.

My wife, Elaine, and I were ambling through the streets of Dachau, grown into a suburb of 36,000, wishing we could divine how the people who passed us felt about the Hitler days. The very name of their town still stood for horror in all the world, yet here it was, a cheerful place, pretty, terraced, with a gingerbread castle that once belonged to the royal Bavarian Wittelsbachs, now offering marvelous concerts. A spotless nation of composers, a city of artists? There once was a school of Dachau painters. The misty moss fields that they memorialized were still there, reminders of another era, like the concentration camp.

A group of small schoolchildren passed us, skipping and giggling. What could they possibly know about Nazis? How rotten should they be made to feel about their forefathers?

# 33

## THE "NASTY GIRL" TRIUMPHS

Except for the happenstance that Adolf Hitler, the child of an Austrian customs official, lived in this city when he was three to five years old, the Nazi past of Passau (population 50,000) was no different from that of other Bavarian communities; the local people buried those years as taboo.

No one talked about the 400 Jews — doctors, department store owners, even the town treasurer — who were chased into emigration or death; or the anti-Nazi "resistance" heroes who were actually collaborators; or the connection of locals with the mass murder of Russian prisoners of war; or the success of Hitler's home as a well-attended museum.

All this was wished away. Hitler? He never lived in Passau, the historic tourist town on the Austrian border, where the Danube and the Inn Rivers merge. Or so ran the official perception until a feisty, small, blonde troublemaker, Anna Elisabeth Rosmus, born in 1960, a generation after the outrages, stuck a mirror into the faces of her fellow townspeople.

For her efforts at enlightenment, shopkeepers jeered, called her "Traitor!" and "Jews' whore," and she was spat upon. Her two young daughters were threatened. The town officials castigated her. The newspaper denounced her as a "nest-soiler." Obscene and threatening phone calls did not stop day or night. When she had her first daughter and defiantly gave her a Jewish name, Salome, the location of her hospital room was kept secret because of threats that the baby would be killed. Under the pressure her marriage broke up.

It was a most uneven war, the young woman battling her own town, and yet, surprisingly, she won. En route, she became the real-life heroine of the 1990 Michael Verhoeven film *The Nasty Girl*. It was much the same role of critic and liberator that young Sybille Steinbacher had played in airing the culpability of the townspeople in Dachau.

Rosmus had never met a Jew or cared much about Passau's past when her father, a school principal, one evening in 1980 brought home a circular announcing a national essay contest. The assigned subject was "The Prewar Years in My Hometown," and what interested Anna were not so much the Nazis as their victims. Her parents had raised her to respect the rights of the weak and innocent. Clearly, there had been people in Passau whom the Nazis had preyed upon. What had happened to them?

Answers were difficult to come by. Archives became inaccessible. Old-timers and officials shrugged off questions. Documents were "lost." Memories went unaccountably dead. For four years, Rosmus pursued a lawsuit, finally successful, to compel the city to open its historical files.

A relentless and clever researcher, she developed a network of productive alternate sources. As in Dachau, the Bavarian state authorities proved more accommodating than local officials. State archives yielded data about persecutions. So did the bureaus responsible for restitution payments to surviving Jewish victims. Ultimately, Rosmus enlisted the Israeli archives at Yad Vashem in Jerusalem and hauled in reports from Jewish families who had emigrated from Passau to America and from the extensive resources at numerous Jewish institutions there.

Wherever she appeared in person or in writing, survivors and historians were impressed by the obvious dedication of this young and lonely gentile mother who was making it her business to remember what her townspeople wanted so dearly to forget. She won cooperation and respect by her refusal to get discouraged for lack of official help or to become intimidated by the personal danger that, during one period, compelled the unhappy Passau police to guard her home around the clock.

"I never regretted and I never felt sorry," she said. "I remained cool. I didn't oblige my attackers by permitting them to see that I was hurt." She was, but she never turned herself into a martyr. She understood that her opposition was not entirely motivated by politics. Typical small-town mentality was at work, too, as in the fictional Peyton Place of decades ago.

"The people of Passau consider the kind of aggression they have vented at me as welcome relief from their rather dull, provincial lives," she said. "They still look at me a bit like a bull looks at a red cloth. I get a certain kick out of it."

Other, more tangible compensations kept spurring her on. Her entry in the student essay contest that first set off her crusade won third prize out of 13,000 entries. The work grew into a book, *Resistance and Persecution: The Case of Passau, 1933–1939.* It was published in 1983 and won the prestigious Scholl Prize, which carries a $14,000 cash award and is named for brother-and-sister leaders who were executed for anti-Nazi activities in 1943.

By now, her writing career was under way. In 1988, Rosmus published *Exodus: In the Shadow of Mercy,* a compilation of case histories documenting discrimination against Passau's Jewish families beginning with the nineteenth century. In 1993, she followed up with *Wintergreen: Suppressed Murders,* about the still secret wartime killings of Soviet soldiers in camps of the Passau area.

Not infrequently, her exposés landed Rosmus in court. Even the descendants of personalities from the Nazi period sometimes felt so aggrieved that they sued and occasionally succeeded in curbing some of her writings. She usually had her way, but rarely without having to come up with incontrovertible evidence. The denials that devotees had flocked to the Passau museum honoring Hitler's childhood home did not cease until she managed to produce copies of the guestbooks.

Often, her continuing persecution by her fellow citizens made her want to leave Passau with her daughters, but new causes always drew her back to stay. Her parents, retired and living next door, offered unwavering protection. Her younger sister and brother were supportive. And always, new projects came up to capture her seemingly irrepressible energies.

In 1994, she was completing studies for a master's degree at the new University of Passau. In between, she was off for periodic speaking tours before Jewish audiences in the United States, mostly to raise funds for the Holocaust Museum in Washington. She was also completing research on yet another newly discovered war crime, the shooting in the Passau forests of eight hundred Jews who, in the last weeks of the war, were being transported by rail from Buchenwald to Dachau.

Not everyone who languished in these death trains perished. Rosmus discovered a humanitarian who had never before been recognized: a Passau minister who ran from farm to farm, ringing a bell and persuading farmers to bring water and food to the dying.

Most satisfactory of all, she was savoring victory over her toughest adversary in recent years, Dr. Gerhard Frey of nearby Munich, publisher of the extremist *National-Zeitung* and chief of the ultra-right-wing DVU Party, the Deutsche Volksunion.

Frey had pulled Rosmus into present-day politics because he had a liking for Passau's huge Nibelungen Hall as the meeting ground for his annual DVU Party convention and speaking platform for Holocaust deniers like David Irving. Rosmus, in turn, opposed Frey and his ilk as disgraceful throwbacks to the Nazis. In his newspaper, Frey likened Rosmus to a pig rooting around the swamp of the alleged Brown Past as if for truffles. Finally in 1992, Rosmus mobilized her media contacts and the considerable national following that her books, the *Nasty Girl* film, and her television appearances had created over the years. She took on Frey and his right-wing forces with a counterdemonstration of some 3,000 anti-Nazis, mostly students and activists even younger.

Their banners proclaimed, "Never Again Genocide!" "No Fascists in Passau!" "In With the Foreigners!" "Stop Gerhard Frey!" As a headline attraction, Rosmus brought in another "nasty girl" to help, Beate Klarsfeld of Paris, the veteran hunter of hidden Nazis and war criminals, who was allowed to speak on the Passau streets but not in halls.

Rosmus finally became so incensed about the Frey convention that she attacked him and his followers on national television. They were keeping Nazi ideas alive, she charged. Some of the Frey delegates went around Passau screaming, "Heil!" A few showed up wearing SS insignia. Quite a number had swastika-shaped pretzels hanging around their necks. Frey, himself a lawyer, sued for slander. The charges against him were inventions, he countered; the media paid actors to masquerade as Nazis. Frey's position was rejected in court. He appealed but lost again. It was an embarrassing defeat for him.

By late summer of 1994, when Rosmus left with her daughters for at least two years of further graduate studies in the United States and money-raising trips for Washington's Holocaust Museum, the Passau establishment had conceded defeat and all but announced her canonization.

Along with its manual covering two hundred Passau restaurants, the latest edition of the official guide to the city carried two pages entitled "Vergangenheitsbewältigung" — not usually a feature of the intellectual diet dispensed in such works. The pages, entirely devoted to Rosmus, might have come from her press agent, if she had one.

"With her writings," it declared, "Anna Elisabeth Rosmus achieves courageous and important work for the survivors of the Third Reich, for the victims as well as perpetrators; also, for what today is even more important, for the younger people who did not experience that time . . . so that history can never repeat itself!"

Her departure was "a loss for the city," the send-off said. "Her opponents have no cause to be triumphant, for this author has awakened a consciousness among many readers that will last."

Rosmus may return and she may not. She doesn't think it matters. "I have the feeling my work here is done," she told me in her paper-cluttered bungalow shortly before she left the city. She was, as ever, in a rush. There were many more campaigns to be run, if not in Passau, then beyond.

# 34

## PUBLISHER'S EPILOGUE

Whip Peter Wyden began this book, I truly believe he felt, or certainly hoped, that with the passing years and the demise of the often still unbending, but increasingly elderly, Nazi old guard, the Hitler virus would die out. But I must confess that in the last two years of his life, I detected that his optimism was waning. The fall of the Berlin Wall, rather than solving Germany's problems, only seemed to exacerbate them. Now, more than ten years after the Wall came down, unemployment in the former East Germany still hovers around 17–18 percent. And as we saw in the 1920s and '30s, unemployment breeds not only discontent but, all too often, violence and the tendency to resort to radical solutions. As we have seen throughout this book, over the past decade the majority of violent, racially motivated crimes have occurred in the east. Just how many of these are anti-Semitic and how many simply racial in the larger sense is often hard to determine. But the Hitler virus is not so self-circumscribed that it manifests itself solely against Jews. For one thing, Hitler's maniacal anti-Semitism resulted in the virtual elimination of the Jewish population of Germany: after the Shoah, only 15–30,000 Jews[1] remained scattered throughout the two Germanys, a handful in a few dozen cities, usually living without any communal support from rabbis, with most of the synagogues long ago destroyed or, if still standing, more often than not mere historic relics, a sad reminder of what once had been.

---

[1] Exact figures for Germany's remaining Jewish population are hard to verify, but estimates run from a low of 15,000 to a high of double that figure.

Interestingly, since the demise of the Soviet Union, the Jewish population of Germany has almost trebled: some 55–60,000 Jews have immigrated to Germany, largely from the former Soviet republics. Unfortunately, in the towns and cities to which they immigrated — or, rather, have been assigned, since regional authorities allocate them geographically, sometimes with apparent reason, sometimes whimsically — the support system, the local *Jüdische Gemeinde* (Jewish community) is generally woefully lacking in resources to help them reshape their lives. Still, this new, enlarged Jewish presence, however tiny compared to the country's total population, has been the target of an outsized number of attacks in recent times. In 1999, for example, some fifty-seven desecrations of Jewish cemeteries were noted by the authorities — more than one a week. Their number and their intensity led Paul Spiegel, head of the Central Council of Jews in Germany, to call for a united front against right-wing extremism. "This is not just about people being persecuted. This doesn't just hurt foreigners, Jews, minorities," Spiegel said. "This hurts Germany and our whole society. What is needed is a sharp jolt that sends waves through the German population."

On July 27, 2000, a bomb exploded at 3:06 P.M. in a crowded Düsseldorf train station, wounding ten foreigners. Six of them were Jewish. Though no one took responsibility for the attack, which was made using a homemade bomb or fragmentation grenade, it had all the earmarks of right-wing extremist origin. "Until we can rule out that rightist extremism was behind this, all Jews in Düsseldorf — and all Jews in Germany — are afraid," Spiegel declared. A few weeks later, as there was no abatement in extremist attacks, he went even further, declaring: "If this increase in violence continues, I may recommend that all Jews now living in Germany consider moving to other countries."

Whether Spiegel's advice is heeded or not, it demonstrates the degree to which concern about the continuing Nazi virus, not only in the former East Germany but throughout the country, is higher than it has ever been since 1945. Whether the far-right NPD Party was responsible for the Düsseldorf bombing and other recent acts of violence, there is no question that they are active carriers of the virus, provoking others to act in their name or in the name of their principles. "We believe that the NPD is largely responsible for this right-wing violence," the interior minister of Bavaria, Manfred Weiss, said a day after the bombing. A week later, a memorial marking mass graves near a former Nazi work camp outside Bremen was spray-painted with swastikas and anti-Semitic slogans. And in Lower Saxony that same week, police reported a wave of neo-Nazi graffiti on bus stops, garage doors, and cigarette vending machines. Every week, it seems, a new outbreak of the virus is reported.

The NPD disclaimed any responsibility for this rising tide of racial crimes. Ulrich Eigenfeld, an NPD spokesman, told journalists on the day of the Düsseldorf bombing that his party drew none of its inspiration from Hitler's National Socialism. "We offer very different policies," he said. What are the policies? Opposing immigration first of all. Also opposing the European Union and NATO, both of which diminish Germany's purity. Sound familiar? The special quality of Aryan blood, which should be preserved at all costs. The language may be different: the virus is the same.

As a direct result of the increase in racially motivated crimes in Germany, and specifically the Düsseldorf attack, the federal government, as this book goes to press, is considering taking legal action to ban the NPD. To do so, the government would have to take its request to the Constitutional Court. The interior ministers of Germany's sixteen federal states met in Berlin in August 2000 to consider the recommendation, which Chancellor Gerhard Schröder strongly supports.

Many in Germany, however, question the wisdom of such a move: the Nazi Party was banned in 1922[2] only to resurface all the more potent and eventually assume power. "Attempts to ban right-wing parties would be politically counterproductive," the interior minister of Hesse, Volker Bouffier, said, adding, "it would only create martyrs." Federal interior minister Otto Schily agreed, saying that if the NPD was forced underground, it would be far more difficult to keep tabs on it. Moreover, he noted, if banned the NPD could simply change its name and reincarnate itself.

---

[2]While it was outlawed in most German states, it was tacitly, if not overtly, encouraged in Bavaria, where it had not been banned.

Not all Germans are taking this violence lying down. There have been, and continue to be, anti-fascist protests in Berlin and other German cities. But some of the rallies have been disappointingly small and are often followed by rightist rallies the next day or two. At a Berlin "Stop the Nazi-terror" rally in the late summer of 2000, author Ralph Giordano said, "It is true that Hitler and his followers were beaten militarily fifty-five years ago, but in the year 2000 they're still not politically defeated."

On a brighter note, in Berlin the Neue Synagogue, which was a target of the Nazis on *Kristallnacht,* has been restored and is currently serving the city's 12,000 Jews.

But the truth is, the Hitler virus is not aimed solely, or even primarily, at Germany's Jewish population. Hitler himself had seen to that, having eliminated 99 percent of the country's pre-Nazi Jewish population. Today's Germany is far different from the Third Reich in myriad ways. Despite its imperfections, there has been democracy for fifty-five years. But demographically the new Germany grapples with many of the same problems the pre-Hitler government had to face: high unemployment, a disaffected youth, and an "immigration problem" (read: people of impure blood) of increasing proportions.

Yesterday's outcasts, the Jews and the gypsies, have become in the new Germany the Turks and the Kurds, the blacks, and the "invaders" from the former Soviet republics. The cast has changed, but the racist mind-set remains chillingly the same.

So concerned was the German government with the rising tide of xenophobic attacks in the eastern part of the country that in the fall of 2000 Chancellor Gerhard Schröder made an unprecedented two-week tour throughout the five former East German states to assess the situation firsthand and lend the federal government's full support to the local authorities. During his trip he called for tougher measures against extremism, including increased police protection and stricter penalties for those accused of fomenting radical violence.

Meanwhile, in December of 2000 the Christian Democrats, out of power for two years, have made a bold if disturbing move. Doubtless partly as a result of the capital's move back to Berlin, coupled with their own political frustrations, the Christian Democrats have proclaimed that it's high time for Germans once again to embrace proudly the concept of the German Fatherland. In its last electoral platform, the party also included the notion of *Leitkultur* — guiding culture — the implication of which is "race purity," a clear slap at the roughly seven million foreigners in Germany, mostly Muslims, but also, politically, a clarion call for a new patriotism aimed at those Germans who, for all the obvious reasons, have felt compelled to repress their true feelings over the years.

Chancellor Schröder reacted strongly, implicitly likening the Christian Democrats' latest strategy to the Nazis. "The last time German conservatism gave in to the seductions of National Socialism," he declared, "Social Democrats suffered and died fighting the fascists."

Whether this play on the part of Germany's Christian Democrats is simply a momentary political tactic or a meaningful move to the right, in line with Haider's strategy in Austria, only time will tell. In the meantime, the battle lines between the parties are drawn far more visibly than ever before.

One of the more curious recent manifestations of the Hitler virus occurred in late summer of 2000, when Horst Mahler, the most famous German lawyer of the radical May 1968 "revolution," who is generally considered the founder of the RAF — the Red Army Faction, aka the Bader-Meinhof Gang — announced that he was joining the neo-Nazi NPD. Mahler, who is sixty-four, spent ten years in prison for belonging to a terrorist organization and for armed holdups made in the context of the politics of the RAF. Interestingly, his defense lawyer at the time of his trial was Gerhard Schröder, currently Germany's chancellor. In 1968, the famous incident in which Beate Klarsfeld administered a sharp slap to then chancellor Kurt Kiesenger to denounce his Nazi past, was roundly defended by Horst Mahler, who shared her anti-Nazi sentiments.

Released from prison, Mahler won reinstatement as a lawyer, and over the next two decades made a reputation both as a defense lawyer and a prosecutor, depending on the cases he took on. What, then, made this former leftist leader swing so suddenly and completely to the far right? A combination of anti-Americanism and anti-Semitism, apparently.

"In the old days" — read: 1968 — "our principal enemy was American imperialism," he is reported to have said. "And today it still is: American policy is to balkanize Europe in order to render it non-competitive." He also cites Marx himself as the basis for his anti-Semitism. "As early as 1843," he says, "Marx wrote: 'humanity must liberate itself from Judaism. It's not the Jews we must kill, it's their God, Yahweh.' There is no religion that celebrates hate the way Judaism does."

But clearly Mahler's sudden political shift also derives from the same bugaboo that motivates Jörg Haider: the fear of immigration. "The falling birthrate among Germans," Mahler says, "combined with the fact that the immigrants, who already number six to seven million, are inclined to have large families, means that in fifty years native Germans will be in the minority. That's especially true of the Muslims," he adds. Like Lauck and other right extremists, Mahler is using his Web site to spread the word and urge others among his fellow Germans to follow his example and join the NPD. As a lawyer, he is very careful to phrase his material so that it does not violate German law, which forbids spreading Nazi propaganda.

Mahler apparently sees no contradiction in his swing from left to right. Perhaps the virus was transmitted to him by his parents, both of whom were staunch Nazis, not only during Hitler's reign but well after the war. In any event, given his eloquence and influence, his adhesion to the NPD is one more disquieting sign of the rising neo-Nazi tide in this first decade of the new millennium.


In another attempt to stem the tide of neo-Nazi propaganda, in the late summer of 2000 German officials took steps to prevent local Web sites from spreading their political poison, warning German Internet service providers that they face fines of up to 500,000 deutsche marks — roughly $250,000 — if they host neo-Nazi sites. Düsseldorf district president Jurgen Büssow also wrote U.S. FCC chairman William Kennard, asking him to block neo-Nazi Web sites on American servers. "If a content provider is based in the U.S.," Büssow said, "I can't get at them. But I do not think any Internet provider wants to be known in Germany for spreading Nazi propaganda. It would hurt their business." Acknowledging the basic differences in free speech between Germany and the U.S., Büssow nonetheless felt that there is a legal basis in the U.S. for preventing or stopping hate speech. German interior minister Schily also vented his anger at the use of extremist Web sites to reach an even wider public. "When you look today at the Internet and see the kind of racist and anti-Semitic filth, it's frightening," he said.

His sentiments were echoed by the general secretary of the Christian Democratic Union, Ruprecht Polenz, who wrote an open letter in which he called for stronger methods against extremism on the Net, noting that "the relative anonymity, the speed and the global availability of the Internet are abused by extremists and the very structure of the Web makes it difficult to combat."

In a related incident in Germany's neighbor to the west, in the summer of 2000 the giant Internet provider Yahoo! was sued in Paris for selling Nazi paraphernalia — swastika battle flags, Nazi medallions, etc. — on its auction site. In France, it is illegal to sell anything deemed to incite racism, and as a result two French human rights organizations, the International League Against Racism and Anti-Semitism and the French Union of Jewish Students, filed a lawsuit in April 2000 against Yahoo!, alleging that, by auctioning Nazi-era paraphernalia on its Web site, it was violating French law. On May 22, French judge Jean-Jacques Gomez found for the plaintiffs, ordered Yahoo! to cease its auction of Nazi paraphernalia on its French site, and fined the company 400,000 euros ($350,000) per day that it violated his order, such monies to be paid to the two human rights organizations that had brought the suit. Judge Gomez gave Yahoo! until July 24 to report back on how it intended to comply, and on July 19 Yahoo! appealed. In the meantime, however, it banned auctions of the Nazi material on its French site, though continuing to sell it on its U.S.-based Web site. Jerry Yong, co-founder of Yahoo!, in an interview with the influential Paris-based daily newspaper *Libération,* said on August 1 that while his company would comply with the ban on its French site, he strongly doubted the French courts could prevent French users from accessing the content of its U.S. servers. It is that same logic — and the broader American law in this area — that continues to serve Gary Lauck so well.

In principle, Yahoo! could ignore the French court, which obviously has no jurisdiction over U.S. business. But throughout the summer Yahoo!'s lawyers have not missed a court appearance, perhaps because 40 percent of the giant Santa Clara, California–based company's business comes from outside the U.S.

In a news release on August 1, Yahoo! raised the ante, in essence thrusting the problem onto the shoulders of the various world governments. "This case opens up broader issues on Internet jurisdiction — whether one country has the jurisdiction to regulate the content of Web sites in another country," the release said. Indeed, the French Yahoo! case may well be setting a precedent for companies whose Web sites can be accessed around the world.

In late November 2000, Judge Gomez affirmed his earlier ruling against Yahoo!, which after the May ruling appealed on the grounds that it was impossible for it, or any Internet company, to know the country of origin or nationality of users accessing their sites (Yahoo!'s French subsidiary, Yahoo.fr, refrains from posting any Nazi-related items on its site). Whereupon Judge Gomez appointed a panel of three judges to assess Yahoo!'s allegation. After careful study, the panel reported back that, while a filter of users might never be 100 percent effective, scanning methods were available to accurately detect the geographical location of roughly 90 percent of Internet surfers. As a result, Judge Gomez gave Yahoo! three months — until February 2001, to put a scanning system in place or face a fine of 100,000 francs (about $13,000) for every day it fails to comply.

As this book goes to press, lawyers for Yahoo! were studying Judge Gomez's decision to see whether it would appeal the decision in the French courts or take the ruling to a U.S. court.

"This opens up the question of whether one country has the right to impose its rules on another," a Yahoo! Europe spokesman said. American e-business, like other businesses, are protected at home by Constitutional guarantees of free speech, but Laurent Levy, a lawyer for one of the French plaintiffs, said that in his view Judge Gomez's decision, which he termed "exemplary," unquestionably "resolves the question of borders on the Internet."

What remains unresolved is why, today, so many people around the world are still intent on buying and displaying relics of the Nazi era.

*       *       *

On September 12, 2000, just seven months after it had imposed sanctions on Austria following Jörg Haider's Freedom Party's installation as part of the new coalition government, the European Union formally lifted them. Earlier in the summer the EU had appointed a distinguished panel of three experts to examine and assess the human rights situation in Austria. Their report, while noting that the imposition of sanctions had served the purpose of focusing on the potential dangers resulting from the FPÖ's becoming part of the ruling coalition, it found no instances of the new government's fomenting racism, xenophobia, or anti-Semitism. On the contrary, the report stated, the government had taken concrete steps to fight extremism within its borders. Further, the report recommended lifting the sanctions, which, it said, only tended to infuriate Austrian citizens (implying that they would increasingly tend to drive voters into Haider's camp). The panel's report, however, sounded a thinly veiled warning: it noted that many of the Freedom Party's members continued to use extremist, racist, and anti-Semitic language throughout the period of the sanctions, without ever being reproached or reprimanded. Haider himself, still very much the Freedom Party head despite having installed his deputy Susanne Riess-Passer as vice chancellor, continued from behind the scenes to lash out at his detractors, especially French president Jacques Chirac, who was instrumental in imposing the sanctions in the first place. In early September, he called Chirac "a pocket-sized Napoleon," to which French minister for European affairs Pierre Moscovi responded by saying that no one should equate the end of the sanctions with exonerating the FPÖ.

Be that as it may, Haider's party has doubtless gained many voters during the seven-month-long freeze by the European Union, and he remains a danger that cannot be ignored. He himself has been infected, apparently incurably, by the Hitler virus, and his party, despite its present quietus, remains a source of concern not only for Europe but for the world.

Despite the political failure of the sanctions, one can take a certain comfort in the fact that fourteen European nations did react to an extremist threat — and it was a very real one — swiftly and in concert, doubtless remembering all too painfully how these same countries' failure to react to a renascent, and openly racist, Germany in the 1920s resulted, in the space of only a little more than a decade, in the worst holocaust the world has ever seen.

Whether Haider ever comes to power only time will tell. But as long as he or any of his ilk continues to live and suffer from the Hitler virus, the world will always be at risk. The European Union report lifting the sanctions declared that "it remained deeply concerned about the Freedom Party's role in government and vowed to maintain a 'particular vigilance.'"

In truth, only constant vigilance will prevent the Hitler virus from resurfacing and spreading.

R.W.S.

# INDEX